FINS

ALSO BY WILLIAM KNOEDELSEDER

Bitter Brew

I'm Dying Up Here

Stiffed

Harley Earl, the Rise of General Motors,
and the Glory Days of Detroit

WILLIAM KNOEDELSEDER

HARPER
BUSINESS

An Imprint of HarperCollins*Publishers*

FINS

HarperCollins books may be purchased for educational, business, or sales promotional use. For information, please email the Special Markets Department at SPsales@harpercollins.com.

FIRST EDITION

Designed by Bonni Leon-Berman

Library of Congress Cataloging-in-Publication Data

Names: Knoedelseder, William, 1947– author.
Title: Fins : Harley Earl, the rise of General Motors, and the glory days of Detroit / William Knoedelseder.
Description: First edition. | New York, NY : Harper, [2018] | Includes bibliographical references and index.
Identifiers: LCCN 2018014672| ISBN 9780062289070 (hc : alk. paper) | ISBN 9780062289094 (digital edition)
Subjects: LCSH: Earl, Harley. | Automobile engineers—United States— Biography. | Automobile industry and trade—United States—History. | General Motors Corporation—History. | Detroit (Mich.)—Economic conditions.
Classification: LCC TL140.E23 K66 2018 | DDC 629.2092 [B] —dc23 LC record available at https://lccn.loc.gov/2018014672

18 19 20 21 22 LSC 10 9 8 7 6 5 4 3 2 1

In memory of my father, William Kenrick Knoedelseder Sr.,
and my dear friend for more than fifty years, Terry J. Cowhey,
the two guys who were always there to talk cars with me

CONTENTS

PROLOGUE:
DEDICATION DAY

It was "D-day" in Warren, Michigan—May 16, 1956. The invasion began at midmorning as an armada of automobiles, shuttle buses, and limousines materialized out of the mist all along Van Dyke Avenue and Mound Road several miles outside the city limits of Detroit.

The cause of the sudden traffic surge was General Motors, which was hosting an event for five thousand VIPs and members of the press to mark the official dedication of its new office complex, called the General Motors Technical Center, located on a mile-square plot of onetime farmland in the usually tranquil township of some forty thousand people.

The Dedication Day festivities were to include a sumptuous, chef-prepared picnic lunch, followed by a closed-circuit television appearance by President Dwight D. Eisenhower and a walking tour of the complex guided by CBS News reporter Walter Cronkite, whose network was set to transmit the event simultaneously to smaller-scale "D-day" gatherings at GM offices in sixty-one other cities.

That may seem like an awful lot of hoopla for a new office park, but the Technical Center was unlike any corporate facility ever before imagined. Built over a period of eight years at a cost of $125 million (the equivalent of more than a billion dollars today), it had been conceived by a trio of senior GM executives as a melding of science, technology, and art that would stand as a testament to the seemingly limitless capability of both the company and the country, a lofty ambition that appeared to have been achieved with the finished product.

Twenty-five sleek, low-slung buildings made of steel and glass, the material of automobiles, were set in a lavishly landscaped 330-acre campus surrounding a 22-acre artificial lake accented by four islands of weeping willow trees, a 138-foot stainless-steel water tower, and two dramatic fountains, one spraying a shimmering curtain of water 50 feet high and 115 feet wide and the other, designed by famed sculptor Alexander Calder, shooting twenty-one streams into the air, pulsing, leaping, and falling in a graceful liquid ballet.

A GM press release boasted that the two fountains displaced more water than all the fountains at France's famed Palace of Versailles, prompting *Life* magazine to proclaim the Tech Center "the Versailles of Industry."

Clustered around the lake, offices for the company's four major staff operations—manufacturing, engineering, research, and styling—were demarcated by decorative exterior walls of brilliantly colored glazed bricks—crimson, scarlet, tangerine, royal blue, lemon yellow, chartreuse—reminiscent of those found in the palaces of ancient Abyssinian kings (again, according to a GM press release). Because no contemporary commercial brick maker possessed the technical know-how to meet the architect's specifications, the bricks had been glazed and baked in a giant kiln that GM financed specifically for the task.

The focal point of the Tech Center was the Styling Auditorium, with its gleaming aluminum-covered dome mirroring the sky. Aside from being visually stunning, the 65-foot high dome was a technological marvel, the first of its size to be held aloft by pressure-vessel construction, which basically inflated it from within. The 188-foot span consisted of welded sheets of steel a mere three-eighths of an inch thick—in relation to its total area, as thin as one-thirtieth of an eggshell.

Given an advance look at the facility, *Architectural Digest* pronounced it "an architectural feat that may be unique in our time."

As it turned out, the fancy picnic had to be moved under a huge tent because of the weather—a stiff, cold wind and an intermittent drizzle that weather forecasters warned might turn into a full-blown thunderstorm before the day was out. Luckily, however, the rain failed to arrive as predicted, and shortly before noon the guests began filing into the open, drafty bleachers that had been set up on the west side of the lake opposite the engineering buildings. Bundled against the chill in overcoats, hats, and gloves, the assemblage represented a sizable portion of America's post–World War II brain trust: Wall Street bankers, CEOs of manufacturing firms, presidents of universities, deans of engineering schools, scientists, inventors, architects, philanthropists, government officials (notably, Secretary of Defense Charles E. Wilson, a former president of GM), and senior officers from all branches of the military, including the vice commander of the Strategic Air Command, the chief of the navy's bureau of ordnance, and the army's chief of research and development. Typically for the time, almost all were men; it was nearly impossible to find a female face in the crowd.

After Cronkite explained the wonders of the new closed-circuit-TV technology, a military band played "The Star-Spangled Banner" and four F-86 Sabre jets executed a screaming low-level flyover punctuated by the detonation of an aerial bomb. Harlow

Curtice, the GM president and CEO, stepped to the podium and declared, "We have gathered here today for a momentous occasion."

That wasn't exactly true. The Tech Center—with its four thousand scientists, engineers, technicians, and designers—had been operational for more than six months. So the occasion was really an elaborate bit of public relations. But the "moment" was indeed significant. As the sun began to peek through the clouds that November-like day in May, America was at its apex—the dominant military, economic, and social force on earth. General Motors reigned as the most successful company in the history of business. Detroit was the manufacturing capital of the world and home to the industry that directly or indirectly employed one in six Americans.

"No industry has contributed more to our nation's growth and development than the automobile industry," Curtice said. "Its product has completely changed the face of America and the lives of all Americans."

Curtice's preeminence on the program was made possible by the retirement the month before of Alfred P. Sloan Jr., who had headed GM for thirty-three years and whose organizational brilliance was universally credited with shaping the company into a global colossus. The Tech Center had been Sloan's idea. He was sitting a few feet away from Curtice but had chosen not to speak.

Charles F. Kettering, GM's vice president and director of research from 1920 until his retirement in 1947, followed Curtice to the speaker's stand. Now nearing eighty, "Boss Ket," as he was affectionately referred to around the company, was a legend in the auto industry. A scientist, engineering genius, and inveterate inventor with more than 140 separate patents in his name, he revolutionized the car business in 1912 when his electronic starter replaced the old arm-busting crank starter, which had served as a barrier to women becoming independent drivers.

Sloan and Kettering had built GM together, had grown rich and become philanthropists together, founding the Sloan-Kettering Institute for Cancer Research in 1945. They had also planned the Tech Center together, beginning in the years before the war. But in a rare divergence, they ended up disagreeing strongly about how it should look. Kettering thought most of what passed for modern architecture appeared frivolous, frail, and poorly constructed. He preferred a classic "ageless" look. GM didn't need any "fancy buildings," he told Sloan. "We want solid, functional buildings that don't detract from what we do in them."

Twelve years after that conversation Boss Ket still seemed a bit miffed that Sloan, the real boss, had overruled him. "One thing worries me about this Technical Center," he said. "I'm afraid that the people here may lean too heavily on the facilities and forget that ideas are developed in the mind. If we took all the people away it would be obvious that nothing would come out of the Technical Center."

That was his only downbeat note, however, and his stirring summation brought the technocrats in the crowd to their feet. "Anything you can think of today can be done," he said. "With willing hands and open minds, the future will be greater than the most fantastic story you can write."

President Eisenhower wrapped up the speechifying portion of the program, appearing "live" on a large screen to deliver a five-minute pep talk that someone in either the White House or, more likely, the GM publicity department had titled, in keeping with the theme of the day, "The Rich Reward Ahead." It was a bland performance—rambling, repetitive, and replete with platitudes, concluding with a prediction that work at the Tech Center would bring about "broader freedom and richer dignity for human beings, more rewarding lives, for all Americans and, we hope, through all the world."

The audience wouldn't have cared if the President had recited pages from the Detroit telephone directory. As far as they were concerned, he was the auto industry's best friend. He had come into office convinced by his experience moving armies across Europe during World War II that the United States needed a massive upgrade of its transportation infrastructure. "A modern highway system is essential to meet the needs of our growing population, our expanding economy, and our national security," he said in his first State of the Union address. So he threw the full weight of his presidency behind the passage of the Federal-Aid Highway Act, which committed the government to spend $25 billion building 41,000 miles of interstate highways, the largest public works project in the history of the country. The legislation was set to be voted on the following month, and everyone present believed it was certain to accelerate already booming auto sales and spark an attendant surge in the steel, glass, rubber, and oil industries. Billions more dollars would pour into Motor City.

Of course, no one in the bleachers could foresee that all those new roads eventually would send hundreds of thousands of people streaming into the suburbs to live, siphoning off the inner city's tax base and leaving it unable to provide adequate services for its remaining, less affluent residents. On Dedication Day 1956, it was impossible to imagine a future in which both Detroit and General Motors would file for bankruptcy.

The afternoon's program concluded with an hour-long expedition through the Tech Center grounds, office suites, laborato-

ries, and design studios, with much of the narrative provided by
GM's vice president of styling, Harley Earl, who had not been
introduced or even mentioned by any of the speakers, an odd
omission given the role he played in the events leading up to the
day. He was the third member of the troika (along with Sloan
and Kettering) that conceived and planned the Tech Center, and
was arguably the one most responsible for how it turned out. In
the Versailles of Industry, Harley Earl was Louis XIV. He had
chosen the architect and overseen all details of its execution, approving every color scheme and every piece of custom-designed
furniture throughout the entire complex. From the Antoine Pevsner bronze sculpture *Bird in Flight* near the front entrance
to the brushed-steel handrails leading down the back stairs to
the basement of the Styling Building, the GM Technical Center
looked the way it did because that was the way Harley Earl
thought it should look.

The same could be said of the roughly 50 million cars that
had rolled off the GM assembly lines during his twenty-nine
years with the company. Earl practically invented the profession
of automobile styling. He introduced art into the rigid mechanics of mass automobile manufacturing and thereby changed the
game forever. It was styling, not engineering, that had propelled
GM past Ford to an indomitable fifty-plus percent share of U.S.
auto sales. Earl's sense of how an American car should look,
and what it should embody, pervaded every design studio in
Detroit. His decision to put tail fins on the 1948 Cadillac kicked
off a competition among automakers to see who could out-fin
all the rest, to the point that the rear fender protuberances became the dominant design element of American cars during the
1950s and the subject of a heated public debate, with both sides
claiming them as a metaphor for the state of the nation.

If Harley Earl is known at all to the public today, it's probably as the "father of tail fins." But he was a great deal more than that. Six decades after Dedication Day, automotive historians and car collectors alike will tell you that the American car industry's rise to greatness began and ended with him.

1
PIONEERS

The first great fortunes in America were made in the timber business as the country's immense northern forests were felled, first to clear land for homesteads and later to provide lumber for bridges, buildings, towns, and cities.

Commercial logging began in New England and then moved inexorably west into New York, Pennsylvania, and Ohio, taking down nearly everything in its path. When the first loggers arrived in Michigan in the 1840s, they found a vast expanse of untouched white pine and a network of navigable rivers to transport the cut timber to ports on the Great Lakes. In other words, log heaven.

Detroit, which was founded as a fur-trading post in 1701, developed into a major logging hub in the latter half of the 1800s as timber companies floated islands of logs down Lake Huron to the city's many sawmills, which cut them into lumber for shipment east through Lake Erie and Lake Ontario. Michigan timber thus provided the underpinning for Detroit's rise as an industrial center. Detroit-based lumber barons invested millions in real estate and manufacturing, built vainglorious mansions, donated to art museums, libraries, and colleges, and formed an aristocracy that fostered an image of the city as the "Paris of the West."

All the while, their armies of loggers laid waste to Michigan's pine forest, leaving behind millions of acres of stump-studded, debris-littered land that was unsuitable for farming but fertile ground for dry-season fires that periodically destroyed vast tracts of uncut timber and killed hundreds of people. Most of the cutting went on during the winter months so the logs could be hauled to the rivers over frozen ground by horse- or ox-drawn wagons and sleds. Which meant the loggers spent the entire winter in the forest, sheltered in shantylike log bunkhouses that held as many as a hundred men. The so-called shanty boys— mostly single and in their teens and twenties—worked from dawn until dusk six days a week for twenty to twenty-six dollars a month.

Jacob William Earl was a typical shanty boy. Born in 1866 in Oneida, Michigan, a hundred miles west of Detroit, the son of a farmer, J.W. didn't go to high school. After completing eighth grade, he served as a blacksmith's apprentice for a few years and then went to work in the woods, where he labored first as a lumberjack, the most difficult and dangerous job in logging, and later as a sawmill worker, which paid better—thirty to sixty dollars a month—but required him to provide his own room and board. His time as a lumberman coincided with Michigan's peak as the foremost lumber-producing state in the union, when its output amounted to a fourth of the nation's total, nearly equaling the next three states combined. But the pace of the cutting slowed in 1887 as Michigan's timber resources began to play out. Having consumed an estimated two-thirds of the state's pine forests, the large lumber companies started moving their operations on to Indiana, Wisconsin, and, ultimately, the Pacific Northwest.

At age nineteen, J.W. took a break from logging and traveled with his uncle to visit relatives in Arcadia, California, a sparsely populated agricultural area a few miles north of Los Angeles. After those harsh winters in the northern woods, he apparently was seduced by the scent of the citrus blossoms and the persistent warm sunshine. He never returned to Michigan.

He worked for a while with his uncle, who was a carpenter, then found employment in a small blacksmith and carriage repair shop in downtown Los Angeles. The shop's location, near the corner of Fifth and Hill Streets, turned out to be a stroke of luck because it placed him just a few blocks from the home of Harley and Mary Hazard Taft, a prominent couple whose patronage would prove a turning point in his life.

The Hazard-Taft clan was one of the city's most storied pioneer families. The chronicle of how they'd come to settle in Southern California read like a frontier novel.

Mary Hazard was born in Detroit in 1841, the daughter of Ariel Merrick Makepeace Hazard, a ship captain on the Great Lakes and a first cousin to Commodore Oliver Hazard Perry, who won a brilliant naval victory over the British in the Battle of Lake Erie during the War of 1812, after which he supposedly uttered the famous line "We have met the enemy and they are ours."

When Mary was an infant, her father moved the family to Chicago, which amounted to little more than a village at the time. The Hazards lived in a small log house on the banks of Lake Michigan while "the Captain" plied his trade, piloting ships loaded with Michigan lumber. He became successful enough to own three ships, but all were lost in storms one terrible spring, leaving the family in dire financial straits.

Desperate to restore his family's fortune, Captain Hazard left his pregnant wife and five children behind and headed to California in 1849, seized by "the gold fever," as Mary recalled later in a private journal. He sailed aboard a freighter around Cape Horn and after three months arrived in Hangtown, California, a chaotic, violent mining camp during the Gold Rush, so named because of its frequent hangings and later renamed Placerville. Hazard became a merchant, providing prospectors with dry goods, lumber, and groceries. After two years he had amassed enough money to return to Chicago to fetch his family and lead them to what he hoped would be a golden new life in California.

This time, Captain Hazard chose to travel west over land. The family of eight crossed the Great Plains in two ox-drawn covered wagons he had built in the shape of boats so they could float across rivers. He even fashioned tent poles that were flat so they could double as oars. The journey took eighteen months, impeded by a cholera outbreak, herds of buffalo that stretched from horizon to horizon and held them up for weeks at a time, and several skirmishes with Indians. In one instance, a member of their wagon train was shot with an arrow an inch below his heart as he attempted to keep a band of Indians from stealing their supplies. "We ran to him and managed to get him in the wagon," Mary wrote later. "He pulled the arrow out . . . and came very near dying and suffered for many days." Her brother George recalled that the Indians "robbed us of most all we had to eat and wear. They left Mother and the girls with only what they had on their backs. We could see them going over the hills with Mother's flour sacks, containing clothing and her paisley shawls, flung over their backs."

In Council Bluffs, Iowa, the family watched as a town mob dragged a murder suspect to the spot where his alleged victim lay with his head split open in a pool of blood, and then they "hung him on one of the trees," George wrote in his own journal. "About that time, the sky became overcast with intensely black clouds and those who thought him not guilty said it was because they had hung an innocent man . . . describing it as Black Friday."

On a happier day, June 30, 1853, Eleanor Hazard, the Captain's wife, gave birth to their seventh child, Eugene, in one of the wagons. The Hazard family bible notes that he was "born at the Platte River in the Sue [*sic*] Nation on Nebraska Terrian [*sic*]."

(Fifteen years later, Eugene was helping his older brother Daniel guide another wagon train west when he reached into a wagon to fetch a shotgun to shoot some quail and pulled it out muzzle first "with both barrels discharging into his intestines," according to his brother George's journal. "He died in Daniel's arms. His last words were, 'May God forgive Daniel.'" They buried him there, "under the tree where they had, moments before, just eaten their lunch, and built a rock border around his grave. Somewhere on a hilltop in Arizona." As his sister Mary wrote in her journal, "He was born among the Indians and buried among the Indians.")

The Hazard family arrived in El Monte, California, on Christmas Day 1853, planning to resupply nearby at what was then known as El Pueblo de Nuestra Señora la Reina de los Ángeles (the Town of Our Lady Queen of the Angels) before continuing on to gold country along El Camino Real. But according to Mary's journal, they were "delighted with Los Angeles and gave up the idea of going north." The Captain acquired thirty-five acres of land four miles outside the town, built a large adobe house, and settled into ranching and farming for the next ten years, during which time the Hazards crossed paths with Harley Taft.

◆

The twenty-three-year-old farmer's son had sailed around Cape Horn from Rhode Island in 1849, the same year as Captain Hazard. Census records indicate that he quickly found work in Los Angeles, first as a stable keeper and later as a teamster. According to family records and correspondence, one of the places he worked was the livery stable on the Hazard ranch, where he met and, in 1862, married Captain Hazard's daughter Mary, who was fifteen years his junior.

Fate was not finished with the Hazards. In 1864, "our land was declared government land and we did not pre-empt, so we lost it all," George wrote in his journal. They were forced to move into town, where Captain Hazard and his new son-in-law, Harley, began prospecting for land deals. They hit pay dirt on February 1, 1866, when they attended a public auction of tax-delinquent property and bid on an undeveloped five-acre parcel at the edge of Los Angeles. Located next to a large open pasture that arriving settlers had turned into a rowdy, disreputable camp, it was hardly prime real estate, but the price was right. Harley and the Captain bought the entire block between Fourth and Fifth Streets and Hill and Olive Streets for $9.90.

That piece of land became the cornerstone of the family's prosperity as the town expanded into a city, encircling the block over the next three decades. Captain Hazard and Eleanor lived out their days on the Hazard-Taft homestead. Harley and Mary had six children in their house at 411 West Fifth Street. Their oldest son, Alfred, married and built his own house just around the corner from them at 457 South Hill Street. Three of their children did not survive early childhood, however: Walter died as an infant; Alice and Emily died at age two and three, respectively, in 1885.

Mary's brother Henry, meanwhile, graduated from the University of Michigan law school on his way to becoming Los Angeles's city attorney. He also developed the lot at the corner of Fifth and Olive into the city's premier performance hall, Hazard's Pavilion. Opened in 1887, it seated as many as four thousand people for sporting events, music concerts, business conventions, and religious revivals. The legendary prizefighter Jack Johnson won his first title there as "Colored Heavyweight Champion." In 1889, Henry was elected mayor of Los Angeles.

The Hazard family's remarkable American journey helps explain why Mary and Harley Taft might have seen potential in J. W. Earl. He may have been an uneducated lumberjack from the Michigan woods, but he was also smart, determined, and ambitious, a skilled craftsman who knew his way around horses and wheeled vehicles. Indeed, J.W. quickly rose from employee to partner in the carriage shop, and in 1889 bought out the other man and named the business Earl Carriage Works. All of which impressed the Tafts to the point that they allowed him to court their eighteen-year-old daughter, Abigail, who likely was impressed with his lanky good looks (he was six foot one) and pale blue eyes.

J.W. married Abbie Taft (whose childhood nickname was "Taffy" because her hair color matched that of the candy) on June 21, 1891. A year and a day later, she gave birth to their first child, Carl. A second son was born on November 22, 1893. They named him Harley, after his grandfather. A third son, Arthur, arrived two years later.

Earl Carriage Works expanded as rapidly as the Earl family, with J.W. relocating the business several times as his clientele increased, eventually taking over a large three-story brick building at 1320 South Main Street. Before long, he had several dozen men working for him, designing and building all manner of horse-drawn conveyance, from simple farm wagons to fancy carriages for the wealthy to sleek sulkies for the harness-racing crowd at the nearby Agricultural Park track. Given that Harley Taft listed his occupation as "capitalist" on his 1890 U.S. Census form, it seems likely that the family patriarch invested in his son-in-law's growing business.

The city of Los Angeles was growing rapidly, too. Just across the street from the Taft and Hazard homes, the old settlers' camp had been developed into a beautifully landscaped municipal park (now Pershing Square) with a bandstand for outdoor concerts that drew crowds of locals and tourists out for weekend buggy rides. The corner of Fifth and Hill had turned into one of the city's most prestigious and busiest intersections, which increased the family's property value, but at the expense of their peace and quiet.

So in 1893, three generations of Tafts—Harley and Mary, their twenty-seven-year-old son Alfred, and his wife, Blanche, and their three children—summoned up the family's old pioneering spirit and migrated once again, albeit a much shorter distance than in the past. They bought twenty acres in the Cahuenga Valley, about six miles from Los Angeles near a dirt-street village called Hollywood, where they built a two-story Dutch colonial house in the middle of a lemon grove at what is now the corner of Taft Avenue and Hollywood Boulevard. Their new community consisted of a small general store, a one-room schoolhouse, and a dozen or so Spanish-speaking families who tended the area's strawberry and barley fields and nascent orange and lemon groves. Shortly after the move Blanche Taft gave birth to a fourth child, Sarah, who later would write that she was "the first Anglo-Saxon child born in Hollywood."

The Earls eventually followed the Tafts into this new frontier.

On July 4, 1900, J.W. moved Abbie and the three boys into a large three-story house he had built on five acres that Mary Taft had deeded to Abbie just down the street from the Tafts' place, at what is now the corner of Hollywood Boulevard and Bronson Avenue. With a front gate made of stone and ironwork fashioned at his carriage works spelling out the Earl name, the new home was twelve miles from J.W.'s business—a ninety-minute buggy ride—and a world away from that log shanty in the pine forest.

At age thirty-four, J.W. was not about to settle into the life of a country squire, however. His business was growing, but he knew it faced a looming existential threat: the dawning of the new century was bringing an end to the era of horse-drawn vehicles. The Industrial Revolution had accelerated the pace of American life. Increasingly mechanized manufacturing and a doubling of the population were driving a growing demand for goods that needed to get from point A to point B more quickly, and all along the supply chain horses were holding up the process as coal- and steam-powered trains and ships waited for them to trudge to the loading dock. It seemed that horses no longer fit into the modern urban landscape.

Their slowness wasn't the only problem. America's cities were packed with more than 3 million of them—nearly 200,000 in New York, 80,000 in Philadelphia, 12,000 in Detroit. That many 1,200-pound animals produced an epic amount of manure. The city of New York calculated that between 3 and 4 million pounds of it a day had to be removed from its streets and stables, along with 41 dead horses (15,000 per year). The city of Rochester estimated that its population of 15,000 live horses dropped enough road apples annually to make a 175-foot-high mound of manure, which would cover an entire acre.

In addition to creating an ungodly stench and costing untold millions to clean up and cart away, the manure caused serious public health concerns. By one estimate, three billion flies hatched in urban horse droppings every day, at times resulting in veritable clouds of the pathogen-carrying insects. Between flies and windblown dung dust, horses were blamed for outbreaks of cholera, smallpox, yellow fever, and typhoid, feeding a growing consensus that the beasts should be banished from American cities.

"The vitiation of the air by the presence of so many animals is alone a sufficient reason for their removal," the U.S. commissioner of labor wrote in *Popular Science Monthly*. An editorial in the magazine *Scientific American* stated that the banning of horses "would benefit the public health to an almost incalculable degree."

Fortunately, one man's pile of horse poop proved another man's opportunity. For more than a decade, a generation of mechanically inclined young men had been working feverishly in garages, barns, and machine shops all across the United States and Western Europe, racing to create a self-propelled vehicle that would put the horse out to pasture as the world's primary means of transportation and earn themselves a fortune in the process.

The Europeans jumped out in front in October 1885, when Karl Benz of Mannheim, Germany, conducted a successful test drive of the first gasoline-powered automobile, a three-wheeler he called the Benz Motorwagen. America's car boys spun their wheels for a number of years turning out problematic steam- and electric-powered vehicles until Frank and Charles Duryea of Peoria, Illinois, finally gained traction with a gas-powered vehicle they'd built in a Massachusetts loft. On Thanksgiving Day 1895, the brothers entered their Duryea Motor Wagon in what was billed as "America's first motor car race." Sponsored by the *Chicago Times-Herald*, with a two-thousand-dollar prize, the competition pitted the motor wagon against two American-built electric vehicles and three gas-powered imports built by Benz. The course covered fifty-four miles, from Chicago to Evanston, Illinois, and back, and the motor wagon crossed the finish line first.

The brothers quickly announced the formation of a company that would hand-build thirteen identical vehicles for sale to the public over the next year. Based in Springfield, Massachusetts, the Duryea Motor Wagon Company was the country's first commercial auto-manufacturing operation. Widespread news coverage of the race and the new company seemed to speed up the development of gas-powered automobiles.

At 11:00 p.m. on March 6, 1896, Charles King drove the first gas-powered vehicle on the streets of Detroit, a wooden-wheeled, buckboard-style wagon he'd fitted with a four-cylinder engine. His 5 mph cruise down Woodward Avenue drew a crowd of several hundred cheering spectators, which nearly got him ticketed by a policeman for disturbing the peace and resulted in his being quoted in the *Detroit Journal* saying, "I am convinced that in time the horseless carriage will supersede the horse."

Three months later, at four in the morning on June 4, Henry Ford took a somewhat quieter test drive around Detroit in an experimental gas-powered vehicle he'd built in a brick shed behind his home in Dearborn, Michigan. Ford's "quadricycle" was a metal-frame buggy fitted with four bicycle wheels and propelled by a two-cylinder engine mounted under an upholstered bench seat. Lighter than King's wooden wagon, it reached a speed of twenty miles per hour.

On August 11, two months after Ford's debut, Ransom E.

Olds invited a newspaper reporter along when he took his first gas-powered vehicle for a test drive on the streets of Lansing, Michigan. "It never kicks or bites, never tires on long runs, and never sweats in hot weather," Olds famously boasted of his horseless carriage. "It does not require care in the stable and only eats while on the road."

Out in California, J.W. followed the car boys' exploits through newspaper reports, which he no doubt read with a mixture of excitement, concern, and envy. They were his contemporaries, after all, born in the same Civil War decade. With the exception of King, they'd all been raised on small family farms, an experience that left Ford and Olds with an abiding distaste for horses. Ford, too, had worked in a sawmill before seizing on his life's work. Olds was the son of a blacksmith and had dropped out of high school to apprentice in his father's machine shop. About the only significant difference between J.W. and these early automobile pioneers was his location far from the industrial center of the country.

Between 1895 and 1900, young men with similar backgrounds and skills formed nearly a hundred companies to build gas-powered automobiles, mostly in the Midwest and Mid-Atlantic regions—in Cleveland, St. Louis, Chicago, Toledo, and Buffalo; in Kenosha, Wisconsin, and York, Pennsylvania; in Hagerstown, Maryland, and Hartford, Connecticut; and in more than half a dozen cities in Indiana, where hardwood forests had long provided the sturdy but pliable oak, ash, and hickory that supported that state's robust carriage-building industry. South Bend, Indiana, was home to the world's largest maker of horse-drawn vehicles, the Studebaker Brothers Manufacturing Company, which built a major portion of the covered wagons that had carried pioneers across the western plains.

Detroit didn't have a resident automaker until 1900, when Ransom Olds moved his Olds Motor Works there from Lansing. But with initial funding from several lumber barons, Olds and his fellow Michigander Henry Ford quickly began laying the groundwork for what would become Motor City.

Olds's new Detroit factory was the first ever designed specifically to manufacture automobiles. His plan was to build a vehicle that the average man could afford to buy and maintain, one that would weigh about 500 pounds and sell for approximately $500. "My whole idea was to have the operation so simple that anyone could run it, and the construction such that it could be repaired at any local shop," he said. The result was a two-seat buggy with bicycle-style wheels, tiller steering, and a single-cylinder engine. Called the "curved-dash runabout" because of its rounded tobogganlike front end, it weighed in at 750 pounds with a price of $650.

Olds sold 425 of the runabouts the first year and 2,500 the second, with the sharp increase attributed to the vehicle's performance in a highly publicized endurance run from Detroit to New York City for the 1901 National Automobile Show in Madison Square Garden. The Oldsmobile, as it came to be known, completed the 820-mile trek in seven and a half days, averaging 14 miles per hour and consuming 30 gallons of gas.

Olds took orders for more than 1,000 vehicles at the auto show, and thanks to a production process that was a forerunner to the moving assembly line Henry Ford would perfect a few years later, his factory was soon turning out 20 a day when other automakers were struggling to produce that many in a month, or a year. After a tour of the Olds plant, a reporter for the *Detroit Free Press* rhapsodized, "Rows upon rows of special machinery are humming and buzzing away, bewildering the onlooker with their number. Every step in the process of turning out the finished machinery of a modern car is carried out by a group of these beautiful machines. One little imagines, as he looks at the swiftly running car on the street, the immense amount of detail and careful manipulation that have been necessary on the hundreds of parts before they have all been brought together and adjusted to form this engine of commerce and pleasure."

Olds's simple little runabout became America's first successful mass-produced gasoline-powered automobile, and the first to be immortalized in a popular song, titled "In My Merry Oldsmobile": "Come away with me Lucille / in my Merry Oldsmobile / Down the road of life we will fly / automo-bubbling you and I."

But Henry Ford was riding tight on Olds's tail. He formed the Ford Motor Company in October 1903 and quickly began manufacturing his own runabout in a converted wagon factory on Detroit's Mack Avenue. Like Olds, his plan was to "build a motorcar for the multitudes," as he put it, one that "any person with a good salary will be able to own." His Model A was a two-seater with a two-cylinder engine that propelled it to a top speed of 45 mph. Dubbed the "Fordmobile," it caught on immediately, with more than 1,700 sold in the first fifteen months despite a higher price tag than the Oldsmobile—$750—which Ford planned to lower as soon as a more streamlined production process combined with increased sales to drive down his unit cost.

In the beginning, Ford and Olds were more assemblers than manufacturers. In an effort to ramp up production as quickly as possible, they chose to subcontract for many of the component parts that went into their vehicles rather than make them in-house. In 1901 and 1902, for example, Olds bought two thousand engines and three thousand transmissions built by John and Horace Dodge, machinist brothers who had cut their teeth making bicycles. Olds bought additional engines and transmissions from the Leland & Faulconer Machine Tool Company, as did Henry Ford until he entered into an exclusive arrangement with the Dodge brothers to provide his factory with all its "running gear," which comprised practically the entire working automobile except for the wheels, tires, and body.

The decision by Olds and Ford to outsource critical components shaped the course of the industry. As they expanded operations, their companies became seedbeds for other entrepreneurs who dreamed of creating motorcars. Henry Leland, a master of precision manufacturing and founder of Leland & Faulconer, launched the Cadillac Motor Car Company in 1902, named for Antoine de la Mothe Cadillac, the French explorer who founded the city of Detroit. (Leland would later create the Lincoln Motor Company, named after his hero, Abraham Lincoln.) The same year, David Dunbar Buick, who'd helped develop the overhead valve internal combustion engine, produced his first car. James Packard, Louis Chevrolet, and the Dodge brothers followed, building their own namesake brands and further concentrating the industry in Detroit.

"As a group they were utterly dedicated to the manufacture of motor vehicles to the point where they seemed to have preferred going broke making automobiles than get rich doing something else," wrote automotive historian John B. Rae. "These men transformed the fledgling auto industry and gave the world a new technology of production."

By 1905, Detroit had more automobile companies than any other city in the world. Two thousand miles away, J. W. Earl could see clearly that the future of his company—and the country— lay in cars, not carriages. Los Angeles didn't have the industrial base of Detroit; its economy was driven by agriculture and real estate. There wasn't a single auto manufacturer in town. Still, motorcars acquired by the rich and adventurous and shipped across the country were starting to appear on L.A.'s broad, flat, unpaved streets. By some estimates there were nearly a thousand of them among the city's population of 200,000, and each one represented a potential lost customer for Earl Carriage Works.

J.W. was energized by the advent of the automobile and couldn't wait to get his hands on one, to take it apart, study it, and put it back together, to push it to its limits of speed and endurance. Not just for the thrill, though that was a part, but because he needed to find a way to grab onto this new industry that was barreling straight at him, or it would blow right on by and leave him in the dust.

It would take a few more years, but he would find a way in, aided by his second-born son and the birth of another uniquely American industry.

2

HOLLYWOOD
AND HARLEY

Hollywood, California, was a pastoral paradise during the
first decade of the twentieth century, a sun-drenched
valley of fruit and vegetable fields, vineyards, and citrus
and avocado orchards interspersed with large, beautifully landscaped homes. To the north, flat cropland gave way to rolling
hills topped here and there by the oceanview estates of industrial tycoons escaping the havoc their businesses were wreaking
on cities back east. Lines of pepper trees shaded the main route
through town, Prospect Avenue, and cross streets were named
for the various species of trees—Pine, Palm, Sycamore, Olive,
Poinsettia, Orange, Lemon—that a real estate developer named
H. J. Whitley had planted along each of them.

Trees weren't all that Whitley had planted. Along with the
town's cofounder, Harvey Wilcox, he stood staunchly against the
consumption of alcohol. In selling Hollywood acreage, he ac-
tively recruited conservative white Christian Midwesterners who
shared his anti-booze bent, sending out promotional brochures
that played up the community's affluence and exclusivity, urging
prospects to "buy land and wear diamonds." The result was, in
the words of one historian, "a God-fearing suburb with a country club feel."

That feeling permeated the Hollywood Hotel. Opened in 1903, the gracious thirty-three-room country inn boasted its own electric power generator, water supply, and ice-making machinery, along with a broad veranda overlooking Prospect Avenue where guests could sit in rocking chairs and languidly observe the town's comings and goings. It was, in the words of one writer, "a self-contained oasis of civilized conveniences amid a bucolic wilderness."

"We lived a country life," Sally Taft Teschke recalled in a 1934 article for the *Los Angeles Times*, "almost like that of an English countryside."

Since leading the Taft family out of downtown Los Angeles, Sally's father, Alfred Z. Taft, had become one of Hollywood's most prominent citizens. He'd organized local lemon growers into the Cahuenga Valley Lemon Exchange, which was now shipping railroad cars full of lemons to market. In addition to earning $17,000 a year from his own orchards, A.Z. ran a successful real estate company, Taft Realty, from an outbuilding behind his house. A devout Methodist and ardent prohibitionist, he was the prime mover behind a 1903 ordinance that outlawed the sale or transportation of alcohol in Hollywood. As a result, the town's only bar, the Blondeau Tavern, was shut down, and one well-known local businessman, Philo J. Beveridge, was arrested and put on trial for serving white wine during a private banquet at the Hollywood Hotel. He was acquitted.

"Hollywood was a very moderate and temperate center," Sally Taft Teschke wrote. "No saloons, no pool halls, gambling or card playing were permitted. Perhaps we were strait-laced. But those who wanted to do those things could step over into nearby communities."

Sally and her six siblings, along with her four Earl cousins—

Carl, Harley, Arthur, and Jessica (born in 1903)—were familiar faces to the conductors on the electric tram line that ran between Hollywood and the city. The tram passed right in front of their houses on Prospect Avenue several times a day and often had to stop for the children to remove toys left on the tracks. The kids, in turn, took it upon themselves to keep the tourists on the tram from picking souvenir oranges and lemons off their families' trees.

Hollywood apparently wasn't quite bucolic enough for J.W. Every June, he packed up the entire family and embarked on a camping vacation in the rugged Tehachapi Mountains near Bakersfield, a two-and-a-half-day journey by horse and wagon. They pitched their tents in the canyons of Bailey's Ranch, owned by a longtime buyer of farm wagons from Earl Carriage Works, and spent most of the summer among the bears, bobcats, and mountain lions, living off the supplies they brought with them and whatever game they could shoot and cook, an experience not unlike J.W.'s time as a shanty boy in Michigan. It was almost as if he were making sure his children didn't come to think of themselves as privileged, even as his growing prosperity assured them they were.

As each of the Earl kids entered their teens, they began working part-time at the shop, where more and more of the work involved automobiles. A scant five years after the curved-dash Oldsmobile wowed attendees at the National Auto Show, the car had gone from a novelty to a necessity in the minds of many Americans. A 1906 article in *Harper's Weekly* magazine went so far as to say, "The automobile is essential to comfort and happiness." From a few thousand at the beginning of the decade, the number of cars on the nation's streets was heading toward half a million by the end of it. With demand far exceeding supply, they were sold as fast as they came out of the factory, on a cash-only basis with no warranty and no network of dealerships offering customer care. As a result, the nation's blacksmith and carriage shops became the first responders for auto maintenance and repair.

In 1908, the year that Henry Ford introduced the Model T, J.W. changed the name of his business to Earl Automobile Works. He had no intention of turning it into a mechanics' garage, however, as evidenced by the disclaimer on the front of the company's catalog of products and services: "No Motors or Engines Sold or Repaired." The forty-five-page booklet included a foreword by the proprietor, addressed to "Our Trade."

"The most successful companies in the world are the ones that take the greatest interest in their goods even after they've gone into service," J.W. wrote. "This book is submitted to you with the assurance that to all the goods hereinafter shown we take pleasure in extending the Earl Guarantee of satisfaction."

All the goods shown were aimed at improving on the bare-bones vehicles the mass manufacturers were offering their customers and as such they provide a snapshot of the state of the American automobile in 1910.

Few cars came equipped with windshields. Earl's brass-framed "Adjustable Glass Fronts" sold so well at fifty-five dollars that major manufacturers began ordering them by the thousands.

Most cars rode on wooden-spoke wheels that were similar in appearance to wagon wheels and nearly as fragile. "No one will dispute the fact that the majority of serious accidents are caused by the breaking of the wheels," according to the booklet, which touted the benefits of sturdier Earl-made wheels in the language of an ex-lumberman: "second-growth hickory, extra select in quality, double seasoned and double dried."

Factory-installed upholstery often was not colorfast. "You know how aggravating it is to have a light-colored suit spoiled by the color rubbing off the leather and adhering to it?" the catalog asked. The answer was Earl's Blue Ribbon Leather Dye No. 1. At seventy-five cents a pint, it was "sufficient for a five-passenger car."

The bulk of the booklet focused on what J.W. hoped would become the company's main business: designing and building automobile bodies. The mechanical engineering of cars was progressing rapidly—left-side steering wheels had replaced tillers, engines had moved from under the seats to under a hood in the front of the vehicle—but car bodies had not developed much beyond their horseless carriage stage. They still were constructed mostly of wood and bolted onto the chassis as a container for driver and passenger seating but not fully integrated into the whole of the vehicle. The big automakers (Ford, Dodge, Packard) jobbed out their body manufacturing, providing drawings and specifications to established carriage makers such as Brewster & Company in New York and the C. R. Wilson Company in Detroit. Smaller would-be body makers like Earl Automobile Works hoped to attract orders from the mass manufacturers through their custom-design work for well-to-do clients looking to upgrade or personalize their vehicles.

"We have the facilities and men to make any style of body the most critical customer may desire," said the catalog. "It will be just what you want, not what someone else wants you to buy."

By all accounts, J.W. was a gifted *carrossier*, with an eye for elegant detail and clean flowing lines. He was a proponent of the "torpedo" style, which he called the "definite trend in body designing." He advised his customers that the more streamlined bodies "do away with all external projections, resulting in a refinement and general smoothness that greatly adds to their appearance, accessibility and cleanliness."

J.W. put his money where his mouth was when it came to his own car. His first was a seven-passenger 1910 Chalmers touring car with a 112-inch wheelbase and a price tag of $2,750 (about the same as a nice house). But he found the large car impractical for commuting to and from work, so he bought a sleek 1911 Mercer roadster for about $2,250. The bright orange two-seater was one of the most eye-catching cars on the streets of Los Angeles, and possibly the fastest. With a 300-cubic-inch engine and detachable fenders, running boards, and lights, it could be turned into a professional racing machine in about twenty minutes. The Mercer County, New Jersey, manufacturer claimed the little car was capable of hitting seventy miles per hour, but J.W. soon learned it could go faster than that, thanks to his son Harley.

As Harley recalled more than half a century later, "My father made a very tough steel which was in demand by race drivers for steering knuckles, and that led to my hanging out around the racetrack in Santa Monica, where the crop of young drivers of that time included Ralph de Palma and Barney Oldfield."

Harley wanted to try his hand at racing and fortunately he knew just where to find a fast car. According to an oft-told family story, the teenager took the Mercer out one weekend and brought it back with the speedometer stuck at eighty, the highest it registered. When J.W. asked him about it, Harley supposedly shrugged and said he must have hit a bump or something. The following Monday a customer at Earl Automobile Works commented, "Harley sure knows how to drive that Mercer." When J.W. asked what he meant, the man told him that Harley had driven the car in a 100-mile race that weekend, and had won.

Another version of the story had it that J.W. learned of the race and Harley's victory by reading about it in the newspaper. Words were exchanged between father and son, but Harley continued with his high-speed hobby.

Of all J.W.'s children, Harley was the one most badly bitten by the automobile bug. Art gravitated to the upholstery department at the family business and little Jessie, who wanted to be an artist, would sit for hours in the third-floor paint department watching a master pin-striper named George Bernard practice his painstaking craft. But Harley, like his father, was drawn to designing automobile bodies. His talent for it first became apparent in the summer of 1910.

"Harley was sixteen and I was fourteen," his brother Art told journalist Michael Lamm in a 1980 interview. "We were up at Bailey's Ranch, camped in this canyon. It started to rain, and we ended up having a big flood. The whole canyon flooded and it filled up this hollow with clay. Harley and I made little saws out of wood and we went over to the clay, and Harley started designing cars out of clay. . . . He'd pick up a big chunk of clay and would work it down to the sort of car he wanted. I guess we had twenty or thirty of these little cars of different sorts, roadsters and touring cars."

Another downpour quickly dissolved Harley's creations, but the idea of modeling automobile bodies from clay stuck in his head, and what he had discovered in that mud puddle in the Tehachapi Mountains would one day have a profound effect on the development of the American automobile.

A year later, a chance encounter on a Hollywood street radically altered the Earl family's quiet country life. Developer H. J. Whitley was walking along the newly named Hollywood Boulevard (formerly Prospect Avenue) one afternoon when he noticed a stranger looking somewhat lost and confused. Whitley asked whether he could help. The man introduced himself as David Horsley and said he was a principal in the Nestor Film Company of Bayonne, New Jersey, and he was looking for a rental property to house a motion picture production studio.

Whitley had some experience with motion picture people. A crew from the Biograph Film Company recently had spent two days in Hollywood shooting a seventeen-minute film called *Love Among the Roses*, directed by D. W. Griffith and featuring a teenage Mary Pickford. Biograph was one of a number of motion picture companies from back east that had moved to the Los Angeles area in the last two years. Seeking to take advantage of the perpetual sunshine for filming, they'd established production studios in Glendale, Santa Monica, Long Beach, and downtown. Believing that a film studio might attract new home-buyers and businesses to Hollywood, Whitley escorted Horsley to the long-vacant Blondeau Tavern, where the filmmaker noted that the large rear courtyard could accommodate a production stage. Horsley agreed to lease the property for thirty dollars a month.

The next day, a Nestor film crew and a troupe of actors shot a comedy in an orange grove at the corner of Hollywood Boulevard and El Centro Avenue, and Hollywood was never the same. Within a few months, at least a dozen more motion picture companies traveled up the bumpy road through the Cahuenga Pass to establish operations in Hollywood. "They popped up like gypsy encampments full of soldiers of fortune and vaudeville performers down on their luck," according to local historian Gregory Paul Williams.

They shot their short, silent films outdoors on wooden platforms under tented sheets of muslin to filter the sunlight. Because actors had to provide their own wardrobes, the streets soon swarmed with vagabond performers dressed as cowboys and Indians, Roman soldiers and slave girls, biblical kings and belly dancers. It was as if the circus came to town and stayed. The newcomers took over the Hollywood Hotel, which had expanded to more than one hundred rooms, and ignored the house rules against alcohol consumption and sex among the unmarried. Concerned locals coined a derogatory term for them, calling them "movies" (because they worked in so-called moving pictures) and posting for-rent signs and ads that warned, "No Dogs. No Movies."

But the "movies" just kept coming. In December 1912, fledgling director Cecil B. DeMille arrived with a large crew from New York's Jesse L. Lasky Feature Play Company, including well-known Broadway leading man Dustin Farnum. They acquired studio space at the corner of Selma Avenue and Vine Street for seventy-five dollars a month and proceeded to shoot *The Squaw Man*, based on a hit Broadway play that had starred Farnum. The feature-length film was a huge success, enabling the Lasky Company to buy the surrounding block. DeMille built a home down the street from the Earls, becoming the first "movie" to take up permanent residence in town. Along with D. W. Griffith, he began churning out westerns in the surrounding hills, which soon reverberated with the sound of galloping hooves and faux gunfire. Crowds of townies and tourists spread picnic blankets on the hillsides to watch masked outlaws rob stagecoaches and painted Indian warriors attack wagon trains.

For the Taft and Earl kids, it was an exciting change from the bee-buzzing quietude of their early childhoods. "We delighted in watching movies in the making," Sally Taft Teschke said. "And soon the excitement began to spread to the parents." It helped that the studios started paying the townsfolk for the use of their houses and property. "It was quite thrilling to see your own home on the screen, and to comment on how poorly the neighbor's home looked in certain scenes," Sally said, adding somewhat ruefully that the rental money "was a subtle poison that soon broke down all barriers against the studios." She apparently drank the poison eagerly, however, when the studios needed extras for crowd scenes: "I appeared in three pictures before my teachers and parents caught on. And when my shame was discovered, you may be sure that the penalties were in accord."

Some of the community's anti-movie prejudice was allayed by a young actor's real-life act of heroism one morning in 1914 when a truck collided with the tram on Hollywood Boulevard and the truck driver's leg was severed. Witnesses said the man surely would have died if Lon Chaney had not ripped off his own shirt and used it as a tourniquet to stop the bleeding.

From the beginning, the sober citizens of Hollywood stood little chance of fighting off the advance of the studios. With the country's hunger for motion pictures beginning to rival its appetite for motor vehicles, holding back the march of progress, of technology, proved impossible. The Nestor Film Company became Universal studios and the Lasky Company grew into Paramount. And as the studio buildings went up, the pepper trees along Hollywood Boulevard came down and the citrus groves started to disappear.

The Birth of a Nation marked Hollywood's official passage from sleepy hamlet to motion picture capital. D. W. Griffith's three-hour post–Civil War epic was shot in 1914 on a then monumental budget of $110,000. The director ordered the construction of an antebellum town and slave quarters on vacant land at the head of Hollywood Boulevard and hired hundreds of white actors in blackface to play slaves. Decidedly racist but undeniably a technical and artistic masterpiece, the film went on to earn an astonishing $18 million, an amount that no film would surpass until Disney's *Snow White and the Seven Dwarfs* in 1937.

After that, motion picture money rained down hard on Hollywood, with predictable results. Griffith's follow-up, *Intolerance*, was filmed at a then mind-boggling cost of $1.9 million, which allowed him to hire Italian artisans to create a facsimile of the ancient Babylonian palace of Belshazzar and to stage 3,500 extras along three full blocks in the center of town for a single scene. The extras were paid a previously unheard-of two dollars a day. During the production, a British actor playing the role of Jesus Christ became involved in a sex scandal with a fourteen-year-old girl and was deported back to England.

The loosening of morals that accompanied the motion picture invasion surely troubled J.W., who served as a governing member of Hollywood's Methodist church. At the same time, however, the increasingly extravagant productions were the best thing that ever happened to his business. When DeMille and Griffith needed Roman chariots, Napoleonic carriages, stagecoaches, or covered wagons, they turned to Earl Automobile Works, which soon had several hundred craftsmen on the payroll and no meaningful competition anywhere on the West Coast.

Working part-time in the body shop while attending nearby University of Southern California, Harley got to know some of his father's new motion picture clients, including DeMille, who quickly took a liking to him. The director was then in his early thirties and no doubt sensed a kindred spirit in the nineteen-year-old, a fellow showman in the making. It was impossible not to notice Harley. At six foot five, he was almost freakishly tall for the time, with piercing blue eyes and a manner of speaking that combined country colloquialism with a Jimmy Stewart–like stammer to charming effect. Instead of saying he was surprised, he might say, "I liked to fell over." And he could cuss a blue streak when he wanted to, which was most of the time.

Harley's size combined with his fierce competitive streak to make him a standout on the track team at USC, where his exploits—including a pole-vaulting record and a legendary errant hammer throw that caused spectators to dive for cover when it sailed beyond the field and into the grandstand—attracted the attention of the local press, giving him his first taste of celebrity.

Harley idolized DeMille and studied the way he carried himself. He admired the director's panache, his confidence and sense of personal style, which often extended to wearing jodhpurs and carrying a riding crop while making a film. Harley, too, was a bit of a peacock, with a flair for the dramatic. But what bound the two men together ultimately was their shared love of automobiles. Like many early filmmakers, DeMille viewed them metaphorically, not as self-propelled conveyances but rather as expressions of mankind's dreams and desires. It didn't escape him that the motion picture and the motorcar were born in the same year, 1895, and the subsequent rise of both industries reflected, as he put it, "the love of motion and speed, the restless urge toward improvement and expansion, the kinetic energy of a young, vigorous nation."

In some of the earliest motion pictures, automobiles drove the narrative, literally and figuratively. Biograph's 1903 short *Runaway Match*, for example, depicted a young couple fleeing from a suburban mansion in a hired car and racing to the church pursued by the bride-to-be's angry father in a chauffeur-driven limousine. In the decade that followed, dozens of "elopement" films showed "poor but worthy young men demonstrate their adaptability and vitality by hiring or borrowing motorcars in order to carry off the daughters of rich men," according to a scholarly study of American films before 1921, published in *Michigan Quarterly Review*. In these films, "the motorcar itself has inspired temptation, freedom, status and a new identity," the author wrote, noting that the title *Runaway Match* "reminds us of the match between what would become Hollywood and Detroit." Harley and DeMille were the embodiment of that match, and their friendship honed Harley's view that the automobile business was really just another form of show business.

Harley took a break from Earl Automobile Works in 1914, when J.W. sent him off to Stanford University in Palo Alto, California, ostensibly to study law. He joined a fraternity and the rugby team, but his school year was interrupted. On October 8, his mother, Abbie, was coming out of gallbladder surgery in the hospital when suddenly she began coughing up copious amounts of blood from a clot that had developed in her lung. Within minutes, as J.W. looked on helplessly, she died. It was their son Billy's sixth birthday. She was forty-one.

Harley returned to Stanford after his mother's funeral but his mind was not on academics. In the course of a rugby game, he was badly cleated in the leg by an opposing player and the wound became infected, eventually developing into blood poisoning. Stanford put him on a train back home, where his condition worsened to the point that doctors were talking about amputating his leg. "But he fought it and wouldn't let them," his sister, Jessie, recalled decades later. "He came out of it all right but he lost practically a whole year."

When his leg healed, he took another stab at Stanford, but

once again troubling news from home distracted him from his studies. Business was still booming at Earl Automobile Works, but barely two years after Abbie's death, J.W. was about to remarry. The bride-to-be, Nellie Mae Black, was a thirty-five-year-old widow who had traveled throughout South America with her late spouse and never tired of talking about it. According to Harley's siblings and cousins, she was jealous of J.W.'s relationship with his children, especially eight-year-old Billy, whom she treated badly.

That clinched it for Harley, who doted on his baby brother. He dropped out of Stanford short of a degree and returned to Hollywood determined to help his father and family. He went back to the family business with a new energy and, thanks in part to Cecil B. DeMille, a clear-eyed view of his future.

He had pictures of cars in his head. He saw them in his dreams.

3
THE
COMPETITORS

America's carmakers turned out nearly two million vehicles in 1919, enough to make automobile manufacturing the nation's number one industry, employing 651,000 people with wages topping $2 billion.

The person most responsible for those numbers was Henry Ford, whose Model T accounted for more than half of new car sales and as much as two-thirds of all cars on the road. At the dawn of the 1920s, Ford was the most important figure in the American industrial landscape, and not just because of his car.

In the years since he tested his first hand-built vehicle on the streets of Detroit, the former Michigan farmboy had transformed manufacturing. Building on Ransom Olds's idea of a factory production line that passed in-process vehicles from workstation to workstation, Ford had overseen a years-long development of a motor-powered chain conveyor belt at his sixty-acre Highland Park plant that moved chassis and body assemblies ceaselessly from worker to worker as a synchronized system of tributary conveyors fed component parts and subassemblies into the flow, resulting in an uninterrupted stream of completed cars rolling off the end of the mile-and-a-half-long line at the rate of one every twenty-four seconds.

Launched in 1914, the so-called endless chain assembly line was a breathtaking technological breakthrough that gave the Ford Motor Company a huge advantage over its competitors. It cut the company's per-car production time by more than 90 percent, increased output tenfold, and made possible a price cut from $780 to $360. Henry Ford was so pleased with the achievement that he pledged to give everyone who purchased a Model T in 1915 a rebate if the company sold more than 300,000 cars. At year's end, 308,313 customers received rebate checks totaling $15 million. The following year, 1916, the Highland Park plant produced 734,800 cars.

Ford knew from the start that his employees would likely resent the new production process. Up to that point, cars had been built by teams of skilled workers and craftsmen, with each team responsible for at least whole sections or component systems, if not entire vehicles. But the endless chain concept, in which each line worker performed a single repetitive task, would not only end the "organic unity of labor," it would also put management in complete control of the pace of production, making workers, in effect, slaves to the relentless line.

So, in an effort to head off resistance from the factory floor, Ford announced that the company would begin paying workers $5.00 a day for an eight-hour shift. That amounted to more than double the standard industrial wage in America ($2.34 for a nine-hour shift) and equaled the weekly wage for a factory worker in England.

The new compensation policy and mass-production method—quickly dubbed "Fordism" by its critics—had an immediate and profound effect on the industry. To compete on price, other carmakers were compelled to adopt Ford's practices, at great cost. Some companies went out of business; some managed to survive only by merging with others. Pioneering automotive names such as Duryea, Chalmers, Biscoe, Maxwell, and Winton passed into history as the number of U.S. automakers dropped from over 300 to less than 100.

At the same time, masses of unskilled workers from all over the United States, particularly the rural South, streamed into Detroit, doubling the population to nearly one million between 1914 and 1919, making it the fastest-growing city in the country. Twenty thousand workers found employment at the Dodge plant in Hamtramck, four miles from Highland Park, after brothers John and Horace began making their own cars in 1914. Hailed by the *Michigan Manufacturer and Financial Record* as "the two best mechanics in Detroit," the Dodges adopted many of Ford's mass-production methods, but not the five-dollars-a-day pay policy, preferring a piece-rate system. They operated their factory in a somewhat more humane fashion than Ford's, however, running the assembly line at a slower pace. They also maintained a free clinic on the premises with a full-time medical staff on duty around the clock, and even provided workers with cold beer on hot summer days.

The Dodges chose not to compete with Ford on price. Their debut offering was an $800 five-passenger touring car that featured the first-ever all-steel body and quickly earned a reputation for durability, thanks to the U.S. Army. During an expedition against Mexican bandit Pancho Villa in 1916, three Dodge touring cars participated in America's first motorized military action when they carried a young army lieutenant named George S. Patton and fourteen other soldiers on a daring raid against a small contingent of Villa's forces in Chihuahua. The running gun battle resulted in the death of three of Villa's men, whose bodies Patton supposedly strapped to the hoods of the cars and drove back to the headquarters of his commander, Brigadier General John J. "Black Jack" Pershing. The general was so impressed with the vehicles' performance in battle that he subsequently requisitioned 250 of them for his staff officers to use on the battlefields in France during World War I, though he chose a Cadillac as his own official vehicle.

Weirdly, Villa died driving a Dodge seven years later when assassins riddled his roadster with bullets. The car survives to this day, bullet holes and all, on display at the Museo Histórico de la Revolución in Chihuahua.

The Dodge brothers became millionaires many times over and spent their *nouveau* riches as if trying to erase the memory of their boyhoods mired in barefoot poverty. Horace commissioned a 243-foot yacht, the largest private vessel on the Great Lakes; John built a $4 million Grosse Pointe mansion that boasted 110 rooms and 24 baths. They bought their way into Detroit high society by making large donations to the symphony orchestra and the state Republican Party, despite their hard-earned reputations for drunken, boorish behavior. John once forced a saloonkeeper to dance on the bar at the point of a pistol, smashing dozens of glasses against the mirror during the terrified man's performance. On another occasion, he and a companion attacked a prominent attorney who had two wooden legs, knocking him to the ground and kicking him viciously.

The Dodge brothers never came close to threatening Ford's preeminence. The Hamtramck plant produced 144,000 cars in 1920, the year both brothers contracted influenza while attending the National Auto Show in New York. John died a few days later at age fifty-five, but Horace remained chronically ill and despondent about his brother's death, until he died of cirrhosis of the liver eleven months later at age fifty-two.

In the face of fast-rising Fordism, the Packard Motor Company, too, chose not to compete head-on with Ford, but rather to stick with the artisanal style of production practiced in Europe, where motor cars still were made almost exclusively for the wealthy. At Packard's 3.5-million-square-foot plant on Detroit's East Grand Boulevard—considered one of the wonders of the industrial age when it opened in 1903—teams of skilled mechanics and craftsmen continued to assemble cars largely by hand, incorporating beautifully sculpted bodies from the most prestigious coach builders in the country and lustrously finishing them with ten to twenty coats of hand-applied paint in rich colors that helped make every Packard a memorable work of art.

With the introduction of its Twin Six (twelve-cylinder) model in 1915, Packard firmly established its reputation as Detroit's premier producer of luxury automobiles, ranking alongside Peerless Motors of Cleveland, Buffalo-based Pierce-Arrow, and Britain's Rolls-Royce. Priced between $2,750 and $5,000, the 400-horsepower Twin Six was hardly a car for the multitudes. The doomed Russian czar Nicholas II was among the worldwide upper-class clientele that snapped Twin Sixes up as fast as they came out of the factory. Which was not very fast. Even with eleven thousand workers, the Packard plant produced only thirty-five thousand Twin Sixes between 1916 and 1923. During the same period, Ford manufactured nearly seven million Model Ts.

Obviously, Henry Ford didn't lose any sleep over Packard or Dodge, or any of the other smaller manufacturers. While they were making thousands or tens of thousands of cars a year, he was thinking in terms of millions. The astonishing breadth and scope of his ambition could be seen in the new manufacturing facility he launched in 1920 on two thousand acres of bottomland at the confluence of the Rouge and Detroit Rivers in Dearborn. The Rouge River plant, or "the Rouge," as it came to be known, was the linchpin in Ford's plan to become totally self-sufficient in all aspects of carmaking. Toward that end, he acquired hundreds of thousands of acres of forests, iron mines, and limestone quarries in Michigan, Minnesota, and Wisconsin; coal mines in Kentucky, West Virginia, and Pennsylvania; and a rubber plant in Brazil. The company's own railroad and its fleet of Great Lakes freighters transported the natural resources to the Rouge, where 120 miles of conveyors fed it all into separate plants for making iron, glass, sheet metal, radiators, tires, transmissions, and engine blocks.

With 15 million square feet of floor space and more than eighty thousand employees, the Rouge's various plants eventually manufactured virtually every part that went into making the Model T, leading automotive historian David L. Lewis to call Ford's monster facility "easily the greatest industrial domain in the world, without parallel in sheer mechanical efficiency."

The massive industrial enterprise also produced one of the largest personal fortunes on earth. Henry Ford's approximately 55 percent share of the company's stock (the remainder was held by his wife, Clara, and son, Edsel) paid him annual dividends averaging $39 million, and his net worth was estimated at $1.2 billion. Not even John D. Rockefeller was richer.

By the early 1920s, the Ford Motor Company was approaching monopoly territory with an estimated 62 percent market share while its closest competitor, General Motors, held a mere 12 to 15 percent share. GM was the brainchild of William C. Durant, a charismatic businessman who turned to auto manufacturing in the early 1900s after building his Durant-Dort Carriage Company, based in Flint, Michigan, into the largest vehicle manufacturer in the United States. A multimillionaire at age forty, he was hailed as "the king of the carriage makers."

Billy Durant was no less ambitious than Henry Ford. He, too, was a proponent of mass manufacturing and a firm believer in controlling every aspect of the process through ownership of key suppliers. But unlike Ford, whose company was based on producing a single, unchanging vehicle at the lowest possible price to consumers, Durant envisioned a car company that offered an array of makes and models at various prices. Toward that end he'd cobbled together a collection of formerly independent companies, beginning by taking over Buick in 1904 and then adding Oldsmobile, Oakland, Cadillac, Chevrolet, and half a dozen others that would not survive (Marquette, Ewing, Welch, Rapid, Sheridan, and Scripps-Booth). The auto "divisions" operated autonomously within the GM corporate structure, with their presidents reporting directly to Durant.

Durant also acquired a dozen or so automotive parts and accessories companies. He bought the Hyatt Roller Bearing Company of Newark, New Jersey, for $13.5 million, mostly in the form of GM stock. As part of the deal, the firm's chief executive and principal owner, Alfred Sloan, joined GM as head of the United Motors Group (composed of parts and accessories subsidiaries) and member of the board of directors. Durant paid $8 million ($3 million of it in GM stock) for Dayton Engineering Laboratories Company (Delco) of Dayton, Ohio, the firm that produced the first electronic "self-starter" for Cadillac. Again, the deal included the exclusive services of the company's founder, Charles Kettering, who became the head of GM's research division.

In his biggest such deal, Durant paid $27 million for a 60 percent interest in Detroit-based Fisher Body Company, which had been providing about three hundred thousand bodies a year to GM and other major companies, including Ford. Founded by brothers Frederick and Charles Fisher, who were joined later by their younger siblings William, Lawrence, Edward, and Alfred, the company continued to operate independently but built bodies exclusively for GM. In 1926, GM paid $200 million for the remaining 40 percent of the company.

In assembling all the pieces of General Motors, Durant proved himself to be a daring and visionary entrepreneur. But he was a terrible administrator—impetuous, disorganized, unpredictable, and either unwilling or unable to delegate authority, attributes that led his two most experienced division heads, Cadillac founder and president Henry Leland and Buick president Walter Chrysler, to leave GM in a huff to start their own companies. Leland launched the Lincoln Motor Company and intended to compete with Cadillac in the luxury car market.

Durant was also an inveterate gambler whose reckless forays into the stock market ultimately led to his downfall and almost destroyed the company. When the U.S. economy experienced a short, sharp recession in 1920, a decline in car sales caused a precipitous drop in GM's stock price, from $420 a share to $20. In a desperate attempt to shore up the price, Durant secretly began buying up shares on 10 percent margin through friends and private syndicates, pledging his stock as collateral in loans to buy more, which was not illegal at the time. When the price continued to drop, he was undone. GM's bankers and board of directors stepped in and bailed out Durant and the company to prevent the total collapse of the stock. They stopped the price slide at $12, but Durant lost a personal fortune of $100 million and was forced to resign from the company he'd created and always referred to as "my baby."

For all its stock woes, GM was still the second-largest manu-facturer in the United States (behind Ford), worth $350 million, with eighty thousand employees spread across thirty-five cities and annual sales of nearly $600 million. And as car sales climbed back to record levels over the next two years, the company's new VP of operations, Alfred Sloan, developed a broad plan to bring order to the unruly behemoth that Billy Durant had built. The main problem, as Sloan saw it, was that the five automobile divisions operated *too* autonomously, with little regard for the best interest of the corporation as a whole. He cited as an example the "irrationality" of individual division heads setting price ranges that either overlapped or, in the case of Oldsmobile and Oakland, were virtually identical. Which meant the divisions were competing against one another for the same customer, an indication, Sloan said, that GM had "no clear-cut concept of the business."

By the time Sloan was named president in 1923, he had instituted an executive committee to rein in the division heads and had overhauled the pricing structure by segmenting the automobile market along socioeconomic lines, with each of GM's five divisions focused on a different segment. Chevrolet (with cars priced at $600–$795) was priced for the blue-collar workingman in need of basic transportation. Oakland, later named Pontiac ($900–$1,200), appealed to the middle-class merchant or manager able to spend a little more for a modicum of comfort and quality. Oldsmobile ($1,200–$1,700) aimed for the rising executive looking to show off his new status. Buick ($1,700–$2,500) targeted the well-to-do established professional, a doctor or lawyer. And Cadillac ($2,500–$5,000) spoke to the wealthy gentleman for whom quality was paramount and price of no importance. (Female drivers would not factor into the company's marketing plans for several more decades.)

In his 1924 annual report to shareholders, Sloan put forward the new price structure as an organizing principle that would guide the company into the future. "The ideal for which the corporation is striving is to have a car for every purse and purpose," he said.

The pricing revamp lessened competition among GM's divisions, but it didn't solve the problem of competing with Henry Ford, whose massive production capability and sales volume allowed him to produce a Model T profitably at a price several hundred dollars less than the cheapest Chevrolet. Indeed, Ford appeared to be "unbeatable by any ordinary means," Sloan admitted later in his memoir. "No conceivable amount of capital short of the United States Treasury could have sustained the losses required to take away volume from him at his own game." Still, Sloan thought he saw a chink in Ford's armor.

As the world's preeminent industrialist, Ford remained defiantly committed to his original business model of building a simple, durable, and economical car with no extras, no trimmings, no color even, only black, because black paint was the cheapest and dried the fastest. But in an industry that was evolving rapidly, his stubborn resistance to change was beginning to put his company at a disadvantage. Cadillac had introduced Charles Kettering's revolutionary electronic starter in 1912, but Ford did not make it available on the Model T until 1920, and then only as an option. GM began offering its customers financing through its General Motors Acceptance Company (GMAC) in 1916, and within five years was financing two-thirds of the cars it sold. But Ford refused to get into so-called captive financing for more than a decade because he thought buying a car on time was foolish. "It always seemed to me that putting off the day of payment for anything but permanent improvements was a fundamental mistake," he explained. In 1924, Kettering's GM research department and DuPont Laboratories introduced a breakthrough in automobile paint called Duco, a lacquer that held more pigment than traditional varnish and enamel paints, dried much faster, didn't fade in sunlight, and allowed for the economical application of a wide variety of deep, rich colors. Most of the auto industry quickly adopted Duco, but not Ford, who stood pat with his basic black enamel.

Ford's intractability blinded him to some fundamental changes that were occurring in the industry. Thanks in large part to the success of his Model T, the market was approaching the point where every American who could afford a car already had one, and new car sales were beginning to level off. "The growth in the motor vehicle market depends on the ability of the lower income brackets to purchase used cars, not necessarily new ones," said the National Automobile Chamber of Commerce.

As Alfred Sloan later wrote in his memoir, "When first-car buyers returned to the market for the second round, with the old cars as a first payment on the new car, they were selling basic transportation and demanding something more than that in the new car. Middle-income buyers, assisted by a trade-in and installment financing, created the demand, not for basic transportation, but for progress in new cars, for comfort, convenience, power and style. This was the actual trend of American life."

And the trend did not favor Ford's static business model. Sloan put it concisely: "Mr. Ford's concept of the American car market did not adequately fit the realities after 1923."

Sloan and his GM executive committee began discussing the idea of competing with Ford's unchanging product by putting out a constantly changing product. They knew that consumers were replacing their cars, on average, once every seven years.

What would make them do it more often, say, every five years? Or three?

The most obvious answer was better-looking, more stylish cars. The typical mass-produced auto of the time was—again, thanks to Ford's Model T—a nondescript, somber, clunky-looking contraption with all the sex appeal of a bank clerk in a cheap, ill-fitting suit. It wouldn't be hard to produce a more attractive vehicle than that. Packard and Pierce-Arrow were doing it all day long. The real difficulty, the GM executives knew, lay in doing it on a grand scale at a reasonable cost. How could they make a Chevrolet with the sleek hand-finished look of a Packard but without the high price tag? And then, how could they change the look every couple of years or so without bringing the factories to a halt for retooling?

In one such discussion, Lawrence Fisher, who had just been named to the executive committee as president of the Cadillac division, talked about his recent visit to California to meet with the state's largest Cadillac dealer. While in Los Angeles, he'd met a young car designer who was "doing amazing things" making custom car bodies for movie stars.

"I think we should talk to him about coming to work for us," he told Sloan.

4
THE
CADILLAC
KID

Harley Earl's name may not have meant much to the president of General Motors, but he was something of a celebrity on the West Coast—the boy wonder of the California car business. The *Los Angeles Times* had trumpeted his professional debut at the 1919 Los Angeles Auto Show: "Perhaps the most startling local models at the show are those built by the Earl Auto Works, whose sensational Chandler and Marmon are attracting huge crowds. These cars are designed by Harley J. Earl, a local man who only three or four years ago was broad jumping for the University of Southern California and who has sprung into prominence as a maker of motor fashions almost over night."

Both cars had been built for wealthy clients, according to the *Times* article, which couldn't have been more celebratory if it had been a paid advertisement:

The gray Marmon four passenger sport model, sold to a New York banker for $7,000, is something of a tribute to local builders, the said banker preferring to go to the expense of having the car built out here then shipped East because he liked the way they build their automobiles on the Coast. The Chandler town car, in blue, is the classiest thing of its kind ever shown on the Coast or any place else. It is surely distinctive, being a low slung creation; so low that a good sized man can stand alongside and look right over the top, yet there is sufficient room inside to keep one from being cramped. Earl claims there is six inches of clearance between his head and the top when sitting down, and Mr. Earl is a young man of considerable altitude.

He was also a young man with considerable social connections, notably his former Stanford classmate Norman Chandler (no relation to the car), whose father, Harry Chandler, owned the *Los Angeles Times*. The newspaper became an unabashed booster of Harley's career, following up a few months later with a similarly gushy report that Harley had designed a new automobile that "seems to surpass even the wonderful creations of the recent automobile show." This one was for E. L. Doheny Jr., the local heir to an immense oil fortune. A satin-finished gray four-passenger body mounted on a Pierce-Arrow chassis, the car boasted English wire wheels and side-mounted coach lamps "by the Tiffany Company of New York" that added a "very foreign touch," according to the newspaper, which pronounced the vehicle "pretty nearly the classiest creation of the year."

Doheny was so happy with what Harley created that he posed for a publicity photo seated behind the wheel with his smiling designer sitting next to him. The *Times* published the picture with the caption, "If you wouldn't like to own this car, you can't be satisfied." (A decade later, Doheny and his personal assistant were found shot to death in Greystone, his fifty-five-room Beverly Hills mansion, a crime that remains one of Los Angeles's great unsolved mysteries.)

The fact that J. W. Earl wasn't mentioned in either of the *Times* articles spoke to the changes that had occurred in the Earl family and business since Harley dropped out of Stanford after his mother's death.

J.W.'s remarriage in 1916 created a fissure in the family that grew worse when his new wife, Nellie, gave birth to a son, Henry, a year later. Fair or not, the older Earl offspring saw their stepmother as a controlling, hypercritical harpy who had bewitched their fifty-one-year-old father and aggressively favored her own child. Billy bore the brunt of her opprobrium, though his sister, Jessie, did her best to shield him. The three older boys— Harley, Carl, and Arthur—were less affected by the new family tensions because they were now grown men and no longer lived in the big house on Hollywood Boulevard. Harley moved out not long after J.W. and Nellie's wedding and married Sue Carpenter, a stunning blonde who had graduated from Hollywood High School several years behind him and then attended USC.

Harley, Carl, and Art continued to work with their father at Earl Automobile Works, with Harley operating as second in command. "Those were the days when Santa Barbara and Pasadena were great winter resorts," Harley recalled nearly four decades later. "Well-to-do people would come from all over the country and a lot of them drove foreign cars. They began to bring them to me when they'd develop trouble and I'd patch them up. But first I crawled all over them and took down every dimension. I was thinking of what I'd like to build for myself. Before long, I began to get a good idea of what it took to make a good-looking car that was also comfortable."

He also developed a process for making factory-built cars look custom-made by repainting them more interesting colors and adding wire wheels, nickel-plated radiator shells, side-mounted extra tires, and trunk racks. He called it "dolling them up."

In 1918, J.W. became ill and was unable to work for six months. While he was away, Harley took over the shop and transformed it. "When my dad came back, we must have had half a million dollars' worth of special bodies in our place," he recalled. J.W. was "fairly irate" when he found that Harley had turned his business into "a glorified hotrod shop," according to the *Detroit Free Press*.

A few doors down the street from the Automobile Works on the stretch of South Main Street that had become known as "Auto Row," Cadillac dealer Don Lee had been paying close attention to the goings-on at his neighbor's shop. Lee was GM's exclusive Cadillac distributor in the state of California, with dealerships in San Francisco, Sacramento, Oakland, Pasadena, and Fresno in addition to Los Angeles. As such, he had a clear-eyed view of the luxury car market.

Cadillac had earned a reputation under its founder, Henry Leland, for unsurpassed engineering and outstanding styling and comfort. But Lee was keenly aware that many wealthy car enthusiasts viewed GM's luxury offering as a poorer man's Packard or Pierce-Arrow, a step or two down from the hand-finished excellence of those competitors. And now superwealthy buyers like E. L. Doheny Jr. were looking for something even more eye-popping than a Packard. They'd order a Cadillac chassis from Lee, have it delivered to Earl Automobile Works, and then pay two or three times the price of a Cadillac to have Harley create a one-of-a-kind body that was guaranteed to elicit "oohs" of appreciation on the street.

Two months after the Doheny photo in the *Times*, Lee made a bid to buy the Automobile Works. The terms of his offer remain unknown, except that it was contingent upon Harley's remaining in place as chief designer. J.W. accepted the deal at a price that allowed him to retire comfortably at the age of fifty-three. "Dad felt he was too old to start a new activity," Harley explained. Earl Automobile Works became Don Lee Coach and Body Works with the mere hoisting of a new sign on the building. The only other change was the foreword to the shop's sales brochure. "Gone are those picturesque days of the gilded coach, the dappled grays and the silver mounted harness," it now read. "Gone, too, are the top-hatted coachman, the old family victoria and the high-backed carriage."

Gone as well was J.W.'s old-fashioned "Earl Guarantee of Satisfaction," replaced by his son's more contemporary assurance that Don Lee designers stood ready "to express your tastes and ideas so that your coach may be an expression of your own individuality."

No one in 1920s America expressed their individuality more extravagantly than Hollywood's silent film stars. Show-offs by nature and flush with more money than they'd ever imagined making, they flocked to Don Lee, where they formed a sort of salon of exotic-car lovers with Harley as their host—charming and larger than life, an artist at home in the world of welders and mechanics.

"They'd come in with a Rolls Royce or a Bentley and say, 'I want a sports car made,'" Harley told the *Detroit Free Press*. "I'd take them through my plant, get an idea what they wanted and then do a sketch."

One of his earliest celebrity patrons, Mary Pickford, asked him to design a roadster body on a Cadillac chassis for her growing collection of expensive cars. It seems that under all the curls and lace, "America's Sweetheart" was a car fanatic, a habitué of racetracks and auto shows who became a familiar sight bombing around Los Angeles in a flashy cream-colored Maxwell roadster she named Fifi.

Pickford's husband, Douglas Fairbanks, her sister, Lottie, and their ne'er-do-well stuntman-actor-producer brother, Jack, became Harley's customers, as did her good friend Mabel Normand. Hailed as "the queen of comedy" for her appearances in numerous Keystone Cops movies, Normand wrote, codirected, and starred in a car-racing movie called *Mabel at the Wheel*, in which she did her own driving while being filmed by a camera she mounted on the front of the car. Off screen, she was a self-proclaimed speed demon who owned both a Stutz Bearcat and a Mercer Raceabout similar to the one Harley had driven to win that 100-mile race his father only found out about after the fact, except that Normand's Mercer was fitted with a dressing table and makeup mirror that folded into the driver-side door.

Cowboy star Tom Mix had an income of $17,500 a week and a reputation for profligacy that put his peers to shame. The former ranch hand rarely ventured into public view without donning his signature high-peaked white felt Stetson and full cowboy regalia, and he wanted a car that lived up to his image. So he asked Harley to rustle him up a white roadster with a silver-studded western saddle designed into the hood. None would call it classy, but the car served Mix's purpose. "They use them for publicity, you know," Harley once said in an attempt to explain his famous customers' idiosyncratic styling choices. (Twenty years later, Mix was at the wheel of his prized yellow Cord convertible when it ran off the road and flipped over on a stretch of Arizona highway. A suitcase filled with cash and jewelry dislodged from the backseat and struck him in the head. He reportedly climbed from the wreckage, took two steps, and dropped dead from a broken neck.)

Publicity cut both ways, of course. Comedian Roscoe "Fatty" Arbuckle, whose million-dollar-a-year studio contract made him the highest-paid performer in Hollywood, ordered three cars from Harley, including a Pierce-Arrow-based seven-passenger touring car with a frame cast in bronze, an iridescent blue-purple paint job, and white tires that measured four feet in diameter. Like its owner, the car was outsized—seven feet high, with a 168-inch wheelbase and an 825-cubic-inch engine. The gray leather interior had inlaid mahogany cabinetry and a secret compartment under the rear footrest for hiding now federally prohibited alcohol. But it did not contain, as was rumored at the time, a bathroom.

The Arbuckle Pierce-Arrow took nearly a year to complete—six weeks just for the twenty-one coats of paint—but it quickly became the most talked-about car in Hollywood, if not America, and Harley made sure the name of its designer appeared in the captions of newspaper photographs. "I guess altogether Arbuckle must have sold 100 cars for me," he recalled later. (Arbuckle had to sell the car to help pay his legal bills when he was charged with manslaughter in the death of actress Virginia Rappe, who died of a ruptured bladder following a wild party in his San Francisco hotel suite. After three sensational trials, the comedian was acquitted in April 1922, but the scandal killed his career.)

Actresses Pauline Frederick, Ann May, Blanche Sweet, Viola Dana, and Mary Miles Minter soon joined Harley's client roster, as did Wallace Reid, the silent screen's reigning heart-throb. A onetime writer for *Motor* magazine and an aspiring race driver, Reid starred in four car-racing movies between 1919 and 1921—*The Roaring Road, Double Speed, Excuse My Dust*, and *Too Much Speed*. He owned a series of high-powered, high-priced cars, including several Marmons, a Duesenberg, two McFarlans (known as "the American Rolls-Royce"), and a sleek Stutz that sported a robin's egg blue paint job and a horn that sounded out "Yankee Doodle."

Reid had a reputation for reckless driving. After a night of drinking in 1915, he totaled his Marmon when he crashed into a car carrying a family of five on the Pacific Coast Highway, killing the father and seriously injuring the mother and one child. His passenger, movie producer and director Thomas Ince, sustained a broken collarbone and internal injuries. Suffering only minor injuries, Reid was jailed and charged with manslaughter, but D. W. Griffith bailed him out and a grand jury ultimately failed to indict him. Eight years later, at the age of thirty-one, Reid died from the effects of alcohol and morphine addiction.

All in all, they were a young and fast crowd that brought a lot of excitement and attention to Harley's business. But his most valued celebrity patron continued to be his old friend and show business mentor, Cecil B. DeMille, for whom he designed a body for a Locomobile chassis the director had purchased for $12,500. Favored by East Coast aristocracy, Locomobiles were considered the best-built cars in America, each one made to order by a team of six highly trained mechanics that went through the company's factory in Bridgeport, Connecticut, selected the needed parts, and then assembled it by hand. DeMille's chassis originally was intended for a Locomobile the U.S. Army ordered for General Pershing to drive in France, but World War I ended before the chassis and body were joined. Although DeMille famously maintained a fleet of vehicles, he made sure everyone in

Hollywood knew the Earl-designed Locomobile was his favorite, proudly driving it along Sunset Boulevard every day on his way to and from the studio.

In the first year of running his own operation at Don Lee, Harley oversaw the design of three hundred car bodies. His reputation spread beyond California as the dealership began exhibiting his works at auto shows around the country, where the cars were noted for their "raked" windshields, side-mounted extra wheels, and bright two- and three-tone paint jobs. His designs "rarely showed reserve or restraint," according to automotive historian Michael Lamm. "What they did show was a certain sporting flair and a lot of good-humored self-confidence which was a fairly accurate mirror of the designer himself."

Life was good for Harley and his wife, Sue. They were building a country English-style house on a hilltop lot they bought from DeMille, whose gated mansion was a few hundred yards down the street. They became members of the Los Angeles Country Club, where Harley played golf several times a week, for pleasure and business. In the winter of 1922, he got a phone call from Andy Baldwin, a fellow club member who had been a classmate of his at Stanford.

"Could you have lunch and play golf at the club the day after tomorrow?" Baldwin asked. "I have a competitor of yours coming out from the East."

"Fine. Who is it?" Harley asked.

"You'll see," Baldwin replied.

Baldwin introduced him to his mystery guest at the clubhouse two days later. It was Fred Fisher. "Well, I liked to fell over," Harley recalled. "Competitor! I had this little hole-in-the-wall with about 400–500 men and he was, of course, the head of the fabulous Fisher brothers."

Fred and his brothers had turned a $30,000 loan from their uncle into the world's most successful coach-building company, with more than sixty plants now producing nearly half a million car bodies a year for General Motors. He and Harley played golf together several times a week for the duration of Fred's five-week winter vacation, and continued the practice every year for the next three years.

Harley and Sue completed their house and bought the lot next door for her parents to build a home. Sue gave birth to their first child, a boy they named William Orville after Harley's little brother. And business continued to boom, as the dutiful *Los Angeles Times* reported: "Manager Harley Earl of the Don Lee Coach and Body Works has increased his force in the paint and top departments and is now in a position to handle sixty per cent more business."

In the summer of 1925, Don Lee placed an order with the Cadillac factory in Detroit for 100 chassis. The plan was to use them with a series of five-passenger sedan bodies that Harley would design. But the unusually large order attracted the attention of Cadillac's new president, Lawrence P. Fisher, who decided that before he shipped that many chassis to the West Coast he wanted to go out there and see what was going on.

The Fishers were a tight-knit band—fiercely loyal to one another and devoted to their widowed mother, sober, conservative, fervently Catholic, and faithfully married. Except for Larry. The fourth-oldest, he was the gregarious fun-loving Fisher, a committed bachelor known for his sartorial flamboyance (compared to his dark-suited, homburg-wearing brothers at least), his raucous nights on the town, and his lavish, sometimes days-long parties at his 22,000-square-foot waterfront mansion, Grayhaven, which had a boathouse big enough to entirely enclose his 110-foot yacht. He was, in modern parlance, a player. As an unidentified Fisher family friend told Michael Lamm, "He once chartered a couple of private railway cars, loaded them with champagne and broads and went off to Chicago for a big hairy weekend. That's the kind of guy he was."

At the same time, Larry was perhaps the brightest and most capable of the brothers. As head of the Cadillac division, Fisher faced a pressing problem in 1925: Packard had just blown by Cadillac to become the bestselling luxury car in America. He believed the reason was styling. Why else would Packard, with no better engineering and a much higher price, be outselling his brand by a margin of two to one? He shared Alfred Sloan's opinion that under the aegis of Fisher Body, GM cars had become stodgy-looking, unimaginative, and boring.

Fisher's trip to California that December turned out to be one he would never forget. For starters, Don Lee and Harley Earl set up a series of social events and parties in his honor that featured an ample supply of bootleg booze and beautiful starlets. At one such soiree, Harley and Fisher were drinking and talking about automobile styling when Harley supposedly boasted, "I can make a car for you, like your Chevrolet, look like a Cadillac."

That wasn't exactly the solution to Fisher's problem; he needed a Cadillac that looked like a Packard. But he liked Harley's cocksureness. "If you can do that," he replied, "you've got yourself a job."

A subsequent visit to Don Lee Coach and Body Works convinced Fisher that Harley could indeed do what needed to be done. He was particularly impressed with Harley's use of modeling clay to build full-scale models of cars that were painted and trimmed in such detail they looked as if you could open the door, climb in, and drive off. In all his years in coach building, Fisher had never seen anything like them.

Fisher came back from California with a glowing report on Harley's operation. In addition to the clay modeling, "Mr. Fisher saw Mr. Earl lengthen a wheelbase by cutting the frame and inserting an extra piece," Alfred Sloan recalled in his memoir. "The result was a long, low custom body that pleased many famous screen personalities.

"Also [Mr. Earl] was designing the complete automobile, shaping the body, hood, fenders, headlights, and running boards and blending them together into a good looking whole. This, too, was a novel technique."

GM's Cadillac division was on track to introduce a new car in 1927, the LaSalle, named after the French explorer René-Robert Cavelier, Sieur de La Salle. The car was envisioned as a smaller, lighter Cadillac that would appeal to a younger buyer. Powered by a 75-horsepower, 303-cubic-inch V-8 engine, the "blood brother to the Cadillac" would be priced between $2,500 and $2,700, which placed it strategically between the lowest-priced Cadillac and the highest-priced Buick, where it was expected to compete directly with the Packard Six. The only thing that hadn't been settled on was the body. As Sloan described it, "The idea was to approach the design with a new concept in mind: that of unifying the various parts of the car from the standpoint of appearance, of rounding off sharp corners and lowering the silhouette. We wanted a production automobile that was as beautiful as the custom cars of the period." But GM's in-house body men had fallen short.

"Up until this time, Fisher Body Division had been the absolute dictators of body design and zealously guarded their prerogative," recalled Ernest Seaholm, Cadillac's chief engineer from 1921 to 1943. "Theirs was a simple approach—a full-size line drawing on a blackboard, take it or leave it."

For the first time, Alfred Sloan and Larry Fisher chose to leave it. With Sloan's approval, Fisher called Harley in Los Angeles just before Christmas and asked whether he'd like to try his hand at designing the new line of cars. Fisher had already taken the liberty of calling Don Lee and arranging for Harley to take a three-month leave of absence from his duties at Lee's Coach and Body Works.

On January 6, 1926, Harley boarded a train for his first trip to the car capital. When he arrived, he was taken to a body shop in the back of the Cadillac factory on Clark Avenue and introduced to the team of men Fisher had assigned to help him—two Cadillac "body engineers" and a master woodworker and clay modeler. Ninety days was not much time to design a new line of cars, so Harley turned for inspiration to a Spanish-French luxury car that cost six times what GM planned to charge for the LaSalle.

"The Hispano-Suiza was the apple of my eye," he told the *Detroit Free Press* later. "All the chic people who appreciated cars drove Hispanos." He borrowed heavily from the car's design, particularly the front end with its distinctive radiator and winged hood ornament, admitting, "I stole a lot of stuff. You could tell I was looking at a Hispano."

Working from sketches, he came up with a single design for four different body types—a roadster with a rumble seat, a convertible coupe, an open touring car, and a sedan—and built a full-size clay model of each, forgoing his signature bright colors in favor of basic black.

On the day of the unveiling, Fred and Larry Fisher came to the Cadillac plant to look at the models first. They returned later with Alfred Sloan, who had come from GM's New York headquarters, where he spent most of his time, and other members of the GM executive committee, including Charles Kettering. Harley stood off to the side and watched nervously while the group examined the work and talked in low tones. As he recalled the scene, "They walked around and around the models and finally Mr. Sloan said to the Fishers, 'Get Earl over here so everyone can meet him.' Then he said, 'Earl, I thought you'd like to know that your design has been accepted.'

"I was just like a quarterback who has just thrown a pass for a touchdown. It gives you a sense of confidence you've never had before. Mr. Sloan said, 'Larry, I think we should send Mr. Earl to the Paris Auto Show.' Fisher replied, 'Mr. Sloan, I already have his ticket.'"

Sloan sailed to Europe with Earl, and by the time they got to Paris the two men had bonded, which was surprising given that they seemed to have so little in common. Having attended prep school at Brooklyn Polytechnic Institute and graduated Phi Beta Kappa from the Massachusetts Institute of Technology in only three years, Sloan was the quintessential nerd, a "prissy" kid who grew into a prissy adult, in the words of one biographer. The *New York Times* described him as "a functional, frill-less man" who rarely drank, seldom socialized, never played golf or engaged in any sports because he thought they were "a waste of a man's time," and often ate lunch alone in his office, consuming "a homemade sandwich, which he had brought with him, neatly wrapped in paper, in his coat pocket." He was cautious, solemn, and reserved to the point that his GM colleagues nicknamed him "Silent Sloan," and the closest he ever came to swearing was occasionally blurting out the euphemism "horse apples." He had a genius for organization but nary an artistic bone in his body. No one ever called him a showman.

Sloan did have one thing in common with Harley, however. He, too, was a dandy, though his sartorial style was as different from Harley's as the East Coast was from the West. The *New York Times* noted that Sloan's daily business attire consisted of "a dark, double-breasted suit, a high starch collar, conservative tie fixed with a pearl stickpin, a handkerchief cascading out of his breast pocket, and spats."

After Paris, Harley returned to Los Angeles and resumed his duties at Don Lee Coach and Body while GM began the tooling, manufacturing, and assembly processes that would turn his clay models into the real thing. A month later, in May 1926, he was out on the golf course when he was told there was a phone call for him in the clubhouse, from a Mr. Sloan in New York.

Sloan had Fred and Larry Fisher in his office and they wanted to know if Harley would be interested in consulting on the design for the 1928 Cadillac and maybe even GM's other divisions. If so, they'd like him to come to New York for discussions at his earliest convenience. Earl was on the train the next day. Four days later in Sloan's office, Sloan and the two Fishers broached the idea of establishing a corporate styling department at GM, with him in charge. What did he think of that? "I think it's a great idea," Harley replied. "Then we'll do it," Sloan said.

Despite the understanding that Harley would be joining the GM organization, they initially played it publicly as another temporary consulting assignment with Cadillac. Back in Los Angeles, Harley asked for and was granted a six-month leave of absence from Don Lee Coach and Body Works, and the company clearly expected him to return at the end of that time. He would be gone at least until November, reported the *Los Angeles Times*, which couldn't resist engaging in a little local booster- ism. "Earl will not admit that Detroit can equal Los Angeles as a place to live, but he does admit that his work at the Cadillac factory . . . is interesting in the extreme," the newspaper reported, adding, "But they are betting at Don Lee's that he will head back for Los Angeles when snow begins to fly in Detroit streets."

Harley had no intention of ever going back to his "little hole-in-the-wall." In June, he boarded the California Limited with Sue and Billy. They posed for a family picture on the train's rear platform, waving goodbye to Los Angeles. It had been nearly three-quarters of a century since his Detroit-born grandmother, Mary Hazard Taft, crossed the country in a covered wagon, a difficult, dangerous journey that took eighteen months. The Earl family made the trip back in three days, in the comfort and security of a Pullman sleeper and club car. When they arrived at Detroit's Michigan Central Station, they were driven directly to their new home—Larry Fisher's luxurious penthouse suite at the Whittier Hotel, overlooking the Detroit River and Canada beyond.

Harley spent the next six months in the relative seclusion of the Cadillac experimental body department on Clark Avenue, several miles from GM headquarters, working with Cadillac's executives and body engineers on the design of the 1928 models. "When we got to Detroit, [Larry] Fisher told them, 'Write it all down for him, every detail, and tell him to interpret what we say,'" Harley recalled. "That was rather like saying to an architect, 'Here, fellow, you've just fallen into some money. Start building your dream.'"

It was too late in the process for Harley to have any real impact on the body design for the 1927 Cadillac models, which were set to debut at the New York Auto Show in January. But Fisher showed him the sketches anyway and asked, "What can we do with these cars?" Harley responded, "Let's paint them up so they look like something. Put a lot of color and some wire wheels on them and doll them up."

Cadillac had never offered customers more than three color choices, but in October 1926 the company announced that its '27 models would be available in five hundred different color and upholstery combinations. The Don Lee dealership even mounted a weeklong exhibition of brightly colored two-tone models to illustrate the possibilities. The show's highlight, a cream-colored Cadillac roadster with khaki fenders and orange wheels, had Harley's fingerprints all over it.

The LaSalle was supposed to be introduced in January 1927 at the New York Auto Show, the industry's traditional venue for unveiling new models. But because of the late start with the body design, the car wasn't ready and the debut had to be pushed back to the Boston Auto Show at the Copley Plaza Hotel several weeks later. Boston didn't pack the promotional punch of New York, however, as demonstrated by a photo session the company set up on the street in front of the hotel. Ten Cadillac managers and executives were gathered to pose with a beautiful new roadster. Harley was among the group, standing in back and a head taller than the rest. The show was to mark his debut, too, as the company was finally letting it be known that he had been named to head a new design department at the corporation. Several uniformed police officers were hired to hold back the crowd that was expected to gather at the sight of the new car parked at the curb. But no crowd showed up; passersby did not stop to get a closer look. "Knowing Harley, I doubt if he ever again went to Boston," cracked chief engineer Ernest Seaholm, who was seated behind the wheel in some of the photographs.

Despite the cool reception it received in Boston, the LaSalle was everything Alfred Sloan and Larry Fisher had hoped it would be, "longer and lower than other production cars, with sweeping fenders, elongated windows and a novel molding accentuating its horizontal lines," as described by automotive historian David Gartman. "Like the handcrafted luxury classics, Earl's design rounded off all sharp corners, thus replacing the mechanical look of rectilinear lines with the organic appearance of curvilinearity. The whole package, down to the last detail, blended into one harmonious, unified whole that contrasted sharply with the fragmented, assembled look of most production cars."

The LaSalle drew raves from the automotive press when it officially hit the market on March 5, 1927, with one reporter saying it was "about the most beautiful line of cars" he had ever seen. Newspaper articles reported the LaSalle already had placed second in an unnamed "international contest for efficiency and beauty" in Berlin, and that its young designer had "spent the greater part of two years in the study of body design in the United States and in Europe in preparation for the task." Nowhere was the press coverage more positive than in Los Angeles, where the *Times* published an article that opened with this sentence: "Happy as a boy who succeeded in scoring a touchdown for his alma mater, elated over the success that has attended his effort and the reception given his brainchild throughout the world, Harley Earl, the man who designed the new LaSalle, companion to the Cadillac, is back in town for six weeks' well earned vacation and rest."

The article went on to report that Harley had received a "tremendous ovation" at a meeting with Southern California Cadillac and LaSalle dealers. "We designed and planned the LaSalle for the coming generation," he was quoted as saying. Never mind that the car was the spitting image of a Hispano-Suiza.

"We dreamed of it as a fine, flexible American car—distinctly American in its lines, appearance and atmosphere," he supposedly told the dealers. "The public has received it as no new car has ever been received. Drive by the homes of the genuinely elite anywhere in America and you will see these cars displayed before the homes or on the driveways of the best people." The quotes sounded as if someone in the GM publicity department had written them.

Again, the newspaper's editors attempted to put a West Coast spin on the story, ending the article with the manager of the Don Lee dealership saying, "Harley Earl's success in creating the LaSalle and in being chosen to head the designing division of General Motors is just another tribute to California, which is being called upon more and more every day to furnish new talent for the automobile manufacturing organizations back East."

In truth, Harley's new job with GM meant the end for Don Lee Coach and Body Works, which soon would fold without him. It also meant the end of an era for Harley and Sue. As they made the rounds visiting old friends and family on their extended vacation, they were confronted with the reality that they really were saying goodbye to the town where they had been born and raised.

So much had changed. The big house where Harley and his siblings grew up was gone, the victim of a pro-business ordinance passed in 1920 that decreed all residential housing had to be removed from Hollywood Boulevard by March 1, 1925. Mary Hazard Taft, a spry eighty-six years old and twenty years a widow, still occupied the Taft family's original Hollywood homestead just off the now paved boulevard, but J.W. and his wife, Nellie, had moved several miles south to a modest Spanish-style house where they lived with their two children, Henry and

Janelle, Harley's little brother Billy, and his sister, Jessie, who was soon to marry a doctor. Harley and Sue had sold their house down the street from the DeMille mansion to heavyweight boxing champ Jack Dempsey and his actress wife, Estelle Taylor, closing the deal shortly after Sue's parents moved into their new home next door.

The leave-taking surely was harder on Sue than Harley. He was riding a cresting wave of public recognition and looking forward to the challenge and excitement of a job that was a dream come true. Knowing her husband's penchant for working long hours, Sue faced the prospect of raising Billy basically on her own, with no grandparents or other relatives around to help, in a strange, cold industrial city half a continent away from everything she knew.

There is an Earl family photograph that captures the moment. Taken in front of Sue's parents' house during the second week of May 1927, it shows Sue sitting behind the wheel of a new LaSalle roadster with Billy, a towheaded two-year-old wearing a newsboy cap, standing on the seat next to her. Neither of them is smiling.

A few days after the photo was taken, Billy was admitted to the hospital to have his tonsils taken out. In a scene frighteningly reminiscent of what happened to Harley's mother, Abbie, the procedure somehow went awry, and the little boy stopped breathing and died on the operating table.

5
BATTLEGROUND
DETROIT

arley reported to his new job in Detroit on June 14, 1927, barely two weeks after Billy died. He could have pushed back his start date; given the enormity of the tragedy, Alfred Sloan surely would not have objected. But Harley needed to work, to lose himself in a swirl of shop activity, with customers calling and creative decisions crowding all other thoughts from his head.

His son's death had shaken him to his core, but it seemed to have broken Sue, who was so flattened by grief he feared he might lose her as well. She didn't want to return to Detroit; she hated being separated from her parents and, more achingly, from Billy. She insisted that he be buried in the Carpenter family plot at Forest Lawn cemetery in Glendale rather than Rosedale Cemetery in Los Angeles where Harley's mother, Abbie, and other members of the Earl clan were buried. If she was going to have to leave her little boy behind, then she wanted him to be with her family.

Harley's first week at work didn't go the way he had imagined. His new office turned out to be a cramped space on the tenth floor of GM's headquarters on Grand Boulevard. He had no secretary, no staff, and no studio. For the first two days, he didn't receive a single visitor or phone call: not a word from Sloan, who was in GM's New York office; nothing from Larry Fisher, who worked at the Fisher Body plant on Piquette Street several miles away.

Finally, after three days, William Fisher, the general manager of the Fisher Body division, poked his head in the door and asked, "How are you getting along?" Not very well, Harley admitted. He had only a rudimentary understanding of the company's organizational structure. He was supposed to begin building a staff from scratch, but "I don't know a soul in the building," he said. "I don't know who to call."

Fisher offered one of his own people. "I have a man working for me that goes between plants," he said. "He's been doing it for a couple of years, and he's a very smart young fellow and knows everybody at the divisions and in our plants and subsidiaries. He knows where to find everybody."

He would send the man to him with a sealed letter, Fisher said. "You tear it open and read it and ask him some questions. And if you like him, just write 'yes' on the paper, seal it, and [send] it back up, and I'll take care of it."

Three days later, Howard O'Leary became Harley's administrative assistant, a position he would hold for the next twenty-seven years. A few days after that, on June 23, the GM board of directors officially approved Sloan's recommendation for the creation of a new fifty-person department under Harley's direction.

Sloan's grand plan was for Harley to gradually assume overall design responsibility for every model manufactured by the five divisions and to develop an organizational process that would facilitate frequent styling changes. The GM president believed the company's future depended on its ability to deliver a new look for each of its lines every year, thereby enticing people to trade in last year's model for this year's new-and-improved version.

Most of GM's divisional managers and engineers were cool to the idea of annual models, however. They didn't mind styling changes, so long as they were incremental and not mandated by any fixed schedule, and if styling decisions didn't dictate to the engineering imperative. The introduction of new models had always been attendant to a mechanical advancement—a bigger engine, better brakes, smoother transmission, improved accelerator, or whatever else Boss Ket's boys came up with. Any changes in outward appearance were considered incidental, a nice bit of wrapping. What Sloan had in mind was a radical departure, tantamount to putting the cart before the horse.

Anticipating pushback from the divisions, he soft-pedaled Harley's mission at the outset, telling the executive committee and board of directors vaguely that the styling staff would "study the question of art and color combination in General Motors products." He named the new department the Art and Colour Section, choosing the British spelling to make it sound more important.

"I personally thought it was a sissy name," Harley groused to a reporter years later. "I could just see the fellows [at Don Lee] back in California when I told them I was working with 'Art and Colour.' They would have all taken out their handkerchiefs and started waving."

Sloan set up Art and Colour as part of the GM corporate staff, with Harley reporting directly to him. "I think you had better work just for me for a while until I see how they take you," he said. He empowered Harley only to advise Fisher Body and the auto divisions on matters of design, but gave him no instructions on how to proceed. Nor did he tell the division managers that they had to consult with the new department, though he encouraged them to do so. It was up to them to avail themselves of Harley's expertise, or not.

"Mr. Sloan never gave orders that you had to do anything," Harley explained to writer Stanley Brams. "That was his way of operating. And he made it very clear to me that he would give me a good recommendation, but from there on I was on my own."

Sloan gave him one directive at the outset—design cars that will sell.

Despite all the praise for his work on the LaSalle, Harley wasn't sure he was up to the job. He worried that what had worked so well for him on Sunset Boulevard might not play on Main Street. "I didn't know how to build anything except what pleased me," he recalled in a 1969 interview, "and I didn't know if what I liked would appeal to the public."

Sloan, however, remained confident that his new director of Art and Colour had the creative chops and the charisma needed to bring GM's engineering culture around to the idea that, as the automobile business entered its fourth decade, looks were as important to the average buyer as mechanics and price, if not more.

Harley's arrival in Detroit coincided with a pivotal event in the annals of the industry. After dominating all competitors for nearly twenty years, Ford had seen sales of its venerable Model T hit a wall in 1926, dropping by nearly a third, or almost half a million units. Henry Ford cut the price of his bottom-of-the-line runabout to $260, to no avail. By January 1927, the company had lost nearly half of its market share and its sixty-three-year-old founder was about the only auto executive in Detroit who hadn't seen it coming.

Ford's son, Edsel, who held the title of company president, was among those who had been telling his father for years that their boxy, bolted-together "Tin Lizzie" was mechanically outmoded and needed a major body makeover if the company was to remain competitive. But Henry wouldn't hear of it. As far as he was concerned, the car was perfect. The problem lay with the dealers, he'd argue; they were lazy and inefficient. Or he'd blame the customers, saying they were letting themselves be seduced by competitors' slick advertising into buying needlessly expensive, impractical cars. He predicted that eventually they would realize their mistake and come flocking back to Ford's showrooms.

The father-son disagreements became a source of tension within the company as they escalated into angry confrontations in the presence of other employees, with Henry invariably the aggressor. At one executive meeting, as Edsel argued in favor of equipping the Model T with hydraulic brakes, Henry stood up and shouted, "Edsel, you shut up," and stomped out of the room.

Edsel grew so frustrated with his father's bullheadedness that in 1924 he enlisted the aid of several Ford engineers to build a mock-up of a moderately restyled Model T—less blocky, with a bright red paint job—while Henry was traveling in Europe. Edsel kept their work secret, hoping to win his father over by surprising him with the finished product. But the night before the planned unveiling, Henry unexpectedly walked into the garage where the vehicle was parked and flew into such a rage at the subterfuge that he ripped off the doors, windshield, and top with his bare hands.

Henry's almost irrational refusal to update his car became fodder for newspaper cartoonists and columnists. America's most popular humorist, Will Rogers, poked fun at him. "Ford could be elected President," Rogers quipped. "He'd only have to make one speech: 'Voters, if I am elected I will change the front.'"

Henry finally approved some cosmetic changes to the 1926–1927 models, including lowering the roofline and offering four colors—green, maroon, gray, and blue—in addition to the traditional black. But the improvements proved too little, too late. The market had changed. For the first time, Americans were buying more used cars than new ones, and for less than the price of a new Model T you could purchase a better equipped secondhand Chevrolet or Dodge. For only a few hundred dollars more, you could get a brand-new Chevrolet with all the latest styling and comfort features, and you could mitigate the cost differential by financing it through General Motors Acceptance Company. Ford still didn't offer its own in-house financing. Little wonder that Chevrolet sales surged as the Model T tanked.

On May 25, 1927, Henry capitulated, stunning the country with an abrupt announcement that Ford would immediately cease making the only car that most Americans had ever owned. The next day, he and Edsel made a show of driving the 15 millionth—and supposedly last—Model T off the Highland Park assembly line and then piloted it through the rain to the Ford Engineering Laboratory in Dearborn, where a crowd of several hundred watched as they posed for pictures alongside the other iconic vehicles from the company's glorious past—Henry's original quadricycle and the prototype Model T. (The company actually produced a total of 15,007,033 Model Ts.)

As for the future, Ford said he would soon introduce a new vehicle, another "Model A," but in truth the company had nothing in its development pipeline—not an engine, not a chassis, not even a drawing of what the new Ford might look like. So, in what's been called "history's worst case of product planning," Henry shut down all thirty-six of his assembly plants around the country, throwing as many as 100,000 men out of work and leaving 10,000 dealerships with an inventory of officially obsolete vehicles while he and Edsel and a group of Ford engineers scrambled to come up with a new car that would save them all.

The demise of the clunky Model T, coupled with the successful introduction of the stylish LaSalle, seemed to pave the path to Harley's door for the managers of GM's auto divisions. Chevrolet's chief engineer, O. E. Hunt, was the first to seek an Art and Colour consultation. He needed what Harley called a "face-lifting" on the 1928 models—not a restyling of the body proper, but rather an updating of the radiator shell, headlights, trim, and accent features to create a fresh appearance without necessitating a major factory retooling. Next came Buick, which planned to introduce a new LaSalle-like "companion" car called the Marquette for 1929, priced to fill the gap between its cheapest model and the most expensive Oldsmobile. Then Oldsmobile, too, approached Harley about its planned companion car for '29, the Viking.

With Howard O'Leary's recruiting help, Harley set about assembling a staff. He needed draftsmen, woodworkers, clay modelers, metalworkers, pattern makers, and, most of all, designers, who were in short supply because the industry had never much concerned itself with styling. The few experienced designers working in the industry were employed by a handful of custom coach builders that made bodies for Packard, Peerless, Duesenberg, and other low-volume luxury carmakers. The big companies didn't have designers. No art school in the country offered a course in automotive design; it wasn't recognized as an art or a profession.

While Harley searched the custom body shops in the United States and Europe, O'Leary placed ads in newspapers and general-interest magazines, hoping to draw responses from sculptors, architects, engineers, illustrators, graphic designers, interior decorators, or anyone else with an artistic sensibility and an interest in cars. If they showed any promise, Harley figured he could train them himself.

They would all have to be men, of course, and particularly masculine in their comportment, because Harley worried that any hint of softness or femininity would make it harder for him to get his design ideas across in the hypermale world of GM engineers, some of whom were already referring to Art and Colour derisively as the "beauty parlor" or the "powder room."

"Detroit was macho in those days," recalled Frank Hershey, one of Harley's earliest design hires. "Everything was macho— the Fisher brothers, the Dodge brothers, all those people."

Ideally, Harley was looking for men like himself who'd grown up enthralled with the power and form of the automobile, daydreaming about roadsters and racing cars, drawing pictures of them in the margins of their schoolbooks. Edsel Ford would have been a perfect candidate but for his lineage. He'd been captivated by cars since he was a toddler and his father took him along on one of the first quadricycle test drives. Edsel was only ten when Henry gave him his first car. As a teenager, he studied mechanical drawing at the Detroit University School and began sketching cars while working part-time in his father's office. Instead of going to college, he went to work for the company full-time and was named president at twenty-five, although his father maintained ironfisted executive control of the company through force of will and majority ownership of the stock.

Three years later, in 1922, Edsel persuaded Henry to buy Lin-

coln Motor Company, the struggling luxury carmaker founded
by Henry Leland, for $8 million. Once again, his father named
him president, but this time actually let him run the company as
he saw fit. Out from under Henry's thumb, Edsel proved himself
a capable executive with an eye for design. He directed a stylish
makeover of Lincoln's dowdy L Series cars, improving sales and
turning the brand into a worthy competitor to Cadillac. "Father
made the most popular car in the world," he said at the time. "I
would like to make the best car in the world."

In most ways, Edsel was the antithesis of his father—erudite,
charming, philanthropic, socially active, and politically progressive, with a strong creative bent, a passion for art and
photography, and, as one biographer put it, "a superb sense of
design and unerring taste." He also smoked and drank and enjoyed going out to local jazz clubs—behavior that Henry saw as
signs of weakness and played into his opinion that Edsel wasn't
disciplined or "tough enough" to run Ford Motors. In the aftermath of the Model T fiasco, however, Henry announced that
Edsel would be in charge of designing the new Model A, finally
acknowledging, albeit grudgingly, "We've got a pretty good man
in my son. He knows style—how a car ought to look."

Edsel and Harley were both thirty-three years old when they
took over styling responsibilities at the world's two largest car
companies in June 1927. Edsel was born on November 6, 1893;
Harley, sixteen days later. Neither sensed that they held the future of the industry in their hands. With Ford factories sitting
idle at a cost of $42 million a month in lost revenue, Edsel was
under more pressure. He and his father wanted the Model A
ready for the spring 1928 selling season, which gave them little
time. In an effort to speed up the design process, Edsel borrowed a page from Harley's LaSalle playbook and largely copied

an existing automobile, the 1926 Lincoln he had helped design. Aided by a single engineering assistant and several large blackboards, he created six different models of a car that would sit closer to the ground than the Model T, with a lower roofline, a front grille, a nickel-plated radiator shell, and sweeping, cupped fenders.

His father, meanwhile, oversaw a team of about thirty engineers who focused on mechanical improvements. In the course of considerable trial, error, and argument, Henry approved the adoption of an automatic starter (at last), a modern three-speed transmission, four-wheel brakes, automatic windshield wipers, tilt-beam headlights, hydraulic shock absorbers, and a windshield with laminated shatterproof glass. That last safety feature was added after three of the engineers were involved in a test-drive traffic accident in which one of them, Harold Hicks, was thrown partially through the windshield and badly mangled his forearm on jagged shards of glass. Henry and Edsel quickly decided that safety glass should be included on the Model A as standard equipment, something that no other nonluxury car offered at the time. Hicks commented later that the crash and his injury "probably saved the lives of a good many people."

When it came to the Model A's engine, Edsel and the engineering team argued for a six-cylinder instead of a four because Chevrolet was rumored to be developing a six for its 1929 models. But Henry crankily rejected the idea, saying, "I've got no use for a car that has more spark plugs than a cow has teats."

On August 10, Edsel announced that a prototype Model A had been completed. "The new Ford automobile is an accomplished fact," he said. Of course, there remained the epic task of retooling the thirty-six factories before any more could be built. The Rouge would have to be gutted at an estimated cost of $50 million, "probably the biggest replacement of a plant in the history of American industry," according to the *New York Times*.

All during the Ford shutdown, of course, GM pressed its advantage. The Chevrolet division upped production, redoubled sales efforts, and embarked on a naked campaign to recruit disaffected Ford salesmen and dealerships, succeeding in stealing away more than a thousand of the latter. By June, Chevrolet had produced 700,000 cars, more than its total for all of 1926. Ford countered by plastering its dealer showrooms with banners that read "Wait for the New Ford." It seemed that many people did, as car sales slackened across the board, except for the Chevrolet, which shot past Ford to become the number-one-selling car in America, the first time Ford had been bested since the Model T was introduced.

The press seized on the story, describing it variously as the "Ford auto war" (*Springfield* [Massachusetts] *Daily News*), a "fight for the national automobile championship" (the *New York Times*), and "the most titanic industrial struggle" in U.S. history (Scripps-Howard News Service). Only Charles Lindbergh's pioneering transatlantic flight on May 21 garnered more news coverage that spring and summer. Public interest had reached a fever pitch by December 2, when the Model A made its debut. An enormous crowd stormed Ford's New York showroom, spilling out onto the street and blocking traffic, forcing the company to move the event to Madison Square Garden. Similar scenes played out in Detroit, Los Angeles, Cleveland, and Kansas City as an estimated ten million people, roughly 10 percent of the U.S. population, turned out in the first thirty-six hours to get a look at "Henry's new car," this despite the fact that most dealers didn't even have cars to show, only a short promotional film provided by the company. That didn't seem to matter, as Ford took 400,000 orders the first day, 50,000 of them in New York alone.

Stylistically, the Model A was no LaSalle, but it was a marked improvement on the Model T. Available in an array of descriptive colors—Niagara Blue, Arabian Sand, Dawn Gray, Andalusian Blue, Balsam Green, Rose Beige—with steel spoke wheels and no visible bolts in the body or fenders, the car was dubbed "the baby Lincoln" by Ford dealers eager to play up the new look of luxury that could be purchased for $100–$125 less than a Chevrolet (or $1,500–$3,000 less than a Lincoln or LaSalle). The company had 700,000 orders before the month was out, far more than its factories could fill as they struggled to get back on line after the six-month shutdown.

Despite all the Model A hype, however, it was General Motors, not Ford, that ended the year triumphant, selling a record 1.5 million cars and posting the highest annual industrial profit in history, $235 million. Henry Ford's impromptu model change cost his company an estimated $250 million and its position as the industry leader. It also helped build the case among GM executives for Art and Colour's mission as an agent of continuous, planned, and affordable styling change.

By the spring of 1928, Harley and Howard O'Leary had filled more than half of their fifty budgeted positions and the department's new, larger quarters on the third floor of the GM building bustled with activity, including the constant comings and goings of job applicants. Franklin Quick Hershey was a lanky twenty-one-year-old when he first walked into Art and Colour clutching his portfolio of sketches. Born in Detroit, he had been raised in Beverly Hills by his well-to-do mother, who purchased a new car from Don Lee Cadillac every year when he was growing up.

By age twelve, Frank could identify every make and model of car he encountered, not only by sight but also by sound, thanks to the warm Southern California nights when he slept on the screened porch of his house and listened to the cars coming down the street:

"The Marmon had a hollow, spooky sound, partly because they didn't have any louvers in the hood," he recalled in a videotaped 1991 interview with Alexandra Earl, Harley's granddaughter. "Studebakers were distinctive because their rear axles whined all the time. The Pierce-Arrow had a swishing sound, sort of like it was riding on water, almost like steam, it was so quiet. And I could always tell a Cadillac because they sounded like the valves needed adjusting."

Like Harley, Hershey had attended the University of Southern California and competed on the track team as a long jumper. "But I gave up college to be a car designer," he said. "That's all I ever wanted to be." His mother used her connections to line up a job for him at the Walter M. Murphy Company, a custom coach builder in Pasadena, where young Frank worked on Duesenberg, Bentley, and Bugatti bodies for rich clients, including a number of Hollywood celebrities. Harley hired him on the spot.

Attracted by the good pay and ground-floor opportunity to participate in what promised to be the best-funded artistic enterprise of the time, Hershey and the rest of the young staff quickly ran up against the realities of working for an industrial giant that didn't necessarily take their creative aspirations into account. Instead of crafting beautiful new car bodies, they found themselves designing headlights, hood ornaments, taillights, and bumpers for minor styling face-lifts. Hershey recalled drawing "an awful lot of hubcaps."

The problem was partly institutional. In keeping with long-standing industry practice, GM engineers designed their chassis complete with fenders, running boards, radiators, hoods, and trunks, leaving Fisher Body to design what was once called the coach—the basic passenger compartment with windows, doors, and interior upholstery. Alfred Sloan created Art and Colour hoping to end this outdated, bifurcated process and to place the responsibility for the total outward appearance of all GM cars in Harley's hands. But Fisher's so-called body engineers, some of them former blacksmiths and mechanics, were not about to hand over their hard-won design authority docilely to some new kid from California.

"These were rough-and-tumble guys who'd experienced the hard times of the beginning of the industry," Hershey said. "There were no artists [at Fisher Body]; the chief engineer was doing the designing."

The engineers had personal issues with Harley. For one thing, they didn't like the way he dressed. "His clothes were very expensive," Hershey said. "He'd wear white pants and a dark coat, beautiful ties and beautiful shoes. All these guys always wore dark suits that were not very well tailored because they didn't care about that. But Harley did. He got that from Hollywood. He *was* Hollywood. He dealt with Hollywood people. He dressed like people in Hollywood dressed. So they would laugh at him behind his back. I used to hear them talking about him all the time—'this big sissy from Hollywood telling us how to make a car.'"

The disdain went both ways, as Harley in turn made fun of the engineers' sartorial idiosyncrasies. "Having come from California, he had never run into the kind of people we had in the automotive industry at that time," said designer Clare Mac-

Kichan. "He always [joked] that the engineers would wear big suspenders *and* a belt because they didn't trust anybody." Harley also lampooned them for never taking off their hats. "The factories were not heated," MacKichan explained, "and they'd spend quite a bit of time in the factories, so they wore their hats all the time, and when they came into the styling section they wore their hats because that was their custom. And he would make a lot of fun of that, of course. He had absolutely no respect for ninety-nine percent of the engineering people."

The engineers also resented Harley's close relationship with the big bosses. "Sloan and the Fishers were behind him, but they couldn't control the engineers and their dislike for him," said Hershey. "I don't know if they knew it or not, but the enmity was there, and [the engineers] fought Harley."

The engineers did so quietly by disparaging Earl's design suggestions to the division chiefs, who had the final say on styling changes, citing various technical reasons why this idea or that could not be done or would be too costly. Lacking his own body engineer to counter their arguments, Harley found himself at a disadvantage, but he said nothing to the Fishers or Sloan because he figured they expected him to work things out on his own.

The situation appeared to improve when Buick executives asked for his help with the 1929 "silver anniversary" models, marking twenty-five years since Billy Durant launched General Motors with the purchase of the failing Buick company from David Dunbar Buick, who died in 1929 poor and largely forgotten. They weren't looking for a mere face-lift this time; they wanted whole new bodies for their sedan, coupe, roadster, and phaeton. It was a huge opportunity. Buick was GM's oldest and most profitable division, and the third-best-selling car in America, behind Chevrolet and Ford. A successful restyling of the entire

Buick line would raise Art and Colour's profile tremendously, inside the company and out.

Over the better part of a year, from dramatic, flowing pencil sketches, precise chalk drawings on seven-foot-high blackboards, and, ultimately, full-size clay models, Harley and his staff created a vision of a new Buick that was longer, lower, wider, and more rounded than its predecessors. Just below the so-called beltline, where the windows meet the lower portion of the body, they sculpted a slight roll that ran from the hood all the way around the car. This 1¼-inch curvature would barely be noticeable to the modern eye, but back in the era of uniformly flat side panels, it amounted to a distinctive design feature.

Hearing nothing to the contrary from Buick management, Harley assumed that Art and Colour's styling proposal had been accepted as presented. It wasn't until he saw the first cars out of the factory that he realized Fisher engineers changed his specifications without telling him and, in his view, destroyed the integrity of the car's design. "I roared like a Ventura sea lion," he said in 1954, apparently still smarting from the incident twenty-five years after the fact. "Unfortunately, the factory, for operational reasons, pulled the side panels in at the bottom more than the design called for. In addition, five inches were added in vertical height, with the result that the arc I had plotted was pulled out of shape in two directions, the highlight line was unpleasant and the effect was bulgy."

Put more simply, the changes exaggerated the beltline roll and made the body appear plump, even fat. Walter Chrysler, one of Alfred Sloan's closest friends, apparently couldn't resist some competitive snark. He told a reporter he thought the new models looked "pregnant," a description that quickly spread through the press, and in a matter of a few weeks Art and Colour's debut design effort was widely derided as the "pregnant Buick." Sales were abysmal, falling by more than 25 percent from the year before, enough to drop Buick to fourth place behind Hudson.

Harley was "practically suicidal," according to Frank Hershey, who thought the engineers' actions were a deliberate act of sabotage aimed at undermining the man they had taken to calling "Hollywood Harley."

"That's why they screwed up that Buick," Hershey said. "I think they did it intentionally."

Ironically, while Art and Colour was being blamed for the pregnancy, Buick sales brochures were praising the artistry of the men actually responsible for it: "Built by the Fisher Body Corporation working in cooperation with Buick engineers . . . the new Buick bodies are justly named—Masterpieces by Fisher . . . their lines and distinctive colors establish a new vogue . . . the master work of master craftsmen . . . the crowning achievement of 25 years of leadership in the automobile world." There was no mention anywhere, however, of Art and Colour's role in the restyling.

If the engineers' plan was to damage Harley in the eyes of Alfred Sloan and the Fishers, as Frank Hershey believed, it backfired. Harley went to Sloan, insisting that in order to avoid another such fiasco Fisher needed to run all styling changes by Art and Colour for approval. Sloan agreed, and also signed off on Harley's hiring his own body engineer, Vincent Kaptur, a twelve-year Packard veteran who served from then on as Art and Colour's liaison with Fisher and seemed to be at Harley's side wherever he went.

Sloan likewise didn't blame Harley and the staff when two more cars they helped design—the Buick Marquette and the Oldsmobile Viking—failed to sell. He knew the fault wasn't in the styling but rather in executive management decisions that resulted in the two cars competing against each other in the already glutted $1,000–$1,500 price range. There were larger forces at work as well.

When the Marquette and the Viking were introduced in early 1929, the auto industry and the national economy were in a state of flux. The number of cars in the United States had quadrupled to more than 20 million since the beginning of the decade. Cars were now America's most valuable product, and its number one export. Manufacturing them consumed 20 percent of the U.S. output of steel, 80 percent of the rubber, and 75 percent of the plate glass. Fueling them had transformed the petroleum industry from one that largely produced lighting fuel and lubricants to one that primarily produced gasoline. Cars were rearranging where Americans lived, moving them from the farm to the city and from the city to the suburbs, nurturing new communities that were sprouting up along the nation's improving roadways even as rural railroad towns began to wither beside the tracks. Cars had turned Detroit into the country's fourth-largest city (behind New York, Chicago, and Philadelphia) and arguably its most vibrant. The roar of the Twenties was really the sound of America becoming a car economy.

Which is why the United States had tipped into a recession in 1927, when consumers started buying more used cars than new ones and Henry Ford shut down his manufacturing plants for six months. Ford powered back in 1929, reclaiming its number one spot with the sale of 1.8 million Model As, amounting to a third of the industry total and 400,000 more than Chevrolet, which still managed a record year. The industry, too, set a record—5.3 million cars produced. Still, the overall economy continued to weaken.

After two grueling, frustrating years, Harley had yet to make a real mark on GM; he had not followed up the LaSalle with a similar styling success. But despite his youth, relatively low rank in the organization, and wardrobe choices that made him "stand out like a toucan among grackles," he became part of Alfred Sloan's inner circle. He addressed his corporate mentor as "Mr. Sloan" when others were around, but in private called him "Alfie."

Harley and Sue continued to live graciously in Larry Fisher's Whittier Hotel penthouse, where all the services of a luxury hotel were provided free of charge. Sue appeared to have recovered from her debilitating grief over Billy's death, thanks in part to the birth of another son, James, in May 1928. Still, the pain remained so close to the surface that she and Harley never talked about Billy to anyone, not even family members. His birth and death were not recorded in the otherwise exhaustively annotated Taft-Earl family bible. Indeed, two of Harley's sister Jessie's children expressed surprise recently when they were told the story of Billy's death; they never knew he'd been born. James would grow into adulthood thinking the portrait of the little boy that hung in his father's study was of him.

Harley hired a full-time nanny to help Sue after James was born because his job required many late nights in the studio and an increasing amount of travel. He was among a delegation of seven executives who sailed with Sloan to Germany in mid-October 1929 for talks with that country's biggest carmaker, Adam Opel AG, in which GM held an 80 percent interest. The group was on its way back to New York on October 29, "Black Tuesday," when the stock market crashed.

Like many up-and-coming young men of that decade, Harley had invested heavily in the market, buying on the margins as the economy boomed. The crash wiped him out. Both he and his father lost everything they'd made from the sale of Earl Automobile Works, and then some. At the dawn of the Great Depression, Harley suddenly found himself deeply in debt. All he had left was his job at GM. And who knew how long that would last?

6
ASSEMBLY LINES
TO BREADLINES

The Great Depression hit Detroit and the auto industry head-on, well before the rest of the country felt its full impact.

The big car companies experienced a 30 percent drop in sales almost overnight. Within a year, a third of their dealerships were out of business; after two years, their manufacturing plants were operating at one-quarter of capacity. The situation was even worse for the smaller independent and luxury carmakers, which began folding one by one—Essex, Franklin, Stutz, Marmon, Duesenberg, Peerless, Pierce-Arrow—until of the more than one hundred car manufacturers founded since the turn of the century, fewer than twenty were left. By 1930, GM, Ford, and Chrysler accounted for 80 percent of all production.

The human toll was horrendous. A quarter of a million autoworkers were laid off, about half the industry's 1929 workforce. Ford alone cut 91,000 jobs, and a majority of those who remained on the payroll were working three days a week or less. Hundreds of unemployed, homeless, and hungry people were sleeping in Detroit's Grand Circus Park; some were living in caves dug into the ground and covered over with brush. Men gathered overnight outside the gates of their former factories, huddling around fires and hoping against hope that when the morning broke they would be called to return to the assembly line. On cold nights they kept their feet warm by stuffing newspapers into their worn-out "Hoover shoes," named for the Republican president on whose watch the economy had collapsed. They weren't all autoworkers; layoffs had spread quickly to other industries that fed the car-making beast—steel, rubber, glass, plastic, textiles.

For the proud Midwestern metropolis that so recently rumbled with industrial productivity, it was a dizzying descent into economic chaos. Even as Board of Commerce brochures boasted of "Dynamic Detroit" and "The City of Tomorrow," Mayor Frank Murphy estimated that four thousand children a day were standing on breadlines. And just when it seemed the situation couldn't get any worse, Henry Ford ratcheted up the misery index by shutting down his factories again.

Ford did not learn the most important lesson of the Model T's collapse. In the aftermath, he chose to build another one-off car that he thought could remain unchanged and competitive for as many years as the Model T, if not longer. But despite spectacular sales in 1928 and 1929, the Model A quickly became outmoded, struggling to compete with Chevrolet's fresher styling and new six-cylinder engine. So in August 1931, Ford ceased all production for six months while his engineers worked up a new "Model B" that he decided would be powered by a V-8, an engine with four more spark plugs than a cow had teats.

Ford's second extended shutdown in four years had a catastrophic effect on the economy, as the massive idleness at the Highland Park and Rouge River plants, in the words of Ford historians Allan Nevins and Frank Ernest Hill, "dragged like a dead weight on the city—on the world."

The unemployment rate shot to more than 30 percent in Detroit; it was 80 percent among African American workers, thousands of whom had been drawn from the South by the carmakers' relatively high-paying assembly line jobs. By 1932, the federal government estimated that more than 12 million people were unemployed nationwide, a quarter of the workforce. Michigan was hit the hardest, with 2.5 million unemployed. Laid-off workers overwhelmed Detroit's Department of Public Welfare, which saw its relief rolls quintuple, to the point that it was serving 728,000 people at a cost of $2 million a month and could expend only $5.00 a month per family. It was estimated that three people were dying of starvation in Detroit every day. Mayor Murphy figured the department would need $10 million to help the destitute get through the winter of 1931.

In Henry Ford's hometown of Dearborn, where the Rouge River plant was located, city officials sought his help in allaying the exploding cost of their public relief program. They reached an agreement that transferred furloughed Ford workers living in Dearborn from public relief rolls to a Ford relief program that provided a voucher for sixty cents' worth of food a day at a company commissary—in effect, a free lunch. Except it wasn't really free. Ever the hard-boiled industrialist, Henry insisted that if the workers were later rehired, the relief money then would be deducted from their paychecks.

The Ford welfare barely amounted to a drop in the bucket, however, since the vast majority of the laid-off workers lived within the city limits of Detroit, not in Dearborn, and Detroit was hurtling toward bankruptcy. By Christmas 1932 it was clear to city managers that Detroit would not be able to meet its financial obligations after the first of the year. They turned to the banks for help but learned that—unbeknownst to the public—the city's two most powerful financial institutions, the First Detroit Banking Group and the Union Guardian Group, were dangerously close to insolvency and had applied for rescue loans from the Reconstruction Finance Corporation (RFC), a federal agency recently set up by Congress to deal with the burgeoning problem of bank failures around the country. The RFC already had provided nearly $1 billion to more than five thousand struggling banks, mostly in small towns, but it balked at lending to Union Guardian, whose board of directors was packed with auto executives, including Edsel Ford, its largest single investor. "Why should we bail out Mr. Ford?" the RFC administrators asked.

Indeed, some in the government thought it should be the other way around: the big auto magnates, with all their amassed wealth, ought to bail out the banks. Secretary of the Treasury Ogden Mills told Edsel at a meeting in Washington, D.C., that he and his father had a "duty" to step up and help solve the impending bank crisis in Detroit, starting with the Union Guardian Trust Company, one of the group's banks that was in imminent danger of collapse. During the final weeks of his presidency, Herbert Hoover held separate talks with Alfred Sloan, Walter Chrysler, and Henry Ford in an attempt to get them to deposit funds in Union Guardian Trust to prevent its failure. Ford was considered the key because he had $50 to $60 million in deposits divided equally between First Detroit Banking Group and Union Guardian Group banks. After the discussions, Hoover told the RFC that an agreement had been reached whereby Ford would subordinate the $7.5 million he had on deposit with Union Guardian Trust, in effect lending it to the company, while GM and Chrysler would each deposit $1 million. The $9.5 million would be enough to return the trust to solvency, at least temporarily; however, Ford changed his mind a few weeks later and reneged on his part of the agreement.

President Hoover quickly arranged for Secretary of Commerce Roy Chapin and Under Secretary of the Treasury Arthur Ballantine to meet with Edsel and Henry in the latter's Dearborn office at 10:00 a.m. on Monday, February 13, 1933. According to a written account by Francis Awalt, the Treasury Department's acting comptroller of currency at the time, Chapin and Ballantine told Henry that without his help the Union Guardian Group banks would have to close to prevent a run by depositors, and that could spark widespread panic and lead to a chain reaction of bank closings throughout the state and beyond. But Henry didn't budge, saying he "would not contribute a single dime" to bail out the banks, Awalt wrote, "because he felt that the principle was wrong."

What's more, according to Awalt, Ford told Chapin and Ballantine that if Union Guardian Trust did not open the next morning then he was prepared to immediately withdraw the $25 million he had on deposit with First Detroit's flagship First National Bank of Detroit, a move they believed surely would cause it to fail and bring down the Union Guardian banks as well.

Stunned by the threat, Ballantine pleaded with Ford, telling him that "this would cause vast distress in the State of Michigan as there were nearly a million bank depositors representing the source of support of as many as three million people. All these people would be subject to loss and suffering, and the business of the state would be vastly hampered, if not paralyzed."

Ford responded that if the banking system crashed then it would serve as a lesson to people: "Everybody would have to get to work a little sooner, and that might be a very good thing."

He may have been bluffing, but the President's men didn't want to risk him pulling his money out of First National. After hours of tense meetings and telephone calls to the White House, the Federal Reserve, the Treasury Department, the Commerce Department, and the RFC, Francis Awalt decided that, as comptroller of currency, "I had no choice under such circumstances but to refuse to let the two large Detroit banks [Union Guardian Trust and First National Bank of Detroit] open the next day because I could not let Mr. Ford have preference to the detriment of the other depositors in those institutions." He notified Michigan governor William A. Comstock, who at 1:00 a.m. on February 14 declared an eight-day "bank holiday" in the state, preventing Henry Ford and everyone else from withdrawing funds from Michigan banks. The governor said later that he personally had only thirty dollars in cash on hand when he issued the order.

As many had feared, the Michigan bank closings set off a chain reaction as one state after another declared a similar holiday to protect their banks from runs by panicked depositors. On March 6, thirty-six hours after his inauguration, President Franklin Roosevelt declared a four-day nationwide bank holiday. Three days later, after only thirty-five minutes of debate, Congress passed the Emergency Banking Act, authorizing the RFC to borrow without limit from the Treasury to purchase preferred stock in closed banks and help them reopen. On Sunday, March 12, Roosevelt broadcast the first of his famous "fireside chats" over the radio, assuring Americans that "it is safer to keep your money in a reopened bank than under the mattress."

The next day, Federal Reserve member banks across the country reopened, and by March 15 the crisis seemed to have passed as banks controlling 90 percent of the country's banking resources resumed operations, with more people depositing money than withdrawing.

In Detroit, First National and Union Guardian banks were not among the banks that reopened. Instead, General Motors stepped into the void left by Henry Ford and partnered with the RFC to form a new bank, First Bank of Detroit; GM purchased $12.5 million in common stock while the RFC bought $12.5 million in preferred stock. "Finally it became obvious that the situation required some strong organization capable within itself of assuming the responsibility of affording the essential relief," Alfred Sloan wrote later. "People were suffering. It was not a problem of selection. General Motors was the only organization that had the resources to do the job and General Motors did it."

The Detroit bank crisis signaled the beginning of GM's rise and the fall of Ford. Henry Ford's time had passed. Once seen as a folk hero for putting America on wheels, doubling the industrial pay rate, and initiating the five-day, forty-hour workweek, he was now reviled by the *New York Times* as "an industrial fascist— the Mussolini of Detroit" for a slew of employment practices and public pronouncements that ranged from merely mean-spirited to truly monstrous.

In the midst of the mass unemployment caused in large part by his layoffs, he was widely quoted as saying, "It's good that the recovery is taking a long time. The average man really won't do a day's work unless he is caught and can't get out of it." At the same time, he was employing a security force of some three thousand roughnecks (benignly named the Ford Service Department) that delighted in terrorizing his plant employees by, among other things, monitoring their visits to the restroom and speeding up the assembly line and then summarily firing anyone who couldn't keep up the pace, knowing there were plenty more waiting outside the gates to take their place. The head of the Ford Service was a thuggish ex-boxer named Harry Bennett, who reported only to Henry and later boasted, "I became his most intimate companion, closer to him than his own son."

A virulent anti-Semite, Ford published a newspaper called the *Dearborn Independent* that operated out of a former Ford tractor factory and unrelentingly blamed nearly all the world's problems on "the international Jewish conspiracy." Under the editorial guidance of his personal secretary, Ernest Liebold, the *Independent* specialized in articles that would cause even the most rabid Ku Klux Klansman to blanch, claiming, for instance, that Queen Isabella of Spain had been "a Jewish front for the discovery of America," that Jewish bankers were behind the assassination of Abraham Lincoln, and that Jews were responsible for the popularization of "Negro Jazz," which it called "moron music."

Henry had embarrassed himself on the witness stand in 1919 after he sued the *Chicago Tribune* for $1 million over an editorial that called him "ignorant" and "incapable of thought." Seeking to counter Ford's description of himself as "an educator," the attorney for the newspaper asked him a series of questions that exposed his lack of education beyond the eighth grade:

"Have there ever been any revolutions in this country?"
"There was, I understand," Ford replied.
"When?"
"In 1812."
"Did you ever hear of Benedict Arnold?"
"I have heard the name."
"Who was he?"
"I have forgotten just who he is. He is a writer, I think."

After the testimony, one newspaper described Henry as "a man with a vision distorted and limited by his lack of information." The jury found in his favor but awarded damages of only six cents.

The capper came in March 1932, when several thousand unemployed workers staged a "hunger march" on Ford's Rouge River complex to present Henry with a list of demands that included the rehiring of all workers, a seven-hour workday with eight hours' pay, free medical care for employees and their families, and an end to discrimination against black workers. The Rouge employed roughly 10,000 African Americans, but most were relegated to the hardest, dirtiest, and hottest jobs. Seventy percent of the plant's foundry workers were black.

The march proceeded peacefully under police escort until it reached the city limits of Dearborn, where the combined forces of that city's fire and police departments and the detested Service Department blocked its path. As the marchers pushed through the skirmish line in an attempt to reach the company's employment offices, they were blasted by fire hoses and bombarded with tear gas canisters. When they responded with rocks, Henry's goons opened fire with guns, mortally wounding five and injuring sixty.

"Dearborn pavements were stained with blood, the streets were littered with broken glass and the wreckage of bullet-riddled automobiles," reported the *New York Times*. The more Ford-friendly *Detroit Free Press* called it a "riot" carried out by a "Red [Communist-inspired] mob," but the event quickly became known as "the Ford Hunger March Massacre," making Henry's fall from grace complete.

He'd done more than damage his public image, however. Thanks to his autocratic, capricious management, the company had become increasingly dysfunctional. He disdained college graduates and experts and refused to hire them. He harassed any of his executives who showed promise or gained the loyalty of their underlings, inevitably firing them or driving them from the company, as he did with his extremely capable head of production, William Knudsen, who quit in frustration and went to work as the general manager of archrival Chevrolet. Ford's ideas about running a company were so antiquated that he could have been describing a small-town, turn-of-the-century hardware store when he bragged in his autobiography, *My Life and Work*, that Ford Motors had "no organization, no specific duties attaching to any position, no line of succession or of authority, very few titles and no conferences. We have only the clerical help that is absolutely required; we have no elaborate records of any kind and consequently no red tape." In an obvious dig at Alfred Sloan, he added, "There is no bent of mind more dangerous than that which is sometimes described as 'genius for organization.'"

Once again, he couldn't have been more wrong. Sloan's vision and organizational brilliance got General Motors through the darkest days of the Depression in far better shape than Ford. As GM sales dropped by 40 percent and its stock fell from $73 to $8 a share, the company posted a loss of only $4.5 million on its auto operations in 1932, while Ford lost an estimated $30 million. More important, GM captured 41 percent of the market to Ford's 25 percent. And even as GM shed plant workers by the thousands, Sloan stood steadfastly behind Harley Earl and the Art and Colour staff. "After the crash we all got a letter saying don't worry, as long as General Motors existed, we'd have a job," recalled Frank Hershey.

The Depression turned out to be a springboard for Harley.

Cars had become such an indispensable part of American life that they continued to sell even as the economy cratered, albeit in drastically reduced numbers. In order to stay afloat until the crisis passed, GM needed to draw a larger portion of the smaller buyer pool to its lower-priced (and lower-cost) models. And it didn't take an automotive genius to see that restyling a car was cheaper than reengineering it. Which put Harley in the catbird seat and gave GM a tremendous competitive advantage because no other major car manufacturer had a full-fledged styling department—not even Chrysler, which was challenging Ford for second place, thanks to its acquisition of Dodge and its introduction of the low-priced Plymouth in 1928.

The Art and Colour staff soon grew to more than 125, with the designers easily recognized as they walked around the GM building in the white smock uniforms Harley had them wear. But wisecracks about the "beauty parlor" diminished as their work gained credibility across the divisions. Cadillac's chief engineer, Ernest Seaholm, was an early appreciator of Harley's styling ideas. He asked Art and Colour to collaborate with GM's custom body division, Fleetwood, on the design for the Cadillac V-16 Aerodynamic coupe for the 1933 "Century of Progress" World's Fair in Chicago. The result was a one-of-a-kind promotional show car that boasted a list of styling innovations nearly as long as its 149-inch wheelbase, including a sloping "fastback" rear end, the absence of running boards, pontoon-style fenders, a spare tire tucked away in an integral trunk, a lighted and recessed license plate housing, a gas tank filler hidden beneath the taillight assembly, bullet-shaped headlights, chrome tailpipes, and an exhaust system specially tuned to give the engine a specific tone. Inside, there was walnut trim, "knobs and handles plated in a satin gold finish," and sun visors "shaped like abstract leaves, made of fine cloth and mounted with screws that had heads of imitation pearl." Even the engine, the first V-16 to power an American passenger car, had the earmarks of a Harley Earl production, with the surfaces of its various components detailed and finished in enamel paint, porcelain, polished aluminum, and chrome.

The car was such a hit with World's Fair attendees that Cadillac decided to put it into production with few changes for the 1936 model year. With advertising aimed at "the very rich and very few," management's plan was to build only four hundred of the cars; however, they fell far short of the mark, finding only fifty-some customers for the elegantly appointed, hand-fashioned vehicle. Ernest Seaholm waxed poetic when he later summed up the car as "a dream of the Roaring Twenties, materializing at the time the bottom dropped out of the stock market, advertised for the 'four hundred' who were now in hiding, and finding instead only empty pocketbooks.

"Be that as it may," he said, "it was an outstanding piece of work."

Indeed, auto historians now credit the Aerodynamic coupe with ushering in the modern era of American car design. At the time, it showed GM management how much Harley and his staff could accomplish when they were given a freer hand.

Art and Colour saved the Pontiac in 1933. Having seen an 80 percent falloff in Pontiac sales since the stock market crash, GM was seriously considering discontinuing its moderately priced line. The division had a new chassis and a powerful new straight-eight engine ready to go, but its body engineers were struggling to come up with a new look for the car. So Harley dispatched Frank Hershey to the plant in Pontiac, Michigan, to check out the wooden mock-up of the body they were considering for the 1933 model year. "Go out there and tell me what you think," he told the designer. Hershey reported back that the proposed new model "looks just like the old car." If that was all they were going to do, he said, they "might as well leave it alone."

"All right," said Harley, "you've got two weeks to come up with something better."

Hershey organized a small team and came back on time with a full-size clay model that featured a louvered hood and a radiator grille that he'd flat-out stolen from his favorite British luxury car. "I was in love with Bentleys," he admitted. "So I decided to do a Bentley front end on this Pontiac." The Art and Colour design was accepted and, with the price dropped to $585 and an advertising campaign that prominently pictured the Bentley grille, sales doubled in 1933. As a result, Pontiac got a reprieve that lasted more than sixty years.

Harley's beloved LaSalle faced the same fate the following year, the result of an even steeper decline in sales. According to auto historian Michael Lamm, while Harley was in Europe making his annual rounds of auto shows, designer Jules Agramonte made "a full-sized airbrush rendering on black paper of the front of a car with a tall, slender radiator grille. The grille took its inspiration from that day's track and beach racers."

Agramonte showed the drawing to Harry Shaw, the man Harley had left in charge, and suggested it might be a good design for the LaSalle. Shaw was unimpressed and told him to put the drawing away. But when Harley returned, Agramonte pulled it out and put in up on the board for all to see. "Earl came in and got terribly excited about it, and they were working on it night and day from then on," recalled designer Gordon Buehrig. Harley was so determined to save the LaSalle that he went beyond a clay model and ordered the construction of a wood-and-metal model of Agramonte's proposed body—trimmed, painted, and accurate in every detail, to the point that you actually could open the doors and sit in it—a process that cost as much as $100,000.

Harley unveiled his proposed 1934 LaSalle to a group of pertinent executives he gathered in the Styling Auditorium. He "had the LaSalle mock-up onstage, alone, with the curtains drawn. As he rose to make his presentation, he said, 'Gentlemen, if you decide to discontinue the L'Sawl [as he pronounced it], this is the car you're not going to build.' The curtains parted, and there stood the gleaming mockup of the 1934 LaSalle. The audience sat silent for a moment, and then came to life. Everyone liked the design, and GM quickly approved it."

The LaSalle would live another seven years.

7

A MAN OF
STYLE
AND
"STATUE"

By all accounts, Harley Earl was hell to work for. Reminiscing about the experience decades later, his designers invariably described him as impatient and relentlessly demanding, with a hair-trigger temper and a seemingly bottomless reservoir of profane invective that he drew from whenever he felt the need to tell one of them that his carefully rendered drawing of a taillight "looks like a baboon's asshole."

Just as easily, he could reduce a man to jelly without saying a word. "He had kind of pale blue eyes and when he'd look at you, boy, I'll tell you, he looked right through you," recalled Richard Teague. "He was a terrifying figure," said Bill Porter. Even GM's division managers "were physically scared of him," said Frank Hershey.

No one ever dared to address him as "Harley"; it was always "Mr. Earl," usually contracted to sound like "Mistearl," as if he were some whip-wielding cotton plantation foreman straight out of the antebellum South. Among themselves they referred to him as "the old man," or "the shadow" because he seemed omnipresent, usually arriving at the office by seven in the morning, before anyone else, and staying until nine or ten at night, when he would take a break and then return in the wee hours, sometimes a little tipsy, to look over the work the designers and modelers had done that day. "He'd come in there and sneak around," said Teague. "We always wanted to set bear traps for him at night."

As a committed workaholic, Harley expected the same of his staff, recognizing no boundaries between their professional and personal lives. The work was all-encompassing; eighty-hour weeks were not uncommon. When the crunch was on, weekends didn't exist and neither national nor religious holidays provided any respite. Bernie Smith once worked "a stretch of three months without a single day off, including Easter and Fourth of July, eleven to twelve hours a day."

Bill Mitchell remembered leaving the office with another designer at the end of his first week on the job. "This was Christmas Eve, and he said, 'I'll see you tomorrow.' I said, 'What?' He said, 'Oh yeah, we'll work tomorrow.' And, we did!"

Virgil Exner described a typical all-nighter: "Harley had selected a front-end design sketch of mine to model in full-scale clay—on a crash basis. He and I, along with a modeling man, worked on it until 5 a.m., at which time Harley called a halt, whereupon we 'retired' to an adjoining drafting room and slept on drawing boards until 7:30. We then arose, had a cup of coffee and finished the job for a meeting with Buick executives at 11 a.m."

Irv Rybicki remembered the time Harley appeared in the studio and announced that he was not leaving until they came up with a solution for a particular Cadillac design. Then he sat right next to Rybicki and stared down at the blank sheet of paper on his drawing board, waiting for him to begin.

"I picked up a pencil, and I started sketching," Rybicki said. "I made about three lines, and Earl put his big hand on the pad, wrinkled up the paper and threw it in the [waste] basket. He looked at me and said, 'Let's try again.' Everything wound up in the basket that day."

The intensity took a toll. "It's tough to be creative around the clock," said designer Thomas L. Hibbard. "Overtime was a steady diet—and unproductive in many instances. Employees' family lives fell apart because in many cases evenings for weeks were spent on the job trying to come up with startling innovations to meet a deadline. Those who had the roughest time and were most liable not to make it, of course, were the creative designers."

"The really good guys couldn't take it," said Bill Porter. "He kept the whole place in a state of suspended anxiety . . . and we lost good designers."

Frank Hershey got fed up and went back home to California in 1929, but Howard O'Leary, acting as Harley's emissary, talked him into returning to the staff in 1931. Gordon Buehrig quit twice, in '29 and '33. Ray Dietrich defected to Chrysler in '31, while both Tom Tjaarda and Bob Gregorie jumped to Edsel Ford's nascent styling department in '32. Tom Hibbard quit in '33 and Virgil Exner exited in '38.

They were the lucky ones who left of their own accord. Many more junior staffers were summarily sacked for what sometimes seemed like the slightest of reasons. In the most oft-told tale, Harley walked through the studio at lunchtime one day and discovered a lone soul taking a nap under a drawing board. He woke the poor fellow and informed him that he was fired. From then on, new hires were warned not to hang around the studio during the lunch hour because Harley liked to come through then, and if he started asking questions they couldn't answer, then it might end their careers. He supposedly canned one young man because he didn't like the way he walked, and another for showing up to work wearing an expensive tie that matched one of his own. "I saw him chew some guys out so bad they had to go to psychiatrists," Bill Mitchell told *Automotive News*.

But however much they feared Harley, none of the designers described him as mean-spirited. "He was ruthless," said Strother MacMinn. "I think that's a better way of putting it, because he didn't mean harm to anyone."

According to MacMinn, the summary terminations and foul-mouthed tirades were just Harley's way of maintaining control over a group of creative individuals who, by their nature, "evaded rational management."

"He played all kinds of little tricks and techniques in order to maintain his authority . . . which was good. You have to have that. If you don't, the whole thing goes off in all directions."

Harley may have been "the boss who drove them nuts, drove them to drink and drove them to divorce court," as writer Michael Lamm put it, but he was also the boss who drove them to do their best work. So they endured the bruising criticism and brutal hours as a trade-off for access to the work they so craved. "You loved automobiles above everything else," said Frank Hershey, "even your wife or your children."

Then, too, Harley could be as charming as he was intimidating. And he had one particular trait that never failed to humanize him in the eyes of his employees—a propensity for mispronunciations and malapropisms that put him in a league with Yogi Berra. "Chromium" invariably came out of his mouth as "chronium," and "aluminum" sounded like "alumoornum." Cubic inches became "cubits." Instead of saying, "It's all relative," he'd observe, "It's all relativity, fellas." He regularly substituted "statue" for the word "stature," resulting in howlers like "He's a man of great statue." He sometimes called the beltline a "fence." He once said, in all seriousness, "A car has four wheels and they belong on the ground, not on the roof." Staffers frequently had to turn away and cover their mouths to stifle laughter.

Jim Earl attributed his father's mangled syntax and stuttering to his being "touched by dyslexia." Though it's widely recognized today as a cognitive disorder characterized by difficulty in reading comprehension and verbal expression, dyslexia was rarely diagnosed prior to the 1970s, so the Art and Colour staff didn't know the cause of the boss's struggle with communication, and Harley probably didn't either. The problem was compounded by another impediment that seemed shocking given what he did for a living: he couldn't, or didn't, draw. No one in the department ever saw him sketch so much as a hood ornament.

"When he wanted something it would be very difficult to work with him because he knew what he wanted but he couldn't draw it for you," said Bill Mitchell. "And he would be so impatient with you if you didn't get it."

The impatience likely was born of frustration. Dyslexics can have the ability to see an object from many different perspectives all at once, but their capacity for processing so much information quickly often results in its getting garbled, distorted, or frozen. Harley seemed to picture in his mind how he wanted something to look, but he couldn't show his staff what he saw and often couldn't find the words to describe it either. So he sometimes invented words in the instant, saying, "I want that line to have a *dooflunky*, to come across, have a little hook in it, and then do a little *rashoom* or a *zong*."

Mitchell described the process as chaotic: "He had a chair, like a director's chair in a studio in Hollywood . . . and he would have all these people around him, and everyone would run around like a bunch of monkeys."

Harley would sit for hours concentrating on an actual-size drawing or clay model, while designers and modelers in lab coats scrambled to, as one of them said, "dig out ideas from his head."

"He was really quite a spectacle," said Strother MacMinn, recalling how Harley would sprawl out in a chair and "point with the toe of his shoe and—in a very hierarchical, almost demeaning way—direct the designer, 'Lower that fender line a sixteenth of an inch and let's see what happens.'

"He would refine the design with his impeccable eye. He could really do it, but the scene around him was one of a group of serfs serving their lord and master."

Harley's minute, often conflicting refinements led staffers to joke among themselves that "Mistearl wants it raised down one sixty-fourth of an inch." But even as they chafed under his unceasing judgment, the designers constantly sought his approval by leaving what they considered their best sketches lying on their desks or pinning them on the walls by their drawing boards at the end of the day, hoping he would notice them during his midnight creeps through the studio. He didn't draw and he had difficulty communicating, but "you could show him a wall full of drawings and he'd pick out the best one every time," said Richard Teague. "There's no doubt about it. He really knew a good line when he saw it, and he knew how to get from point A to point B with the modelers in the early days. He could literally look at a car and tell you what was wrong with it, and he was usually right because he had such a great grasp of form and shape."

In one press interview, Harley downplayed his participation in the creative process, insisting that he functioned merely as a "prompter."

"I sometimes wander into their quarters, make some irrelevant or even zany observation and then leave. It is surprising what effect a bit of peculiar behavior will have. First-class minds will seize on anything out of the ordinary and race off looking for explanations or hidden meanings. That's all I want them to do—start exercising their imaginations. The ideas will soon pop up."

He went to considerable lengths to ensure that they could create without corporate interference. After too many instances of middle managers walking into the studio and expressing their opinions about work in progress, he put Art and Colour under lock and key so that only staff and division presidents could enter the studio uninvited. "We were isolated from everything financial," Frank Hershey said. "We didn't have to keep any books; it was all done for us . . . we were run just like a big school."

As headmaster, Harley conducted a nonstop master class in the creation of the modern American car. "The most important part of the design of an automobile is the grille, the face of it," he told his staff early on. "That's the whole design right there." He taught them that a long, narrow hood implied power; the view of it through the windshield, stretching out ahead, gave the driver a feeling of road dominance, which he believed was an important sales feature. He lectured on the "light value" of chrome trim, saying it should be tilted at a 45 degree angle to the horizon to reflect the maximum amount of sunlight into the eye of the beholder while at the same time disguising gaps, seams, and surface flaws in mass-produced bodies. He expounded on his own "highlight rule," which held that a straight, uninterrupted horizontal line extending from the front to the rear of the body just below the windows reflected light and made the car appear longer.

Harley had one rule that was never stated but that everyone came to learn nonetheless: "No one was to get publicity in his department but Harley J. Earl," said Tom Hibbard, who unwittingly violated that rule his first week on the job when he cooperated with a GM public relations man in putting out a press release announcing his hiring while Harley was on vacation. "When Harley returned, he raised hell about it," Hibbard recalled. "In the early days, with few exceptions, pains were taken to see that no individual but Earl received publicity outside the company or got credit for anything they contributed."

Harley believed the practice of "anonymous creativity" and the restricted access to the studios helped shield individual designers from blame if one of their creations failed to catch on with the public, as had happened most dramatically with the "pregnant Buick." But others saw the policies as self-serving, even Machiavellian. Based on interviews with a handful of Art and Colour's original designers, art historian C. Edson Armi concluded that Harley had "isolated the staff through a hierarchical, even dictatorial, chain of command through which all professional contacts passed" and "worked hard to solidify his exterior contacts with directors of Chevrolet, Pontiac and the other car divisions by consciously developing [his own] image of an indispensable arbiter of taste."

In Armi's harsh view, Harley made sure that none of his subordinates developed relationships with the division managers even as he "manipulated and intimidated these divisional managers by flaunting his close friendship with GM President Sloan."

Harley's tight connection with Alfred Sloan was embodied in a button on his desk that put him in direct phone contact with the president's office in New York. No one else in the building had such a button, and Harley didn't hesitate to push it when he needed to prevail in an argument, the most dramatic instance of which reportedly occurred when Harlow Curtice, the newly named head of Buick, came into the studio one day and got into a dispute with Frank Hershey over the proposed design for one of the upcoming models. After Hershey told Curtice that he "didn't know a damn thing about styling," Harley interceded and invited the higher-ranking executive into his office, where he gave a demonstration of his one-touch telephone, placing a call to Sloan.

"Hello, Alfred, how are you?" he said, speaking warmly into the receiver. "How's [Sloan's wife] Irene, all right? That's good."

He quickly got to the point. "Alfred, I'm here in the studio with that sonofabitch Curtice, and he seems to be a little confused. He can't tell who's in charge of Buick and who's in charge of Art & Color. I thought maybe you could straighten out his ass for me."

He handed the phone to Curtice, who supposedly listened silently as Sloan told him, "Let him build anything he wants."

This often repeated story sounds suspiciously apocryphal, but the Sloan phone was a real thing, and multiple sources claim that eventually Harley didn't even have to pick up the receiver to get his way; all he had to do was raise an eyebrow and poise his finger over the button.

Harley's friendship with Sloan, too, was genuine, and it went beyond work. He and Sue regularly socialized with Alfred and Irene, inviting them over for dinner and poker. Sue always made a point of sitting to Alfred's left so she could quickly fold her hand if he bet big because she knew he never bluffed. The Earls also accompanied the Sloans every summer, along with Chevrolet general manager William Knudsen and his wife, Clara, on a monthlong cruise down the Atlantic Seaboard to the Bahamas aboard Alfred's 236-foot, $1 million yacht, *Rene*. Childless themselves, the Sloans doted on the Earls' two boys, Jim and Jerry (born in 1930), and they delighted in Sue, who loved to gamble and wasn't afraid to speak her mind about politics, no matter what the social setting. She once scandalized a group of GM executives attending a formal dinner at the exclusive Cranbrook School in Bloomfield Hills, Michigan, by sashaying into the room proudly sporting a large campaign-style button that disparaged President Roosevelt in language that many in the decidedly Democratic crowd considered uncouth. According to Frank Hershey, the button said, "'Kill the Roosevelts,' or something like that." Her in-your-face gesture set tongues to wagging for weeks at work, but it no doubt further endeared her to Sloan, who despised Roosevelt and thought his New Deal redistribution-of-wealth programs smacked of communism.

"Sue did what she wanted to do and she didn't care what people thought," said her daughter-in-law Connie Earl. "I think Harley liked it because she could say things that he, in his position, couldn't."

Harley's staff would have been stunned to learn that away from work Sue was the driving force in the boss's life. "He was what he was, in large part, because of her," said Connie. "Sue ran the show; what she said, was done."

It was Sue who decided they would not live in Bloomfield Hills, home to a preponderance of up-and-coming GM executives, when they finally moved from Larry Fisher's hotel penthouse in 1931. Instead they chose Indian Village, one of Detroit's oldest upscale residential areas, originally developed by lumber barons and early industrialists and later favored by the Ford family and Ford executives. Harley told people he wanted to live in the Village because its location east of the city adjacent to Grosse Pointe allowed him "to drive to and from work with the sun at my back." The real reason was that Sue wanted them to stay away from the encapsulated social life of GM executives and their wives. So they rented a house on Seminole Avenue, a block south of where Edsel Ford and his wife, Eleanor, lived when they first got married. Sue and Eleanor became friends and played bridge together.

Their social circle may have included the Sloans, the Fishers, and the Edsel Fords, but the Earls lived on a different economic plane. Harley earned $25,000 his first year with GM, less than he'd made in California but, as he joked, "more than any bank president in the country." By way of comparison, Alfred Sloan spent $120,000 annually to maintain the forty-three-man crew on his yacht. Harley missed out on a stock offering that GM had made to its executives just a few months before he joined the company, a last-of-its-kind opportunity that would have made him a multimillionaire, as it did even some middle managers.

"Dad was a hired hand," Jim Earl said recently. "He never had real money, not capital money. Whatever he once had went down the drain in '29. They lived on his salary. And even during his best years there were probably three or four car dealers in the Detroit area that made more than he did."

The market crash left Harley leery of investing, leading him to turn down numerous ground-floor opportunities that others ultimately profited from in his stead. He did not want to risk what he was working so hard for. He'd seen his California relatives, the Taft family, lose the bulk of their Hollywood real estate holdings and his father forced out of retirement and selling real estate to take care of his second family. He was sending J.W. regular support checks and paying down both of their debts to the banks on their stock market losses.

"Money was always a consideration," Jim Earl said. "Dad always turned out all the lights in the house at night."

Which is not to say they didn't live well. In the mid-1930s, $25,000 a year bought an enviable lifestyle. The Earls belonged to the Country Club of Detroit and the Grosse Pointe Yacht Club (though they didn't own a boat). Sue employed a cook, a housekeeper, a "nurse" for the children, and a chauffeur whose duties ranged from driving her and her girlfriends to the racetrack to escorting her and the boys on missions of mercy to Corktown, where they regularly distributed baskets of food to needy families. Also called "Irish Town," this neighborhood was originally populated by immigrants from Ireland's County Cork who had escaped the potato famine in the 1840s. By the time of the Great Depression, the area was crowded with unemployed autoworkers.

Harley's biggest extravagance was his wardrobe. Because of his size, everything he wore, even his hats, had to be custommade. His shoes came from London and were so exquisitely sculpted that "they looked like they had wooden trees in them even when he was wearing them." His shirts were made in Paris and his suits were created either by Basil Durant of New York or Eddie Schmidt of Los Angeles. The latter was known as "Hollywood's tailor" because his appointment-only shop on Sunset

Boulevard catered to a moviemaking clientele that included the era's biggest and most fashionable male star, Clark Gable, who used his services exclusively. During the filming of *Gone with the Wind*, Gable insisted that producer David O. Selznick bring in Schmidt to recut his entire wardrobe because he didn't like the way the studio-provided costumes fit.

Harley's attire combined with his height, his ice-blue eyes, and his seemingly perpetual tan to ensure that he would be the most visually commanding figure in any room he entered. "He wore clothes that nobody wore back then," said Connie Earl. "He'd wear pink socks! He loved color. He'd tell designers what he wanted and he would make himself part of the design. He didn't do it to get people to look at him. How he dressed was one of his greatest pleasures in life."

The way Frank Hershey saw it, the colorful clothes and fearsome demeanor were part of a defensive tactic, a façade Harley constructed to conceal his underlying insecurity. "Oh, he was flamboyantly dressed. He wore bright ties; he wore purple shirts, or whatever. But it was calculated. He *was* projecting an image, but he had to. I mean, he was fighting, he was 'kicking against the pricks,' as the saying goes. And while it seemed to us he was living the life of Riley, he wasn't."

8

"WHAT WILL I TELL MR. SLOAN?"

As the U.S. economy crawled out of the pit of the Great Depression in 1936, General Motors emerged as the dominant force in the auto industry. Having reported a profit in every post-crash year except 1932, the company matched its 1928 production level of 1.7 million vehicles and commanded a 43 percent market share, as Ford dropped behind Chrysler for the first time, to a distant third place.

GM sales had rebounded across all divisions. Chevrolet alone accounted for 27 percent of all cars sold. Pontiac sales had nearly doubled under the hand of Frank Hershey, who designed the distinctive Silver Streak trim, a wide-ribbed strip of chrome that ran down the center of the hood and rear deck and identified the brand for the next twenty years. Even Cadillac, which had hemorrhaged money for five years after the market crash, was back in profit, thanks to a remarkable intervention by a previously undistinguished middle manager.

Nicholas Dreystadt was a forty-two-year-old German-born former Mercedes-Benz mechanic who had worked his way up from the shop floor to become Cadillac's national service manager. Upon learning in June 1932 that members of GM's executive committee, including Alfred Sloan and William Knudsen, were meeting on the fourteenth floor of the Detroit headquarters to vote on whether to kill off the Cadillac due to flagging sales, Dreystadt took drastic action—he burst into the meeting uninvited.

Sloan and Knudsen likely had never seen or heard of Dreystadt before. But suddenly there he was, standing in front of them in a rumpled tweed coat pocked with burn holes from pipe embers, speaking in a thick accent and pleading for them to spare the storied luxury line. Struck by his passion and audacity, the committee let him talk.

He told them he had learned something surprising in his visits to Cadillac service centers around the country, something they probably didn't know. While overall sales were down, Cadillacs remained extremely popular among a small, hidden elite—black entertainers, boxers, business owners, and professionals, people who earned high incomes but were barred from spending it on the usual accouterments of success. They could not join fancy country clubs, for example, or buy homes in upscale (white) residential areas. About the only American status symbol they could acquire was an expensive automobile. But they couldn't buy a Cadillac, at least not officially, because in an effort to appeal to the prestige market, the company had long maintained a policy of refusing to sell to "negroes."

Dreystadt said he had talked to many black owners as they brought their cars in for servicing, and he discovered that they had gotten around the ban by paying white people several hundred dollars to "front" the purchases for them. He wasn't about to tell a room full of rich white capitalists that their policy was unfair or immoral. Instead he argued that it made no economic sense to allow outside parties to profit from the sales of their cars. Why not keep that front money in-house by ending the ban and catering to the black bourgeoisie, actually marketing directly to them?

It was a radical notion; no major American company had done that before. The committee promptly granted a stay of execution for the Cadillac and gave him eighteen months to develop the "Negro market." Within a year, sales had increased by more than 80 percent and the division was breaking even, earning Dreystadt a promotion to general manager and a permanent place in auto industry annals as "the man who saved Cadillac."

Perhaps the best news for GM in 1936, however, was the resurgence of its cornerstone division, Buick, thanks largely to the bond that had developed between Harley Earl and Harlow Curtice since their early contretemps in Harley's office. An accountant by training, "Red" Curtice had risen from bookkeeper to president of GM's AC Spark Plug Division when Alfred Sloan handed him the keys to Buick in 1933. Frank Hershey was right when he said that Curtice "didn't know a damn thing about styling." But Curtice did know what he liked in a car, and his taste ran to big, bold, and fast. He wanted more than anything to blow away Buick's age-old image as the stodgy, respectable "doctor's car." According to an often told story, when he saw the first drawings for the proposed 1936 models, he asked Harley, "Would you want to be seen driving one of these cars?"

"To be honest with you, no," Harley said. "These cars are designed for the Buick market."

"There *is* no 'Buick market,'" Curtice supposedly replied. "Design me a Buick that you would like to own."

That was all Harley needed to hear. When the 1936 models appeared in the showrooms a year and a half later they were rounder and more streamlined than their predecessors, with swept-back windshields and massive vertical-bar "fencer's mask" grilles. A new model called the Roadmaster weighed in at 4,100 pounds, heavier than a Cadillac, and featured rear-hinged "suicide doors" that gave it the look of a gangland getaway car. A smaller, sportier Century sedan boasted a top speed of 100 miles an hour and a zero-to-sixty acceleration of eighteen seconds, which was considered jackrabbit-quick at the time, earning the car accolades as "the first factory hot rod." Buick was named the best-looking car of the year in a public opinion poll conducted by *Sales Management* magazine, and sales bounced back nearly to pre-Depression levels, with Buick ranked as the fifth-best-selling car in the United States.

Harley had been a Cadillac man since he joined the company, largely out of loyalty to Larry Fisher, his GM mentor. But after Fisher retired in mid-1934, Curtice persuaded Harley to switch his company car from a Cadillac to a Buick. Either as enticement or appreciation, he offered Harley a Century chassis and a budget to design and build a one-of-a-kind car for his personal use, a perquisite enjoyed by the industry's two other styling chiefs, Edsel Ford and Packard's Ed Macauley. After ten years in Detroit, Harley was beginning to taste the fruits of his labor.

In January 1937, Art and Colour was renamed the GM Styling Section and took over the top four floors of the newly constructed eleven-story Research Annex B, known as the Argonaut Building, across Milwaukee Avenue behind GM headquarters. The new quarters provided enough space (80,000 square feet) for each of the five design teams—Chevrolet, Pontiac, Oldsmobile, Buick, and Cadillac—to have separate studios for the first time. The top floor contained a specially lighted auditorium with raised revolving platforms for presenting finished clay models to division managers and board members, although the Styling staff preferred transporting the models via a large freight elevator to a garden area on the roof where they could be viewed in natural daylight, to better show off the highlights. Outdoor viewing had its drawbacks, however. On one occasion several clay models melted in the heat, and on a bitterly cold winter day another froze and cracked in half.

Harley's new office on the eleventh floor caused as much talk around the company as his clothes. Designed with the help of Detroit's most expensive interior decorator, William Wright, it featured "dark paneled walls; a high, elaborate, hand-carved, beamed ceiling with touches of gilt; deep oriental carpets; lots of leather; and heavy, muted drapes." At the far end of the room, Harley's massive oak desk was elevated on a dais, assuring that he would sit at eye level with anyone who stood before him. The overall effect was intimidating. "As you walked into that room and had to make the long trek from the door to his desk to receive your audience, you were in a pretty shaky state by the time you arrived," recalled Frank Hershey. "And if you could survive that ordeal, then he knew that you had the guts to do this thing."

Harley wasted no time turning Styling's new home into a secure fortress. Each of the studios was kept locked at all times, and staff members were given keys only to their own studio, the idea being to prevent not only spying by other companies but also unauthorized creative cross-pollination among design teams, who were forbidden to even discuss their work with one another for fear it would lead to a creeping homogeneity, a visual sameness among the divisions. Sloan and Harley believed that GM cars needed to be so distinct from one another and the competition that a twelve-year-old kid would be able to tell from a block away whether it was a Chevrolet, Pontiac, Oldsmobile, Buick, or Cadillac coming down the street.

Internal security was strictly enforced, with elevators stopping only on the eighth and eleventh floors, so that staffers who worked on the middle two floors had to enter and exit on the eleventh, where Harley stationed a "timekeeper" who took down names and had the authority to inspect packages and briefcases coming in or going out. Only Harley, with his master key, could enter any studio any time he wanted. Only he could take a sketch from the Pontiac studio over to the Buick studio and say, "I think you should try something like this." He was the only one who knew what everyone was doing.

Harley came through each studio regularly, if not every day, with no notice except for a phone call from a staffer in another studio warning that he was on the floor, in the hallway, headed in their direction. Then they'd hear his key in the lock, the design chief and his assistant would scramble to meet him at the door, and everyone else would look like they were busier than they'd ever been in their lives. Designer Gene Garfinkle described a typical Harley drop-by. "There would be guys drafting lines with the width of a 2H pencil—tenths of a millimeter wide on a full size drawing—and Earl might have been in the studio three nights before and asked if that fender line could be lowered a little. And as soon as he had that studio door open, I mean, you could hear his voice: 'I thought I told you to lower that line.' He could see it from 40 feet away. He knew exactly where that line was supposed to be; that was the sort of sensitivity he had."

Sometimes Harley would just wander through, looking over shoulders, examining sketches, checking progress on clay models, striking fear into their hearts without saying a word. If he did speak, it was either to the staff as a group or directly to the chief designer; he never addressed lower-ranked staffers individually. "It was like a caste system," said Strother MacMinn. "Even if the designer in question was standing right there, he'd say [to the chief designer], 'Ask him why he did that. Ask why he put this line on the side of the car?' It was as if you did not exist."

Harley's overall responsibilities were expanding rapidly. Sloan named him to the company's new Engineering Policy Group, a committee composed of a dozen or so of GM's highest corporate executives and board members. "It will give you more authority when you talk to the presidents of these different divisions," Sloan told him. Chevrolet added trucks to his client list and Opel, GM's German subsidiary, sought his help in developing a mini-car with a 75-inch wheelbase.

His staff had grown to nearly two hundred at a time when the design departments at Ford and Chrysler employed no more than fifty between them. The Styling Section now included an interior department that focused on developing durable and attractive new fabrics and materials for dashboards, floor coverings, headliners, and upholstery, with the stated aim of fashioning passenger compartments as "harmonious and comfortable as a living room." Styling's color department had teams of experts that researched fashion trends and conducted extensive field surveys to track shifting color preferences among car buyers in all sections of the country. Their findings were regularly incorporated into a large wall map that showed a clear connection between color choices and climate, with black, dark grays, maroons, and dark blues favored in New England states, while lighter colors predominated in the South and California. The research also showed a correlation between color preferences and the economy.

"During periods of reduced business activity, people seem to prefer dark colors, and they swing to lighter hues with the return of good times," Harley said in a GM press release. Deep in the Depression, for example, black cars were the most popular. But as the economy gradually rebounded between 1933 and 1937, color choices lightened in lockstep with the improving public mood. "Certain gunmetal shades [of gray] have gone as high as thirty-five or forty percent of the total production," he said. "This is quite significant because at no time in the history of painting automobiles has any color assumed so big a proportion of the total output." Hinting at brighter days ahead, "Colors that have aluminum powder added to them, creating a somewhat metallic effect . . . have been growing in popularity steadily."

Styling's clashes with division engineers decreased sharply after Harley staged what Alfred Sloan called "a dramatic demonstration" in the Styling Auditorium. Tired of constantly hearing it was structurally impossible to lower a car body to his specifications, Harley brought a Cadillac onto the stage and, in front of an audience that included the division presidents, chief engineers, and several members of the board of directors, he instructed two assistants to lift the body off the chassis. Donning protective masks, the men then cut the frame apart with acetylene torches and quickly welded it back together in such a way that the passenger compartment would sit cradled between the axles rather than on top of them. When the body was lowered back onto the chassis, it sat four inches closer to the floor than the unaltered car. "They had proved a point," Sloan wrote in his memoir. "Not only could the body be lowered but, in its position, it looked one hundred percent better."

Harley had done more than prove a point; he had finally won the grudging respect of GM engineers. They may not have liked him any better than before, but his little display of showmanship told them that he knew what he was doing and had the full backing of upper management, so it was not in their interest to keep fighting him.

The result was nothing short of a sea change. Aesthetics finally began to drive the design process as the engineers acceded to the stylists' artistic visions by moving the engines forward, lowering the body profiles, and facilitating the development of a rear deck large enough to accommodate an integral trunk compartment that would hold a spare tire and luggage. The lowered bodies eliminated all rationale for vestigial running boards, which were relics from the days when passengers had to step up into carriages set high enough off the ground to navigate unpaved, rain-rutted roads.

Harley forced his body engineers "to explore areas beyond what they considered to be feasible; that was part of his technique," said Strother MacMinn, citing as an example the creation of what Harley called the "suitcase fender." As drawn on paper and sculpted in clay, "the front well is very rounded and encases the wheel thoroughly. And as it goes back, it trails behind the wheel and goes downward on a slight angle, and when it gets to the limit of its length, where the door is, it drops vertically." The engineers found it almost impossible to stamp that form in sheet metal in one piece, but Harley insisted on the design and pushed them to find a way to make it happen. "So they stamped it in three pieces and hand welded it," MacMinn explained. "Which was acceptable to Cadillac engineering because they had a large number of craftsmen in the depths of the Depression and they wanted to keep them employed. So they were able to keep them fed, which was a good thing for loyalty and the development of the product, and it was a fender form that nobody else could imitate."

"It was his insistence on doing these things that brought them about," said Clare MacKichan. "They didn't happen because some inventor had this idea. He wanted that to happen. And what he wanted, he got. And in doing it, he developed a very inventive group of engineers."

Harley still had to sell Styling's ideas to the division chiefs, however, and they weren't always receptive. At a meeting with Chevrolet executives, he presented a front-end design featuring headlights that were "faired-in" (streamlined) to the fenders rather than mounted separately on stanchions, which would have been a first for an American car. But the Chevy boys didn't buy it.

"There was Sloan, there was Knudsen, the Fisher brothers, and O. E. Hunt, the chief engineer, and I thought, 'My God, wow!'" designer Bill Mitchell recalled. "O.E. was negative on that light in the fender because he said, 'If you bump the fender, you'd throw the headlight out of kilter.' Earl stood up, his belt buckle [level with] O.E.'s mouth—he's that tall. And he looked down—he'd always look down at him—and he said, 'O.E., why don't you call me a son of a bitch? I could understand that.' And he walked out of the studio quietly, and broke up the meeting."

Mitchell, who was just twenty-three at the time, couldn't believe that anyone would dare to walk out on Sloan and Knudsen. "Oh, [Harley] was powerful," he said. "God, I admired him. He'd just knocked the tar out of anybody."

Harley's reputation within the industry grew as gifted designers left GM and went to work for other automakers, taking with them techniques they'd learned in his employ, tales of his temper, and portfolios stuffed with drawings that had failed to please him. Art and Colour alums Tom Tjaarda and Bob Gregorie worked in tandem on Edsel Ford's 1936 Lincoln Zephyr, which caused a sensation at the New York Auto Show with its aerodynamic "streamline moderne" styling. Gordon Buehrig designed the classic 1936 Cord 810 at the Auburn Automotive Company from sketches he had done several years before for one of Harley's periodic intramural competitions. Harley had tasked five design teams with producing a quarter-scale clay model of a futuristic four-door sedan, with an expenses-paid, weeklong, chauffeur-driven trip to the Chicago World's Fair as the prize. Buehrig's team, working from his sketches, submitted a model with a front end that featured hidden headlights and an unadorned coffin-shaped nose with low horizontal louvers but no grille. Buehrig said later that he was trying to show that, contrary to what Harley preached, the grille or "face" was not necessarily the most important part of a car's design.

It was not a winning strategy. In a straw vote among the teams, the Buehrig model came in first. But the panel of official judges, which included Harley and several of the Fisher brothers, ranked it last. Now, however, the car inspired by that rejected model was being heralded as a groundbreaking objet d'art, its blunt, grille-less coffin nose, horizontal hood louvers, and first-ever retractable headlights causing one automotive writer to rhapsodize, "For sheer taste, for functional correctness and for beauty, the 810 Cord is the best design the American industry has ever produced."

For a man as competitive as Harley, that had to sting, although he may have found some solace in the fact that the Cord was plagued by mechanical problems resulting from its being rushed into the marketplace, and its financially strapped manufacturer, Auburn, discontinued it in August 1937, having produced only 2,320 of the now legendary cars.

Still, the fact remained that GM Styling didn't produce anything as exciting as the Cord or the Zephyr in 1936 and 1937. So Harley had something to prove in 1938.

For that model year, Cadillac was looking for a makeover on its Sixty series, which had been introduced two years earlier as an entry-level luxury sedan, priced at the low end of the Cadillac line, just a few hundred dollars more than the top-of-the-line Buick. With its good looks, new V-8 engine, and more affordable price, the Sixty had proven enormously successful, accounting for more than half of Cadillac's production and helping to drive up the division's sales by 254 percent.

Cadillac general manager Nicholas Dreystadt wasn't as focused on styling as his predecessor, Larry Fisher, and he was far more conservative. All he wanted was a face-lifted Sixty that would attract more first-time luxury buyers. Harley had something more ambitious in mind, however. Eager to pick up the gauntlet thrown down by the Zephyr and the Cord, he and Bill Mitchell, whom he'd just promoted to chief designer for the Cadillac studio, came up with a prototype Sixty Special that featured a new body that sat three inches lower than any previous Cadillac (but with no less headroom), a first-ever rear-hinged, front-opening "alligator" hood, an extended curvilinear coupe-style rear deck never before seen on a sedan, and long suitcase fenders that were sculpted with trailing knife-blade edges that Mitchell likened to the look of "creased pants." They slimmed down the traditionally bulky roof pillars and upper doorframes, allowing for more glass area and greater visibility, and banded the side windows with thin chrome strips that foreshadowed the "hardtop" look that would dominate the industry in the decades to come. They opted for minimal chrome body trim and, in another first for an American production (noncustom) car, eliminated running boards, making it possible for the body to be extended out almost to the width of the wheels, thereby providing extra interior room and comfort for up to six passengers.

The prototype looked so unlike previous Cadillacs that some executives were concerned that they had gone too far. "I remember they had it all finished and were showing it in the auditorium and had the board and all the division heads there," said Frank Hershey. "Harley had to sell it to the board of directors, and he wasn't getting very far."

Dreystadt was among those who worried aloud that the new look was too radical for traditionally conservative Cadillac customers. "Sloan was supposed to be there, too, but he wasn't for some reason," Hershey recalled. "They all knew, though, that Sloan and Knudsen liked it." The executives hemmed and hawed until Harley, in exasperation, played his trusty hole card. "Earl turned, put his hands on his hips, looked down at everybody and said, 'Well, goddammit, gentlemen, what will I tell Mr. Sloan when he asks me?' And that sold it in five minutes."

The Sixty Special quickly became Cadillac's bestselling model, and over the next few years proved to be arguably the most stylistically influential car of the era. Still, Edsel Ford managed to score points against Harley in 1938. His restyled Lincoln Zephyr featured not only the in-fender headlights that Harley had failed to sell to his division chiefs but also the first-ever horizontal grille. By simply turning the '36 Zephyr grille on its side and moving it down below the nose of the car to the so-called catwalk area between the headlights, Edsel's designers forever changed the face of the American automobile.

Harley and Frank Hershey were in Paris for the annual auto

show when Hershey first saw the new Zephyr, which was making its debut at the event. He hurried back to their hotel to show pictures of the car to the boss, who studied them for a moment and said, "Aren't they god-awful?" Hershey didn't think so, and he was sure Harley didn't either. "He wasn't going to admit that Ford got one up on us."

Harley one-upped the entire industry the following year when he unveiled a singular car that was not intended for public sale and didn't even have a proper name. Technically, it was a Buick. Harlow Curtice had provided the chassis and design budget, and Buick's chief engineer, Charlie Chayne, was part of a small team that worked on it for eighteen months in a separate se-cured studio. They dubbed it the "Y Project" in an ironic nod to the experimental "X Projects" that proliferated in the auto-mobile and aircraft industries, but Harley kept referring to it as the "Y-job," and the name eventually stuck. It was to be his personal car, after all.

"I just want a little semi-sports car, a kind of convertible," he told the team at the outset, though he soon decided the Y-job would be a "boattail," a body style defined by a rear deck that tapered to a prow point and long popular among wealthy custom car aficionados. Edsel Ford and Packard design chief Ed Ma-cauley drove boattail roadsters created by their styling staffs; Errol Flynn and Marlene Dietrich tooled around Hollywood in limited-production Auburn Speedsters, the most flamboyant of the boattail breed.

The Speedster was Harley's kind of car—low-slung, with a long, narrow hood that radiated power, four chrome exhaust pipes snaking out of the engine compartment into the front fend-ers, and a raked V-type windshield that made it appear to be speeding even when standing still. Designed by Gordon Buehrig, it was a car that demanded to be noticed. But it was also a car of the past, with a vertical grille and headlights mounted on stanchions—beautifully designed, classic, and outdated. The Indiana-based Duesenberg-Auburn-Cord Company sold fewer than two hundred Speedsters between 1935 and 1937, when it went out of business.

Harley wanted the Y-job to be a car of the future. Toward that end, he pushed the team relentlessly to come up with styling and mechanical features that hadn't been seen or even imagined before, a process so arduous and frustrating at times that they began calling it the "Why job." But the result was a masterpiece of innovation.

Completed in late 1938 at a cost of about $50,000 (twenty times the purchase price of a Speedster), the Y-job boasted a long list of firsts that included a power-operated soft top that stowed beneath a hinged rear-deck panel, power windows, push-button outer door handles, retractable headlights that opened and closed like human eyelids at the turn of a dashboard switch, and front fenders that flowed back through the doors. Between its broad horizontal grille and tapered tail, the car stretched more than 17 feet yet stood only 58 inches high at the top of the windshield (the same as the Speedster). Harley looked like a giant standing next to it. That he could climb in and out with ease was a testament to the underlying engineering. The glossy black finish seemed at odds with his love of bright colors, but it lent a look of sophistication that other sports cars lacked. The Y-job was an exquisitely tailored tuxedo to the Speedster's flashy Hawaiian shirt.

At some point in the design process, Harley discussed with Sloan and Harlow Curtice the idea of giving the Y-job a broader purpose, of using it as the basis of an ongoing program to test styling concepts with consumers far in advance of production. Most car buyers didn't know exactly what they wanted until they saw it sitting in front of them; that's why millions of them packed the auto shows every year. But if the Y-job and other GM "cars of the future" toured the show circuit, Harley reasoned, then attendees could see what might be available several years down the road and the company could log their reactions before it spent tens of millions of dollars retooling factories to build a car, or thousands of cars, the public might reject.

Harley's plan was for the Y-job to make its official debut during the 1939 New York Auto Show at the Waldorf-Astoria Hotel. The event coincided with a GM publicity push to introduce the work of the Styling Section to the automotive press. As part of that PR campaign, the company published a remarkable thirty-two-page booklet, *Modes and Motors*, illustrated in the art deco style, which traced the evolution of art through human history—from the first cave painting in Spain to the Egyptians, the Assyrians, the Babylonians, the Greeks and the Romans, Chinese and Moors, from the Dark Ages to the Italian Renaissance to the Industrial Revolution. The introductory passage reads like something Steve Jobs might have written more than half a century later: "Art in industry is entirely new. Only in recent years has the interest of manufacturer and user alike been expanded from the mere question of 'does it work?' to include 'how should it look?' and 'why should it look that way?' Appearance and style have assumed equal importance with utility, price and operation."

Harley didn't write the text, but his personal experience at General Motors clearly drove the booklet's allegorical narrative, which told of the "artist" who once regarded manufacturers with "thinly-concealed contempt" and thought of them as "rough coarse men whose sole purpose in life was to make money" and who did not "feel the need to have an artist tell them how to design their products."

According to the narrative, "The job of the designer [is] to bring together the science of the engineer and the skill of the artist," noting that finally "the artist and the engineer have joined hands to the end that articles of everyday use may be beautiful as well as useful. Probably in no field have the results of the application of art to the products of industry been more apparent than that of the automobile."

As for the future, *Modes and Motors* concluded, "Certain it is that out of the merger of art, science and industry have come new techniques that have within themselves the ability to create an entirely new pattern and setting for the life of the world."

The Y-job was exhibited at the New York Auto Show, but its debut turned out to be its swan song as well. After the show, Harley shipped the car to his home in Grosse Pointe and began driving it to and from work every day. It was the ultimate vanity vehicle, outclassing anything in Edsel Ford's garage and never failing to draw admiring stares as Harley cruised along Lake Shore Drive, usually with the top down. "His head would stick up above the windshield and he had to duck when he put the top up," said Clare MacKichan. "We'd often see him come in on a morning with a light sprinkle of rain, but the top would be down."

Despite that drawback, Harley loved the car and drove it for years. The national tour of auto shows never materialized, however, due to the ominous turn of events in Europe.

9
HELPING MAKE GERMANY GREAT AGAIN

Adolf Hitler never learned to drive, but he was an ardent admirer of the American auto industry and its founding father. "I regard Henry Ford as my inspiration," he famously told the *Detroit News* in a 1931 interview. "I shall do my best to put his theories into practice in Germany."

His admiration bordered on hero worship. As early as 1922, the *New York Times* reported that the future Führer proudly displayed a life-size portrait of Ford in his office at the Nazi Party headquarters in Munich, where visitors could pick up copies of Ford's anti-Semitic screed *The International Jew*, which was a compilation of articles from his racist newspaper, the *Dearborn Independent*.

To Hitler, Ford was the world's most successful and stalwart anti-Semite. "It is Jews who govern the Stock Exchange forces of the American union," Hitler wrote in his autobiography, *Mein Kampf*.

When Hitler read Ford's 1922 autobiography, *My Life and Work*, he had an epiphany. Germany's automakers were years behind the Americans, still building mostly expensive cars for the upper classes. Only one in a hundred Germans owned an automobile, compared to one in five Americans. But if the German auto industry applied Ford's mass-manufacturing techniques to the production of a car the common people could afford, like the Model T, Hitler figured, then perhaps it could be the key to rebuilding Germany's devastated economy and financing his dreams of European expansion.

As he amassed power over the next few years, Hitler talked constantly about his idea for a *volkswagen*, or "people's car." A former art student and still a frustrated artist, he supposedly dashed off a sketch of how he thought the car should look while eating lunch one day at a Munich restaurant, and gave it to Jakob Werlin, the head of Daimler-Benz. Shortly after becoming German chancellor, Hitler said in a speech at the 1934 Berlin International Automobile and Motor Cycle Show, "It can only be said with profound sadness that, in the present age of civilization, the ordinary hard-working citizen is still unable to afford a car, a means of up-to-date transport and a source of enjoyment in the leisure hours." He broached the subject again two months later during a meeting in his chancellery office with James Mooney, president of the General Motors Overseas Corporation. "The German People have precisely the same desire to use a car as, for example, the American People," Hitler said. "If I hope to increase the number of cars in Germany to three or four million, the price and the maintenance costs of these cars must be compatible with the income of the three or four million potential buyers." He told Mooney he thought the car should be priced at approximately 900 marks (or about $300).

In addition to acquiring all of Opel, GM built a truck-manufacturing plant in the state of Brandenburg in 1935. Meanwhile, Ford established a German subsidiary, Ford Germany

Company, in 1931 (it was later renamed Ford-Werke to sound more German) and built a factory in Cologne. Both American car giants were interested in making the *volkswagen*, but Hitler wanted a purely German company to build the inexpensive little car that could, he believed, make Germany great again. So he gave the job to his friend, automotive engineer Dr. Ferdinand Porsche, the founder of the firm that bore his name. Porsche then teamed up with Jakob Werlin and Robert Ley, the head of the German Labor Front, to form Volkswagenwerk.

On May 26, 1938, Hitler laid the cornerstone of the Volkswagenwerk factory in Fallersleben, Germany. The immense facility was modeled after Ford's Rouge River plant and partly staffed with Ford engineers. The Nazi Party promised it would be "the biggest automobile factory in the world," capable of turning out 1.5 million cars a year. Seventy thousand people cheered as the Führer was driven around in a test car that most Americans today would recognize as a classic Volkswagen Beetle. In his accompanying speech, Hitler dubbed it the KdF Wagen after the Nazi Party slogan *"Kraft durch Freude"* ("Strength through Joy").

Calling the undertaking "something only possible in Hitler's Germany," Nazi propagandists predicted that "hundreds of thousands of people's comrades, above all those who live in big cities and in drab industrial areas and who lead a joyless, colorless life, will now be able to reach the beauties of nature on weekends or after work with their families. They will find pleasure and relaxation. They will feel more like free and independent people. To own a car means to live twice as much!"

(As it turned out, only fifty-four KdF Wagens were built before the factory was converted to military production in 1940. Hitler received one of the cars for his forty-ninth birthday, Japan's

Emperor Hirohito got one, and the rest were distributed among Nazi Party officials.)

Henry Ford's contribution wasn't mentioned on that day in the spring of 1938, but two months later, on Ford's seventy-fifth birthday, Hitler sent two German diplomats to Ford's Dearborn office to present him with the Grand Cross of the Supreme Order of the German Eagle, the highest honor Nazi Germany bestowed on foreigners. The previous year's honoree was Benito Mussolini. Ford seemed delighted as he posed for pictures with the diplomats, who told him the award represented Hitler's "personal admiration and indebtedness" to him.

Despite the Führer's affinity for Ford, General Motors seems to have profited more from its investment in the German auto industry. Under GM's ownership, Opel became the country's largest manufacturer of automobiles and trucks—three times the size of Daimler-Benz, quadruple that of Ford-Werke. By 1938, Opel was producing 40 percent of the vehicles in Germany and about 65 percent of its exports. Its biggest customer was the German military, which purchased six thousand of the company's Blitz trucks that year alone, vehicles that would be used to carry troops, ammunition, and supplies when Hitler launched his *blitzkrieg* ("lightning war") invasion of Poland the following year. Ford was the second-largest producer of trucks for the German army.

Hitler's thoughts upon reading Henry Ford's autobiography proved out. Auto manufacturing had sparked an economic recovery, eliminating the mass unemployment that had afflicted the country in the wake of World War I and boosting the popularity of the Nazi Party. He could not have done it without the help of Ford and GM.

In the run-up to the war in Europe, GM maintained publicly

that its involvement with Opel was purely passive, not operational. But even the Styling Section was involved in the day-to-day operations at Opel. Harley sent Frank Hershey and several others to Opel headquarters in Russelsheim in 1937 to supervise the restyling of Opel's small family car, the Kadett, and its new larger "executive" sedan, the Kapitan. As Hershey prepared to leave for Europe, Harley impressed on him the importance and prestige of the posting. "Are you sure your wife has the proper clothes?" he asked. "You have to have two tuxes. Here's two thousand dollars."

Harley went to Germany a number of times to check on the team's progress. At the conclusion of his first trip he asked Hershey to drive him to the airport in a Kadett.

"You can't get in a Kadett; you're six foot six," Hershey said, exaggerating Harley's height by an inch. "You can't sit in that." Harley was traveling with four or five large bags to accommodate his wardrobe. Still, he insisted, "Get me a Kadett."

Their journey to the airport was highlighted by a shouting match between Harley, who didn't speak German, and two German baggage handlers, who apparently didn't know the meaning of "goddamn sonofabitch," as well as a male bonding moment in the men's room that Hershey would never forget.

"You had to step up onto a platform and stand in front of the urinals," he recalled years later. "So there I am standing next to God. I thought, 'My god, if the guys at home could only see me now they wouldn't believe it.'" Hershey was so nervous he couldn't pee, so he gave up and stepped down from the platform, and just as he passed behind Harley, "he broke wind right in my face, and then he turned and said, 'Did I get you, Frank?' I couldn't believe it. I saw him like nobody else ever saw him, as just an ordinary guy, not the king of General Motors, 'Mistearl.'

I could have called him Harley at that moment and gotten away with it. And no one ever believed that story."

During one of Harley's trips to Germany, he spent a festive evening with William Knudsen, James Mooney, and several other GM executives celebrating Knudsen's birthday at Hitler's favorite restaurant, Osteria Bavaria, a popular artists' hangout in Munich. Such public displays of conviviality became increasingly uncomfortable for GM employees, however, as the Nazis tightened their grip on all aspects of German life.

Swastikas began appearing inside the Opel plant and some of Hitler's most hateful and militarily bellicose speeches could be heard on the public address system. A growing number of employees were disappearing from work without any explanation.

At the end of what turned out to be Harley's last visit to Russelsheim, he took Hershey aside and asked, "Frank, if anything happens, have you got enough money to get out and get home?" Hershey said he didn't. "Well, look, I'll send you some," Harley said. "Where do I send it?"

"You can't send it to Germany because [the Nazis] won't give it to me," Hershey told him. "They will confiscate it." They decided that Harley would wire the money to the Bank of Arnhem just across the border in Holland and have the bank notify Hershey with a telegram saying, "Your grandmother has arrived."

Three weeks later, Hershey heard from the bank and headed for Holland, driving an Oldsmobile. Stopping to spend the night at a hotel in Bonn, he heard movement in the trunk, where he discovered a sixteen-year-old boy he recognized from the office. "He worked in the blueprint room in the foreman's office and he was always smiling and giving me a 'how do you do.'" Hershey didn't know how the boy found out he was going to Holland or what car he would be driving, "but he wanted me to take him over the border," he said. "If [the Nazis] had caught me, they'd have shot me at sunrise. I was scared stiff. I took him in and made him stay the night. And then I bought him a suitcase and something [to wear] that made him look legit, and put him on a train back."

Still sounding uncomfortable with his decision decades later, Hershey told the interviewer that Jews "were trying every kind of way to get out. I think he thought I was the best way to do it."

Hershey returned from Holland with the four thousand dollars that Harley had sent, but it was only a matter of weeks before he was on his way back, this time fleeing with other GM employees in a caravan of twelve Cadillacs, a Buick, and a Pontiac. "We got the call in the morning and we evacuated," Hershey said. The German army was poised to invade Czechoslovakia to enforce Hitler's claim to an area known as Sudetenland, where three million ethnic Germans lived. British prime minister Neville Chamberlain and French prime minister Édouard Daladier were on their way to Munich to meet with Hitler and Mussolini to try to negotiate a peaceful solution, but all of Europe was bracing for war at any moment.

"We got to the Dutch border just as they were putting up the last roadblock. But we finally got out, and we stayed a week in Holland."

The invasion was averted when the Munich Conference ended with an agreement that ceded the Czechoslovakian territory to Germany in exchange for Hitler's promise not to invade the rest of the country. Chamberlain returned to England claiming they had negotiated "peace in our time." To which Winston Churchill famously replied in a speech to the House of Commons, "You were given the choice between war and dishonour. You chose dishonour and you will have war."

Hershey and the other GM refugees returned to Russelsheim, where "all the Germans made fun of us for being scaredy-cats."

A year later, on September 1, 1939, they fled Germany for good when the German army and all those GM-made Opel trucks rolled across the border into Poland, touching off World War II. They escaped across France, where they boarded a ferry in the port of Dunkirk and crossed the English Channel to Dover, dodging floating mines along the way.

When Hershey finally made it back to Detroit, he went up to Harley's office and found that some things hadn't changed.

"I've got $3,800 of the company's money," he said. "What'll I do with it?"

Harley looked at him and replied, "I don't have the slightest idea of what you are talking about."

"It's the money you sent me."

"The money I sent you?"

"Yes, you sent it to the Arnhem Bank."

"Look, I'm busy as hell," Harley said. "Would you get out of this office? And don't ever mention that goddamned money to me again."

Knowing better than to argue with the boss, Hershey and his wife used the leftover money to buy a house.

10

"I WOULDN'T
BUY THAT
SONOFABITCH"

As Harley Earl approached his forty-seventh birthday in the fall of 1940, GM's executive committee voted to make him a vice president.

The promotion marked the first time a designer had reached that rank in the auto industry, or any industry, and it served as a long-overdue public acknowledgment of his pivotal role in the company's phenomenal rise. He had succeeded beyond Alfred Sloan's expectations, revolutionizing the way cars were designed, marketed, and even imagined. Full-size clay modeling was now standard practice throughout the industry.

As America's first and only corporate vice president of styling, he was accorded a new level of respect wherever he went. "When he walked into a room, everything went silent," said Frank Hershey. "They all wanted to hear what he wanted to say." His name was starting to be mentioned in the same breath as Raymond Loewy and Norman Bel Geddes, the two most celebrated figures in the burgeoning field of industrial design. Loewy made a fortune designing everything from refrigerators for Sears, Roebuck, and soda fountain dispensers for Coca-Cola to vacuum cleaners for Electrolux and locomotives for the Pennsylvania Railroad. Bel Geddes, a onetime movie set designer, created the most popular attraction at the 1939–1940 New York World's Fair, GM's "Futurama" exhibit, which cost $7 million to build (the equivalent of $120 million today) and offered fairgoers a simulated eighteen-minute flight over an imagined 1960 American landscape with farmland, forests, small towns, and cities connected by a ribbon of multilevel automated superhighways. With unheralded help from the Styling staff, Bel Geddes had built a one-acre scale-model diorama that boasted nearly fifty thousand miniature buildings, a hundred thousand individual trees—of thirteen different species—and five thousand futuristic vehicles. It drew tens of thousands of people a day to GM's Highways and Horizons pavilion, which recorded 25 million visitors over the fair's two-year run.

Bel Geddes and Loewy had been dabbling in auto design for nearly a decade through consulting deals with Chrysler and Studebaker, respectively, but neither had yet designed a commercially successful automobile, perhaps because they weren't real car professionals and therefore lacked a requisite ingredient, what Bill Mitchell and Harley called "gasoline in the veins." By that metaphor, Harley's vascular system pulsed with pure petrol. The carriage maker's son not only "loved cars more than anything in the world," according to Mitchell, he also seemed to have an unparalleled understanding of the space they occupied in the American psyche. "Your automobile," he'd say, "is the only possession that you can get into a discussion about with a stranger in a bar."

As GM's competitors began expanding their styling departments to keep up with him, they quickly found there weren't enough trained designers and clay modelers to go around, which created a seller's market for anyone with GM experience. Partly to stay ahead of the turnover in his staff, Harley directed company scholarship grants to two leading industrial-design schools, Pratt Institute in Brooklyn and the Art Center School in Los Angeles, both of which added automobile design courses to their curriculum. He even started his own school, calling it the Detroit Institute of Automobile Styling, with a classroom in the General Motors building on Cass Avenue. Recruited through ads in *Popular Mechanics* and other magazines, prospective students had to submit work samples and references. If accepted, they were paid $75 a month to participate in a yearlong program that included training in sketching and clay modeling overseen by members of the Styling staff.

Clare MacKichan had studied art and architecture and held a degree in mechanical engineering from the University of Michigan when he enrolled, along with nine others, in the first class at the institute. "I wanted to design; it was my sole interest," he said. "I don't think Harley ever came to the school, but, of course, we'd heard from him, because he was God, and occasionally we would see him on the street. I'll tell you, there were some times when he looked to be about eight feet tall."

Upon graduation in 1940, MacKichan went to work in the Styling Section, earning $150 a month as a clay modeler's helper in the Buick studio. "For the first time, I could see Harley Earl coming into the room and saying what he wanted," he said, recalling an encounter with the legend late one night when he was working flat on his back under a clay model. "I heard this noise and heavy walking of feet and I looked out and there's Harley dressed in his yachting costume, along with some of the Fisher brothers and some other notable people. And they were coming in from a party at the yacht club, I supposed, at 1:30 or

2:00 a.m., just to see how we were doing." MacKichan didn't speak to Harley "because I wasn't supposed to," he said. "A person in my position would never talk to the man."

MacKichan and his fellow graduates rotated through various positions as they learned Harley's system. The five division studios were self-contained, each with its own layout tables, modeling platforms, clay ovens, staff, and chief designer. The design teams operated on a three-year cycle, creating an entirely new model in year one, freshening it up with a face-lift the following year, and then restyling the fenders, deck, and hood in the third year. As a result, every GM sedan, coupe, convertible, and station wagon looked new and different every year.

But not *too* different. Alfred Sloan told Harley early on that he needed to stimulate the public's appetite for new GM models without rendering the older models unpalatable in comparison. A delicate balance had to be maintained between the new and used car markets, he said, because most people depended on the trade-in value of their old car for the down payment on a new one.

Having learned from the 1929 "pregnant Buick" debacle that the average American car buyer didn't go for abrupt, radical styling changes, Harley developed an ingenious process for delivering gradual, carefully planned change. He introduced major styling innovations—suitcase fenders, for instance—in the Cadillac, then passed them down in succeeding years to the less expensive makes, first to Buick, then to Oldsmobile, Pontiac, and finally, in the fifth year, to the low-priced Chevrolet, where they became commonplace. The trickle-down styling scheme "played upon consumers' desire not merely for progress, but also for social mobility," according to automotive historian David Gartman. "Consumers of the lower makes were persuaded that their cars were getting better because they looked more like Cadillacs, and their lives were getting better as well."

No other styling department operated on such a sophisticated level or produced anywhere near the volume of new models, a point Harley dramatically drove home to the staff the day a young designer was passing around pirated photos of a competitor's unfinished new model. "I don't give a goddamn what they are doing," Harley barked as he snatched the pictures away and tossed them into a wastebasket. "*We* are leading the industry; *they* follow *us*."

In fact, the Styling staff had a long tradition of spying on the competition. They called it "chasing," according to Frank Hershey, who recalled the time in the early days of Art and Colour when he and a friend from GM's photographic department decided "to go and find out what the latest Ford V-8 was going to look like." They drove to Dearborn and parked on a side street, peeked over a shrub-covered fence, and saw old Henry Ford himself driving around in a new Model A V-8. They snapped off a quick round of pictures, jumped back in the car, and hightailed it for the office.

"We got about a mile down the road, and here comes a huge Lincoln with about four guys in it," Hershey told art historian C. Edson Armi. "They ran us off the road and turned us over in the ditch on our side. We climbed out of the car, and they took this big Graflex [camera] and took the film out. But we had hidden the original film under the seat, so they didn't get anything. They smashed the camera, but we had put a new film in the camera to make it look good. They weren't that smart."

Asked if he'd been frightened by the encounter with what

had clearly been a squad of Harry Bennett's goons, Hershey shrugged. "I was young and foolish, and besides, I was so automobile-crazy I'd do anything to see a competition car."

The occasional "chasing" adventures provided a welcome break from the daily chaos and frustration attendant to Harley's creative process. He pushed his design teams relentlessly to come up with graceful new shapes and novel decorative treatments, while at the same time cautioning them not to cross over the line of what the consumer was prepared to accept. "Go all out and then pull back," he'd say. He always seemed to know where that line was, but because he couldn't draw it or describe it, his staff usually had to find it through trial and error, proffering as many as fifteen hundred renderings of a taillight or grille before he saw the right one.

"Earl's real talent lay in his critical eye . . . which was always focused firmly on the bottom line," said David Gartman. "He was an uncanny commercial critic with an extraordinary ability to anticipate the sales success of a design."

In reminiscing about their experiences, several of Harley's designers offered versions of the same incident as an example of his unique style of criticism. It began with a phone call to the Pontiac studio warning that "the old man" was on his way down to check the progress on a clay model. The Pontiac design chief, Bob Lauer, and his assistant had just enough time to position themselves at the door to greet him as Harley let himself in with his key. Across the room, the model had been slicked with water so it glistened. Several modelers stood by ready to make any changes he might order. The designers were all heads-down busy-looking at their drawing boards, but they tracked Harley carefully out of the corner of their eyes as he walked over to the model and circled it slowly, stopping to scrutinize the front, rear, and sides, saying nothing. You could have heard a pencil eraser drop.

"No, Bob," he said, finally. "It's two or three years from now and you are out in Pasadena, and a little old lady comes into the showroom and she's standing about the same distance from the car and she will look it over, and do you know what she will say?"

"No, Mistearl, I don't," Lauer supposedly said.

"She'll say, 'I wouldn't buy that sonofabitch,'" Harley responded. Then he turned on his heel and strode toward the door, saying over his shoulder as he left, "I'll come back."

When he did, so the story goes, the model had been reshaped to his satisfaction.

"You had to have someone at the head of this who would not be satisfied with anything but the best," said Clare MacKichan. "And you didn't know what was best until you tried a hundred things, a thousand things. How do you know what's best until you see all of them? That's why we had the large group we had."

"It was still small enough that it was a family," he added. "And we used to have big annual picnics, which were really great fun and lasted into the wee hours. Harley knew that we worked long, hard hours so he would do things to make up for it. I guess our wives didn't agree with these things making up for it."

The wives certainly wouldn't have agreed with how some of their husbands dealt with pressure during the workday. "There was a group of designers that participated in what was often described as 'nooners,'" said Strother MacMinn. "This means taking off for lunch and going to a place of physical release, shall we say, and maybe coming back around 2:00 p.m., and you'd probably had a good martini lunch in the process as well, so you'd come back fully relaxed, theoretically. But it was a desperate move for a lot of designers."

The pressure they felt wasn't just from Harley. As they worked on what were to be the 1942 models, everyone on the staff was keenly aware they were racing against world events. During the spring of 1940, Hitler's army had swept into Norway, Denmark, Holland, Belgium, Luxembourg, and France, forcing their soldiers to surrender or flee the Continent by boat; a German invasion of Great Britain seemed imminent. The United States was not yet directly involved in war, but all signs said it was just a matter of time. On May 26 President Roosevelt announced in a Sunday-night radio broadcast that he was asking the leaders of American industry to convert part of their production capacity to making aircraft and munitions for the beleaguered British and to build up America's own defense arsenal. He said there was an urgent need for 50,000 warplanes, both fighters and bombers.

Three days later, Roosevelt called William Knudsen and asked him to come to Washington to head up a new National Defense Advisory Commission aimed at enlisting the nation's largest manufacturers in the armament effort. Knudsen seemed an inspired choice for the job. His combined twenty-nine years at Ford and GM made him arguably the world's foremost expert on mass production and perhaps the most respected executive in the auto industry. If anyone could persuade a bunch of filthy rich, highly competitive industrial titans to cooperate, it would be Big Bill.

Knudsen would have to resign from GM to take the new position, which paid one dollar a year, or about $400,000 less than he was making at GM. "This country has been good to me and I want to pay it back," the Danish immigrant explained to his

Employees of Earl Automobile Works in Los Angeles in 1918. Harley helped his father, J.W., build the former carriage repair shop into the sixth-largest maker of auto bodies in the country. *(Courtesy of the Earl family)*

The Earl family in the driveway of their Hollywood home in 1915. Left to right: Bill, Nellie, Jessie, Art, J.W., Carl, and Harley. *(Courtesy of the Earl family)*

Harley behind the wheel of a 1927 LaSalle, the first mass-produced American car styled front to back and top to bottom by a designer. *(General Motors Media Archives)*

Harley's wife, Sue, and their two-year-old son, Billy, just days before the little boy died during surgery to remove his tonsils. *(Courtesy of the Earl Family)*

The dapper young designer sailing to Europe in 1932 for the annual auto shows. *(Courtesy of the Earl family)*

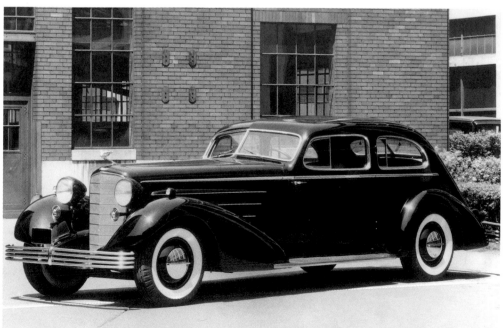

The 1934 Cadillac V-16 Aerodynamic coupe, GM's first one-of-a-kind show car. *(General Motors Media Archives)*

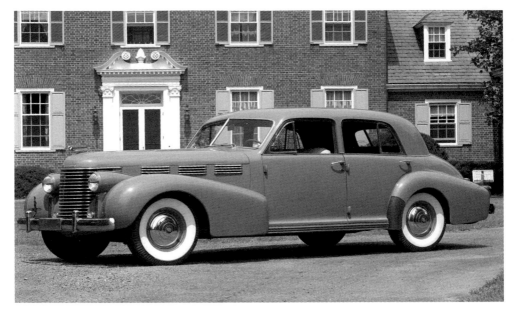

The stylistically influential 1938 Cadillac Sixty Special was the first production car without running boards. *(All photographs: General Motors Media Archives)*

Harley showing off the first-ever "concept car," which he dubbed the "Y-job" and drove to and from work for eleven years.

Unveiled in 1950, the Le Sabre was perhaps Harley's most famous creation.

America's first sports
car, the 1953 Corvette,
was inspired by Harley's
weekend at a road race in
upstate New York.

The 1955 Chevrolet Bel Air was called the "Hot One" for its powerful V-8 and popularity among the burgeoning youth culture. *(All photographs: General Motors Media Archives)*

Harley's brother Art with their father at GM's 1956 Motorama show in Los Angeles. *(Courtesy of the Earl family)*

The Styling staff took tail fins over the top with the 1959 Cadillac, creating one of the defining images of that decade. *(All photographs: General Motors Media Archives)*

Harley looking over new models under the lights of the Styling Auditorium.

daughter, though Germany's invasion of his beloved Denmark, where his three sisters still lived, surely was a motivating factor in his accepting the job.

The President's advisors, including the First Lady, Eleanor, wanted him to set up a centrally directed New Deal–style re-armament effort with a "single commanding figure in charge," a war production czar in today's parlance. Knudsen disagreed with that approach. He was cut from the same conservative Republican cloth as Alfred Sloan, who believed that any gov-ernment intervention in the economy or interference with the affairs of private business was anathema. "If we get into war, the winning of it will be purely a question of material and produc-tion," he told Roosevelt at the outset. The best way to harness the energy of American industry, he argued, "was to clear away anti-business tax laws and regulations" that had held back eco-nomic progress during the New Deal, and to allow companies to deal directly with the military services, deciding for themselves which war matériel they were best suited to bid on, and how to produce it. The point, he said, was to reduce Washington's inter-ference in the production process to a minimum. To the surprise and irritation of his advisors, Roosevelt went with Knudsen's vision of a voluntary, decentralized production effort, and the seeds of the modern military-industrial complex were sown.

Sloan was furious at Roosevelt for poaching his chief operat-ing officer and at Knudsen for agreeing to it. "They'll make a monkey out of you down there in Washington," Sloan warned his longtime friend and colleague, at the same time letting Knud-sen know that if he went to work for the President there was no coming back to GM.

The day Knudsen left GM to assume his new responsibilities in Washington, D.C., a reporter asked him, "Can you build those fifty thousand planes the President is asking for?" Knudsen responded, "I can't, but America can." His reputation in Detroit was such that in a matter of weeks he personally enlisted the cooperation of every significant automotive manufacturer, most notably Ford president Edsel Ford, who committed his company to building six thousand Rolls-Royce engines for Britain's Royal Air Force and three thousand for the U.S. Army Air Corps. The agreement was announced with great fanfare in America and greeted with jubilation in the United Kingdom. Three days after approving it, however, Edsel's father, Henry, changed his mind and reneged on the RAF engines, believing that Roosevelt was deceitfully attempting to move the country into a foreign war that he believed could be avoided.

Flabbergasted, Knudsen hurried to Dearborn to reason with his old boss. "Mr. Ford, this is terrible about those motors," he began. Ford cut him off. "You are mixed up with some bad people in Washington," he said. "I won't make motors for the British government. For the American government, yes; for the British government, no."

"But, Mr. Ford, we have your word that you would make them," Knudsen sputtered, his face reddening with rage. "I told the President your decisions and he was very happy about it." The thought of disappointing the President he loathed apparently moved Ford to repudiate the entire agreement. "We won't build the engines at all," he snapped. "Withdraw the whole order. Take it to someone else."

On September 7, 1940, Germany commenced a terrorizing two-month aerial bombardment of London. With the population huddled nightly in makeshift basement bomb shelters and RAF Spitfire fighter planes locked in a desperate battle with the Luftwaffe in the sky over the city, Prime Minister Winston

Churchill wrote to Roosevelt pleading for more planes to defend his country.

The ongoing London Blitz was at the top of Knudsen's mind on October 15, when he delivered a speech at the New York Auto Show. Speaking to five hundred auto executives gathered at the Waldorf-Astoria Hotel, he said that between building up its own defenses and providing military aid to Great Britain, the United States faced "the greatest production problem of any country in modern times."

He talked about America becoming "the arsenal of democracy," a term FDR promptly appropriated, and ticked off what was needed in addition to the 50,000 warplanes: 130,000 engines, 9,200 tanks, 300,000 machine guns, 400,000 automatic rifles, 1.3 million regular rifles, 380 navy ships, 33 million shells, clothing, and other equipment for 1.2 million soldiers. He said the task would require eighteen billion man-hours, and starting that month Washington was going to push through defense contracts at a rate of $600 million a week. "Talk to your men. Make them feel that it is their responsibility as well as yours. Ask them what they think of a civilization that drives women and children to live in cold and wet holes in the ground.

"The first half of 1941 is crucial," Knudsen said in closing. "Gentlemen, we must out-build Hitler."

Within six months, automotive manufacturers had entered into military production contracts with the United States, Great Britain, and Canada totaling more than $3.5 billion. Despite Alfred Sloan's misgivings, GM led the pack with over $500 million in defense contracts, including one for its Indianapolis-based Allison division to provide engines for a top-secret new fighter plane called the P-38 Lightning.

In the spring of 1941, Harley heard through the GM grapevine that one of the P-38 test planes was being housed at Selfridge Field, an army air base thirty miles north of Detroit. So he pulled some strings, possibly with Knudsen, and took several of his top designers, including Frank Hershey and Bill Mitchell, on a field trip to check it out, thinking the plane's supposedly radical design might provide some styling inspiration for the staff.

Because of the plane's top-secret classification, they weren't allowed to walk up to it or photograph it; they could only view it from a distance of thirty or so feet. But that was close enough to get the idea. None of them had ever seen an aircraft like the P-38. With an unusually wide 52-foot wingspan, it didn't have a conventional single fuselage but rather twin booms that flanked a small bullet-shaped, glass-domed pilot's compartment, called a nacelle. Each boom housed a 12-cylinder, 1,100-horsepower Allison engine, and tapered from a shark-snout front end into a rounded vertical rudder in the rear. The effect was that of a sleek, aerodynamic insect, like a flying spider.

Frank Hershey was particularly taken with the plane's twin tail rudders. He thought about them all during the drive back to the city and immediately began sketching them on his drawing board at the studio.

"I fell in love with those tail fins," he told Harley's grand-daughter fifty years later. He was trying to incorporate them into a rear fender design when the time for thinking about such things ran out.

11
DETROIT'S
WAR

I t all happened quickly.

At 7:55 a.m. on December 7, 1941, more than three hundred Japanese warplanes, launched from four aircraft carriers that had sailed unseen across 3,800 miles of ocean, swooped down on Pearl Harbor on the Hawaiian island of Oahu and laid waste to America's Pacific fleet, destroying or damaging nineteen navy ships, including eight battleships, and more than 300 planes, while killing 2,403 servicemen and civilians. The attack lasted seventy-five minutes.

Congress declared war on Japan the next day. Three days after that, Japan's allies, Germany and Italy, declared war on the United States, which reciprocated a few hours later.

With a badly damaged navy and an army that ranked as the world's eighteenth largest, behind Holland, the United States appeared woefully unprepared to fight a war on three continents against three opponents that had been building up their military capability for years. The Axis powers had more than 6 million men under arms, compared with America's less than half a million, an imbalance that moved Hitler to mock, "What is America but beauty queens, millionaires, stupid records and Hollywood?"

As an admirer of Henry Ford and a self-proclaimed student of his mass-manufacturing techniques, the Führer should have known better. The industry that Ford and Ransom Olds founded at the beginning of the century now encompassed more than a thousand manufacturing companies and contained the world's largest pool of mechanical and engineering talent, which made America the best-equipped country on earth to mass-produce the instruments of global warfare.

"When Hitler put his war on wheels, he ran it straight down our alley," said the army's supply commander, Lieutenant General Brehon "Bill" Somervell, after returning from a post–Pearl Harbor tour of Michigan automotive factories to assess their war production capability. "When he hitched his chariot to an internal combustion engine, he opened up a new battlefront—a front we know well. It is called 'Detroit.'"

From the outset, President Roosevelt was counting on the auto industry to manufacture 75 percent of the aircraft engines, 80 percent of the tanks, a third of the machine guns, and all of the trucks the military would need to take the fight to the enemy. As *Fortune* magazine put it, "Detroit must now become the main plant in the Arsenal of Democracy."

Thanks largely to William Knudsen's eighteen months of cajoling, the industry was fully on board. "This is our war," Chrysler chairman K. T. Keller told eight hundred executives attending the first meeting of the Automotive Council for War Production at Detroit's Masonic Temple on January 24, 1942. Naming George Romney as its managing director, the council pledged that the industry's theretofore brutally competitive companies now would cooperate in the war effort to the point of sharing research and production techniques. Packard chairman Alvan Macauley, the father of company styling chief Ed Macauley, told the attendees, "The job now is to clear the decks for the expanded war work that the government will require in the drive for victory."

They all knew what that meant. Car manufacturing was consuming huge amounts of iron, steel, glass, rubber, and other materials badly needed by the military. So, on February 1, 1942, after functioning for two decades as the driving wheel of the American economy, the auto industry shut down. By government decree, no new civilian vehicles could be manufactured for the duration of the war, and the manufacturers' unsold inventory of more than half a million 1942 models was to be stored in warehouses and carefully doled out to military personnel and civilian workers deemed critical to maintaining public safety—police, firefighters, doctors. Further restrictions included the rationing of gas to three gallons per week and the imposition of a national "victory" speed limit of thirty-five miles an hour. The latter was not intended to save gasoline, which was plentiful and cheap, but rather to preserve rubber, most of which came from a part of the world that Japan's military controlled.

The scope and swiftness of the transformation from car economy to war economy was breathtaking. Within weeks, Packard assembly lines were rolling out 1,000-plus-horsepower airplane engines instead of Clipper sedans. Hudson workers were making antiaircraft cannons and armor-piercing artillery shells at the brand-new $21 million Naval Ordnance Plant in Warren, Michigan. Chrysler started building 28-ton M3 tanks at its new $20 million Detroit Arsenal Tank Plant even before the factory walls were fully up. Chrysler president Keller operated a bulldozer himself to help clear land for the more than one-million-square-foot facility, which he predicted would outproduce all Germany's tank plants combined.

The Ford Motor Company began building an airplane factory near the tiny town of Ypsilanti, thirty miles west of Detroit, on 1,450 acres where Henry Ford had grown soybeans and apples for twenty-nine years and maintained a summer camp for disadvantaged young men whose fathers were killed or wounded in World War I. The company promised that the Willow Run plant—named for the stream that ran through the property, which Henry demanded be allowed to run undisturbed beneath the factory—would be the largest of its kind in the world, capable of turning out B-24 "Liberator" bombers at the rate of one per hour.

Over the course of the war, General Motors would produce nearly as much war matériel as all the other car companies combined—$12 billion worth, or 41 percent of the industry's total. With all of its ninety-four factories dedicated to the effort, GM manufactured 2,300 different products for the military, ranging from tiny ball bearings to 30-ton tanks, in numbers that were astonishing—119,522,000 artillery shells, 1,900,000 machine guns, 3,142,000 carbines, 206,000 aircraft engines, 854,000 trucks, 190,000 cannons, 85,000 tanks—establishing the company as America's preeminent industrial contributor to the war. "If the corporation ever had a supreme moment, a period of unqualified contribution to the commonweal," wrote journalist Ed Cray, "it was during the years of 1940 through 1945."

The contribution wasn't only in matériel. Nearly 120,000 GM employees joined the military, including Harley Earl's two favorite designers, Frank Hershey and Bill Mitchell. Clare MacKichan would have joined up, too, but high blood pressure disqualified him. He left Styling when the work slowed and layoffs seemed likely. With all the government money pouring into Detroit, he had no trouble finding a new job. He signed on with a company that needed tool designers. The work wasn't nearly as fulfilling as designing cars, but it was guaranteed for the duration of the war, and with ample overtime, "it paid much better," he said.

Harley tried to retain as many people as he could, working to ensure that Styling had enough defense work to keep them out of the draft. He named his interior design chief, Steve McDaniel, to head up a new Wartime Production Studio, which turned out thousands of detailed drawings, diagrams, and illustrations for military manuals and guides. When the military sought help in developing a more sophisticated form of camouflage, he contacted friends in the Royal Canadian Air Force in Ottawa. "You've got pilots coming back here for a rest after the [North] African campaign, haven't you?" he said. "Would you mind letting them come down if we paid the expense, and let them lecture to us in our auditorium? I'm going to start a camouflage school, and I want to find out some things."

After hearing the Canadian fliers explain how the Germans attempted to hide airfields, towns, and buildings from their bombers, he ordered the locks changed on the Styling Auditorium to make it top-secret secure and proceeded to turn the space into a smaller version of GM's "Futurama" exhibit at the New York World's Fair. Modelers constructed a scale-model city complete with miniature factories, houses, cars, and scenery, then interior department staffers experimented with ways of concealing it from the eyes of enemy pilots. "Colored cloth was used, paint effects, blending of backgrounds, all the techniques that were known and some that hadn't been imagined before," according to Stanley Brams. They checked the results by climbing up on tall stepladders and peering down on the mock terrain through reducing glasses that mimicked what pilots might see from altitudes up to 20,000 feet.

Harley went so far as to change the name of the Styling department to the Camouflage and War Service Section. But after producing a twenty-two-page pamphlet titled *Camouflage Manual for General Motors Camouflage School*, the project was abruptly canceled after the military developed intelligence that the enemy was using infrared technology that countered the effect of camouflage.

He had more success with a project that hewed closer to Styling's original mission. The U.S. Ordnance Corps approached Buick about developing a new class of armored vehicle for the army. Called the M18 tank destroyer, it was to be track-driven, like a tank, with a 76 mm gun mounted on a rotating top turret, and it needed to be considerably lighter, faster, and more maneuverable than the heavily armored German tanks it was intended to take out. Harley assigned his Oldsmobile studio chief, Art Ross, to design the M18, which Buick engineers dubbed the Hellcat. Working from Ross's detailed designs, they built two prototypes with gun turrets that could swivel 360 degrees, and tested them at GM's proving grounds in Milford, Michigan, where they proved capable of reaching speeds of 60 miles an hour (German tanks topped out at 25 mph), climbing low walls, fording six feet of water, and ramming through the walls of buildings. The army quickly approved the Hellcat for production at Buick's Flint, Michigan, plant, but changed its name to the Wildcat.

Some months later, after the first M18s arrived for training exercises at Fort Hood, Texas, a general's aide called Harley. "We have the Wildcats you fellows designed," he said. "Now we'd like an armband for an outfit like ours whose mission is to crush the tank." Buick designer Henry Lauve created a shoulder-patch logo showing a snarling black panther with tank tracks clamped in its teeth, encircled by the army's tank force motto, "Seek. Strike. Destroy."

M18s were widely deployed during the Allies' slog across Europe following the D-day invasion. Five Wildcats from the 704th Tank Destroyer Battalion ambushed a column of more than thirty German tanks in September 1944 and knocked out nineteen of them. Three months later, during the Battle of the Bulge, four Wildcats joined in an attack on Germany's Second Panzer (Tank) Division as it neared the Belgian town of Bastogne, where American forces were surrounded and defiantly refusing to surrender. In what became one of the most famous anecdotes of the war, Brigadier General Anthony C. McAuliffe, the commander of the besieged American troops, responded to the Germans' surrender demand with a succinct written refusal: "Nuts!"

The Wildcats were credited with slowing the panzers' advance long enough for reinforcements under the command of General George Patton to reach the trapped Americans. It's a safe bet that Art Ross and Harley never expected to be credited in military annals as the designers of such a vehicle.

Harley's staff continued to shrink as his designers enlisted or were drafted, until only thirty-five remained from a prewar high of nearly a hundred. He busied himself overseeing the design of instrument panels for tanks and airplanes, dividing his time between his office and studios downtown and airplane hangars at Wayne County Airport and Selfridge Field. He was constantly called upon to serve as host to visiting generals and admirals, easily winning them over with his man's-man charm, salty language, colorful apparel, and imposing physique. He had no worries about losing his job. Although he was just one of twenty-nine GM vice presidents, none had a closer relationship with Alfred Sloan, who believed Styling had been the key to the company's rise before the war and would be equally if not more important after it ended. Sloan had recently lost two close friends and automotive mentors—first Walter Chrysler, who succumbed to a stroke in 1940, and then Bill Knudsen, who committed the sin of going to work for Roosevelt. With them gone, the GM chairman turned more and more to Harley for counsel in areas beyond styling, even bringing him into early discussions with Charles Kettering about building a new GM headquarters complex outside the city after the war—just the three of them quietly imagining what the company's role in America might be in the second half of the twentieth century.

After years of renting, Harley and Sue bought a house in Grosse Pointe Farms in 1942, a white stone mansion formerly owned by millionaire industrialist J. B. Ford Jr., the heir to a glass fortune and no relation to Henry Ford. The new house had a large marble entrance hall, high ceilings, six bedrooms, five bathrooms, and maids' quarters. Sue employed a housekeeper and cook who lived in, plus a personal maid, one or two "cleaning ladies," and a laundress, but no chauffeur. At seven o'clock every morning, she drove to the Red Cross blood bank downtown, where she was in charge of volunteer workers. She also initiated and supervised the annual Christmas bazaar for Planned Parenthood, then in its infancy and focused primarily on promoting birth control to combat overpopulation, as controversial an idea in heavily Catholic Detroit at the time as legalized abortion would be thirty years later. An Episcopalian, she simply thought there were too many unwanted babies being born.

The Earl boys were privileged but not pampered. Jim and his younger brother, Jerry, supported the war effort and earned extra spending money by cruising the neighborhood on their bikes to collect old newspapers, which they carted in bulk to collection centers set up to help with a national paper shortage. In the late summer of 1943, Sue took fifteen-year-old Jim and his friend David Robb on a trip to see one of her oldest friends in Newport, Rhode Island. Newport was a navy town and the harbor was full of destroyers and frigates. The boys spent much of their time walking the streets trying to spot battle ribbons on the throngs of sailors and marines, most of whom didn't look much older than they thought they did. When they got back home to Detroit, David persuaded his older brother to drive them to Windsor, Ontario, where they attempted to enlist in the Essex Scottish Infantry Regiment of the Canadian army. As much as they thought they might be the key to winning the war, they were relieved when the recruiting sergeant gently turned them down.

The following summer, Jim and another sixteen-year-old friend landed jobs at a factory that made tank parts, earning a whopping seventy-five cents an hour, which pointed up a dramatic turnabout from the not-so-distant days of the Depression when thousands of unemployed men huddled around trash-can fires outside the gates of padlocked manufacturing plants.

Thanks to the war, Detroit's employment rate was nearly 100 percent, with more government contract jobs available than there were able-bodied men or women to do them. To meet manpower needs at its Willow Run plant, Ford Motors sent recruiters to Kentucky, Tennessee, Texas, West Virginia, Missouri, and Arkansas, and hired workers from Egypt, Iceland, New Zealand, Panama, Turkey, Chile, and Cuba. Ford's various war plants reportedly employed 4,390 blind or deaf workers, 111 deaf-mutes, 3 armless men, and 10 legless men.

When Cadillac general manager Nicholas Dreystadt contracted to manufacture sophisticated electronic airplane bombsights, the division's personnel manager, James Roche, told him it would be impossible because the city's workforce was utterly depleted. There were no unskilled workers left, he said, let alone the kind of trained mechanics it would take to machine the bombsights. Dreystadt was undeterred. "It's got to be done," he said, "and if we at Cadillac can't do it, then who can?"

So they went looking for workers on the Lower East Side of the city just north of the river, in an area where few GM executives ever ventured. Early French settlers called it "Black Bottom" because of its rich, black river-bottom soil, though most modern-day Detroiters thought the name derived from the fact that 90 percent of the city's black population lived there. Whites referred to it as "the colored district."

Dreystadt knew Black Bottom, especially its vibrant commercial sector, known as Paradise Valley, where well-heeled white patrons looking for a memorable night on the town were more than happy to sit in mixed-race audiences at the Paradise Theater to see the likes of Count Basie, Billie Holiday, and Bill "Bojangles" Robinson or feast on fried squash under glass in the Ebony Dining Room of the Gotham Hotel, where heavyweight boxing champ Joe Louis always stayed when he came back to his hometown. It was in Paradise Valley, with its 350 black-owned businesses, that Dreystadt discovered the well-to-do black entrepreneurs and professionals who helped him save the Cadillac division during the Depression.

In the early 1940s, the lure of wartime jobs drew several hundred thousand additional migrants to Detroit from rural Michigan and the southern states, creating a housing shortage throughout the city, but particularly in Black Bottom, where an estimated fifty thousand African American arrivals increased the number of residents to a teeming two hundred thousand, all crammed into sixty square blocks bounded by the Detroit River on one side and fiercely segregated white neighborhoods on the other three. Not surprisingly, Black Bottom became a tinderbox of racial tension, and when the federal government attempted to ease the crisis by building a public housing project in a bordering white neighborhood, the whole thing exploded.

An estimated twelve hundred whites turned out to protest the project's opening and tried to block black families from moving into their new homes. The confrontation turned violent and led to scores of arrests, mostly of blacks. Months of gang fights, vandalism, police beatings, and more arrests followed, culminating in what was then the worst race riot in U.S. history. On Saturday evening, June 20, 1943, a false rumor started in a Black Bottom social club: a group of white men supposedly had thrown a black woman and her baby off the Belle Isle Bridge, which connected Black Bottom to a popular recreational island park in the middle of the Detroit River. A furious mob stormed out of the club and moved along Woodward Avenue, breaking windows, looting businesses, and assaulting whites.

They were met at the corner of Davenport Street by a white mob motivated by another false rumor: that blacks had killed a white sailor and raped his girlfriend. An estimated ten thousand people ultimately converged on the intersection, and before the melee was brought under control the next afternoon with the help of six thousand federal troops, thirty-five people were dead—twenty-five of them black—nearly a thousand were injured, and thirteen hundred had been arrested—again, most of them black.

In that charged environment, Nicholas Dreystadt found the

last untapped workforce in Detroit. Along Hastings Street, a seamy Black Bottom thoroughfare lined with blues bars, gambling dens, pool halls, strip clubs, and brothels, he recruited two thousand black prostitutes to make the bombsights in his factory. He hired their madams, too, figuring they "knew how to manage the women," according to Peter F. Drucker, who was in the midst of conducting a management-approved study of GM's corporate systems and practices at the time and included an account of the Cadillac women in his memoir *Adventures of a Bystander.*

Most of the women had never held a legitimate job and were largely illiterate. Dreystadt didn't have time to teach them how to read, so he "went to the workbench himself and machined a dozen of the bombsights," Drucker wrote. "When he knew how to do it, he had a movie camera take a film of the process. He mounted the film frames separately on a projector and synchronized them with a flow diagram in which a red light went on to show the operator what she had already done, a green light for what she had to do next, and a yellow light to show what to make sure of before taking the next step." In a matter of a few weeks, the women were turning out better work and in larger quantities than skilled machinists had before them.

For his efforts, Dreystadt was called a "whoremonger" and a "nigger lover" to his face and behind his back and subjected to constant cracks about Cadillac's "red light district."

"These women are my fellow workers, and yours," he would respond angrily. "They do a good job and respect their work. Whatever their past, they are entitled to the same respect as any one of our associates."

He pleaded with leaders of the United Auto Workers (UAW) to keep at least some of the women on after the war. "For the first time in their lives, these poor wretches are paid decently, work in decent conditions, and have some rights," he said. "And for the first time they have some dignity and self-respect. It's our duty to save them from being again rejected and despised."

But the union's white, largely fundamentalist Christian membership didn't like the idea of working next to women of any color, much less black prostitutes. So as the young men began returning home from the European conflict, one by one Dreystadt's Black Bottom recruits were let go. Rather than return to their former profession, "many tried to commit suicide and quite a few succeeded," according to Drucker, who described a devastated Dreystadt sitting in his office with his face buried in his hands, sobbing, "God forgive me; I have failed these poor souls."

◆

At the same time as the riots, another long-simmering conflict bubbled over in a different part of town; author A. J. Baime dubbed it "the battle of Dearborn."

Edsel Ford knew he was racing against time to get the Willow Run plant up to its promised goal of producing one B-24 bomber per hour, or about 700 a month. However, only fifty-six planes had been built, which alarmed William Knudsen and President Roosevelt because the military was counting on thousands of them to pound the Germans in North Africa and Europe. Newspaper editorials characterized the Willow Run situation as a national embarrassment and began referring to the plant as "Will It Run."

Part of the problem was that Edsel had not foreseen the government's gas rationing and driving restrictions when he picked the site of the plant, mandates that made it impossible for employees to commute daily between Detroit and the town of Ypsilanti, twenty-seven miles away. Which meant that at least forty thousand plant workers would need to find housing in a small farming community that had none available. So before the plant could become fully operational, Ford and the government had to build a camplike community that dwarfed the neighboring town. "Bomber City" (later changed to Willow Village) took a year to complete and cost an estimated $100 million.

Another problem was Henry Ford. The increasingly erratic company chairman and majority shareholder continued to allow his thuggish factotum, Harry Bennett, to fire experienced executives according to whim and run roughshod over plant employees, to the point of sparking fistfights and wildcat work stoppages. At one point Edsel received information that Bennett was overseeing the organized theft of as much as $12,000 worth of military equipment a day from the Rouge River plant and was selling it to an outside fencing ring. He turned the information over to FBI director J. Edgar Hoover, who placed an agent from the bureau's Detroit office inside the company to conduct an investigation.

Under the pressure of trying to counter the machinations of his father and hit a production goal that many considered unattainable, Edsel grew gaunt and began experiencing severe abdominal pains. His colleagues and friends worried that he was working himself to death, but when they urged him to slow down or take time off, he responded, "The war can't wait." He reached a breaking point in early April 1943, when the company's head of purchasing, a trusted thirty-year employee, told him that Bennett had allowed a local mob boss to obtain the lucrative fruit concession at the Rouge plant and gain an ownership interest in a Ford dealership. "There were people that we were asked to put on the payroll for no apparent reason except to pay a debt of some kind," the man said, "people that had to be paid for something they never did." After Edsel angrily confronted Bennett, his father decided the best thing to do was fire the purchasing manager.

After that incident, one of Edsel's closest associates found him slumped on the couch in his office, worn down and in tears. "The best thing for me to do is resign," he said. "My health won't permit me to go on."

As his friends had feared, Edsel was indeed dying, but not from stress. Six months earlier, he had undergone surgery for what his doctors thought was ulcers but turned out to be cancer. They removed half of his stomach. He quickly returned to work, getting through the days with painkillers and the nights with sedatives while telling people he was "making fine progress" in his recovery. Neither his father nor his children knew the seriousness of his illness. But a subsequent procedure revealed that the cancer had spread to his liver, and the doctors told the family there was nothing more they could do. Henry refused to believe it and angrily ordered them to return his son to health "because that's what you're here for." Upon hearing the grim prognosis, Edsel's second oldest son, Benson, declared, "Grandfather is responsible for Father's sickness, and I'm through with him!"

A few weeks later, Edsel left work early, went home to his Grosse Pointe estate, and never left. He died there in a makeshift infirmary on May 26, 1943, sixteen years to the day after he and his father had driven the last Model T off the assembly line. He was forty-nine.

President Roosevelt sent a condolence note to Edsel's widow, Eleanor, the same day. "A powerful force has been lost to the war effort," he wrote. "He had devoted his superb abilities wholeheartedly to the defeat of the Axis powers and his passing in this critical time in our history is a grievous loss to his country's effort and to the cause of the United Nations. My heart goes out to you and to all of the family in deepest sympathy."

Calling Edsel "one of the most tragic figures in American business history," historian David L. Lewis eulogized, "He was more than talented; he was creative. He was more than hardworking; he had an extraordinary sense of responsibility to his company and community. He was an excellent administrator, and he commanded the affection, respect, and loyalty of his associates. Unfortunately, his father, far from rejoicing in and making constructive use of these qualities, restricted and nullified them in his unceasing effort to remold his son into a tough, hard-hitting executive."

A few days after Edsel's death, at a board meeting with his widow, Eleanor, present in his place, Henry made the stunning announcement that he would be stepping back into the role of chief executive, a position he had not held in twenty-four years. Incensed at the old man's timing and tactlessness, Eleanor reportedly shocked the room by blurting out, "You, Mr. Ford, you're the one who killed your son," a sentiment shared by the entire family, including Henry's wife, Clara.

With Edsel gone and an often addled Henry back in charge of daily operations, Franklin Roosevelt entertained the idea of nationalizing the company to ensure the flow of critical equipment to the military. But he held off in the hope that Edsel's eldest son, Henry Ford II, could wrest the reins of the company away from his grandfather and gain control of the dangerously dysfunctional company. First, however, the twenty-five-year-old navy ensign had to be granted an early discharge. On July 26, two months after his father's death, Henry II received a letter from the secretary of the navy relieving him of any further obligations to the military. "The services you will render as a private individual will surpass any work you could possibly do in your present situation."

As the newly installed executive vice president of the company, Henry II tried to get his arms around its myriad problems, but by the spring of 1944 he'd become so frustrated with the constant sabotage by his grandfather and Harry Bennett that he was threatening to resign, sell his stock, and advise Ford dealers all over the country to jump ship. "This thing killed my father, but I'll be damned if I'm going to let it kill me," he reportedly told a close associate. "I'm going to get out before it does." Instead, his mother and grandmother joined together to get the old man out.

Eleanor conspired with Clara to arrange a closed-door confrontation with Henry at the couple's Fair Lane estate. With Clara present, Eleanor gave her father-in-law an ultimatum—either he turned the company over to Henry II, or she would sell all of her and Edsel's shares of Ford stock and his relations with his grandchildren would cease. Frail, experiencing intermittent episodes of dementia, and engulfed by grief and guilt over Edsel's death, the seventy-nine-year-old patriarch gave in and officially resigned from the company.

A month after D-day, in July 1944, Willow Run hit its bomber-an-hour production goal, and by war's end it had provided the military with nearly nine thousand B-24 Liberators.

12
THE BIRTH
OF FINS

Navy lieutenant Frank Hershey received a medical discharge in the fall of 1944 and became the first of Harley's senior designers to return from the war. The reunion must have been emotional, given their long mentor-protégé relationship, but it's unlikely either man let on. Harley's display of affection consisted of naming Hershey chief of the Cadillac studio until Bill Mitchell completed his tour of duty as a naval officer.

Harley began gathering up other staffers who had been dispersed to various projects scattered among different GM divisions, including a small group of designers the company had interred in somewhat shabby quarters at 40 West Milwaukee Avenue because their age or national heritage disqualified them, in the eyes of the government, from involvement in defense work. In a wry reference to the military classification that deems a person unfit to serve, they had taken to calling themselves the "4-F Club."

Fierce fighting continued in Europe and the Pacific, but the momentum of the war had shifted in favor of the Allies and the mood on the home front was optimistic. People were starting to talk about what life would be like in "the coming peace," and automobiles were no small part of the conversation.

Nearly three years into the production shutdown, cars had become a precious commodity. Half of the 26 million passenger vehicles that had been on the road in 1941 now were more than seven years old. Wrecked and worn-out cars were being scrapped at the rate of 4,000 a day. Of the approximately 500,000 1942 models the government had ordered set aside for the military and essential civilian personnel, only 47,000 remained. And the shortage would only worsen with the war's end, when as many as 10 million servicemen and -women returned to civilian life en masse, a vast horde seeking jobs, housing, and America's preferred means of transportation.

In an article titled "Your Car After the War," the *Saturday Evening Post* quoted Harley as boldly predicting that the number of automobiles in America would reach 50 million by 1952. "The car of the future will be functionally designed and so is likely to change greatly in overall appearance," he said. "The thing we have all been trying to do for years is to erase the static look of cars. We are convinced the public wants low, racy styles." He scoffed at the notion that postwar automobile design would mimic that of aircraft design, stating flatly, "The only thing the car and the plane have in common is the principles of aerodynamics." He also declared that "comfort will be demanded at all times and will have to be provided at a lower cost per car pound," and said he doubted that postwar economics would move Detroit to start building smaller cars, explaining in his inimitable fashion, "They don't make chairs or beds smaller during depressions. Then why shrink the car?"

GM president Charles E. Wilson proposed to do exactly that,

however. Having assumed the chief executive position with Chairman Alfred Sloan's blessing at the beginning of the war, Wilson announced on May 15, 1945—two weeks after Hitler blew his brains out in his Berlin bunker—that Chevrolet was developing a smaller, lower-cost car, which, he believed, would stimulate the postwar car market. "The higher the prices of automobiles, the fewer will be sold," he explained to the *New York Times*. "If people cannot raise the money or credit for new cars, they will simply get along with their old ones. They proved they could do it during the war."

As envisioned, the new car would be a four-passenger sedan, eight inches shorter and $50 to $100 cheaper than a standard Chevrolet, with a sticker price under $1,000, not unlike Hitler's prewar KdF Wagen. Dubbed the Cadet, it was still in "the idea stage," Wilson said, and would not go into production "until a considerable period of time after the close of the war with Japan."

Even with the chief executive's enthusiastic backing, the Cadet was a long shot, however, because most members of the executive committee opposed it. Harlow Curtice was among those who shared the industry's long-standing bias against so-called European-style small cars. He believed that size mattered to the American motorist and few would be persuaded to sacrifice hip room and horsepower for the sake of a small price cut from a full-size sedan. Sloan thought the project made no economic sense. With experts predicting a pent-up demand for at least 12 million new cars in the first two years after the war, a number that far exceeded any previous annual output, the market probably wouldn't need stimulation; buyers likely would be standing in line to snap up whatever came out of the factory. In which case, every Cadet the company made instead of a full-size

Chevy would represent a $50 to $100 loss. The project proceeded anyway, primarily because Chevrolet general manager M. E. Coyne backed it and GM's decentralized system gave division heads unfettered authority to develop new products up to the point of setting up an assembly line, which required executive committee approval. Harley assigned a design team to help Chevrolet engineers create a Cadet prototype, and the company provided them with studio space in a dreary downtown building they nicknamed "Cockroach Canyon." He was just happy to have his men back and working on a car.

Bill Mitchell rejoined the Styling staff in late August 1945, soon after Japan's surrender. He'd barely settled back in as chief of the Cadillac studio when the UAW shut the company down with a nationwide strike; nearly 200,000 GM plant employees walked off the job demanding a 30 percent pay increase. Union leaders had forsworn such actions during the war "for the good of the country," lest they impede the military production effort. But now they moved quickly to make sure their members got a slice of the postwar American pie. Nearly 3 million hourly wage earners—electrical, oil, steel, and railroad workers; lumbermen, coal miners, meat packers, teamsters, and longshoremen—staged walkouts during the first six months of 1946, in what the U.S. Bureau of Labor Statistics called "the most concentrated period of labor-management strife in the country's history."

The GM strike differed from those of the 1930s, when the economic desperation of the Depression frequently erupted into violent clashes on the picket lines. This was a peaceful "stay-at-home" strike, enforced only by skeleton-crew picket lines that the company made no attempt to breach. After nearly five years of full employment, relative labor peace, and government-guaranteed profits on military production, GM could well afford to meet the UAW's wage demand, and the union had ample funds set aside to help its members weather a protracted work stoppage. Negotiations dragged on for 113 days and sometimes veered into broader socioeconomic issues. During one bargaining session, for example, UAW president Walter Reuther argued that without the pay increase autoworkers would not be able to buy the cars they're making, which would spell trouble not only for the company but for the country as well. "Unless we get a more realistic distribution of America's wealth, we don't get enough to keep this [industrial] machine going," he said.

GM's assistant personnel director shot back, "You can't talk about this thing without exposing your socialist desires."

"If fighting for a more equal and equitable distribution of the wealth of this country is socialistic," Reuther replied, "I stand guilty of being a socialist."

The strike locked the Styling staff out of their studios for the duration, but some of them managed to keep working nonetheless. Frank Hershey had a sixty-acre farm called Winkler Mill in Rochester, Michigan, thirty miles north of Detroit, and he invited the Cadillac design team out to help him on a project. He was now chief of the Special Car Design Studio, considered a plum assignment because it wasn't dedicated to a specific auto division, which meant less meddling by management, or, as Hershey put it, "Nobody stops you from doing what you are doing."

He'd been working on the rear fender design idea that had first come to him before the war, when Harley led the field trip to Selfridge air base to see the P-38 fighter. Looking at the plane's twin tail rudders that day, Hershey immediately thought of fins on sea creatures—slicing through the water's surface as a shark moved in on its prey, flashing silver-blue in the sun when a sailfish rose out of the ocean in full flight, waving a languid goodbye just before a whale disappeared into the deep—heart-stopping images long embedded in his imagination. It struck him that fins were wondrous creations of nature—beautiful, sleek, and shiny, streamlined and symmetrical, the embodiment of power, speed, maneuverability, and stability, everything that a modern automobile should be. And yet no one had designed them into the body of a car, until now.

In the basement of the farmhouse, two designers, three modelers, and a sculptor began turning Hershey's sketches into three dimensions on a quarter-size clay model. "We would lay out ideas on the board, and Harley would come out and we'd make changes," Hershey said. "He came out all the time." When the strike ended in March 1946—with the union agreeing to an 18.5 percent pay increase—the work was transferred to the Styling studios, where Harley, Hershey, and Bill Mitchell agreed that Cadillac, the company's traditional style leader, should get the first fins treatment.

With the exception of Studebaker, carmakers decided not to introduce fully redesigned new models in 1946, 1947, and 1948, but to offer instead face-lifted versions of their 1942 models, which had barely hit the showrooms when the production ban went into effect. It wasn't a tough call. GM put the cost of reconverting its factories to passenger car production at $700 million, with a three-year timetable for reaching full capacity. The wisdom of the decision was borne out when car-starved consumers began gobbling up every made-over '42 model the manufacturers produced, oftentimes paying extortionate fees to dealers above and beyond the company-suggested purchase price.

The hopped-up demand helped kill the Cadet because it backed up the opinion of the naysayers on the GM executive committee who had argued that the smaller car wasn't needed and would only displace sales of the company's larger, more profitable models. "The proposed Chevrolet lighter car project has been indefinitely deferred," the company announced, citing its "desire to devote all of the productive facilities and available materials of the Chevrolet Motor Division to meet the overwhelming demands of the motoring public for the established line of Chevrolet vehicles." The four Cadet prototypes Styling helped build were scrapped, and the work product "was simply locked away and forgotten . . . written out of GM's and Chevrolet's history," in the words of journalist Karl Ludvigsen.

It wasn't a time for looking back. The United States had emerged from the most violent and destructive event in human history as the most powerful nation on earth. As British historian Robert Payne wrote after a 1948 trip to America, "She sits bestride the world like a Colossus; no other power at any time in the world's history has possessed so varied or so great an influence on other nations. . . . Half of the wealth of the world, more than half of the productivity, nearly two-thirds of the world machines are concentrated in American hands; the rest of the world lies in the shadow of American industry."

As Detroit's car-making machinery roared back to life, the captains of steel, oil, rubber, and glass were licking their chops. "Never in all the history of Christendom had there been such a rich market awaiting businessmen," said author Ed Cray.

And never had a company been in a more enviable position than General Motors. As the top industrial contributor to the war effort, the company was now the preeminent member of America's budding military-industrial complex, with significant manufacturing assets in Great Britain and Germany, whose economies were about to receive $12 billion in U.S. aid through the Marshall Plan. In the automotive arena, GM had no serious competitor anywhere in the world. Its traditional archrival, Ford, had limped from the war a shell of its former self. Having failed to turn a profit for fourteen years, the once supreme carmaker was losing $10 million a month and hemorrhaging experienced executives, including Edsel's longtime confidant and styling collaborator Bob Gregorie, whose abrupt resignation left the new twenty-six-year-old CEO, Henry II, without a design chief as he struggled to breathe life back into the nearly moribund company. According to Ford family biographer Richard Bak, morale at Ford "was lower than the keels of the lake carriers hauling iron ore to the Rouge."

The atmosphere at GM was euphoric by comparison, particularly in the Cadillac division, which saw sales more than double between 1946 and 1947, with orders for 96,000 more cars than the factory was able to produce. "Cadillac fever is of epic proportions," declared automotive writer Eugene Jaderquist, who reported that in Los Angeles the chic Sunset Boulevard nightclub Ciro's had reserved its main parking lot for Cadillacs only, and dealerships were experiencing a new phenomenon called "the pool" in which a handful of people chipped in to buy a single Cadillac. "Ownership rests with the group as a whole, but actual use of the car rotates in whatever manner the members have been able to agree upon." In other words, a Cadillac timeshare.

"As far as can be discovered, only Cadillac enjoys this tribute," Jaderquist said. "Pools don't consider the big Chryslers, Lincolns or Packards."

In Detroit and New York, meanwhile, GM executives were discovering they could buy a Cadillac at cost from the company, drive it for a year, and then sell it for more than they paid for it.

Fortune magazine reported that Cadillac's growing popularity persuaded the corporation to pour more money into its luxury line, reasoning that "if there were going to be more customers than cars, they might as well be generous with the division that could return the most dollars per pound of steel." At some point the decision was made to move up the introduction of the first fully redesigned postwar Cadillacs to 1948, ahead of the rest of the industry.

All of which helped create a higher-than-usual level of curiosity at GM's Detroit headquarters about what the Cadillac styling team was doing behind their locked studio doors. The few executives who were given a peek came away with mixed opinions. President Charles Wilson liked Hershey's fins, but Cadillac general manager Nicholas Dreystadt, predictably, did not. Dreystadt, however, soon was promoted to general manager of GM's largest division, Chevrolet, and the man who replaced him, John Gordon, was younger and more open-minded. When Bill Mitchell invited Gordon into the studio to see a full-scale clay model, Gordon brought along Cadillac's chief engineer, Ed Cole, who liked the fins. But Gordon wasn't sure. He supposedly sat on an overturned wastebasket and stared at them in silence for ten minutes. Finally, he shook his head and said, "Too tall," suggesting they cut three-quarters of an inch off the top. According to Michael Lamm, Cole stayed behind after Gordon left and agreed with Mitchell that the fins were just right. So Mitchell instructed his clay modeler "to make the far fin an inch or so taller than the one nearer the viewer. Next day, when Gordon returned, he said, 'See, didn't I tell you it looks better lower like that?'"

Harley was ambivalent. He had encouraged the tail fins concept from the beginning. He appreciated the creative spark that caused a young designer to look at a warplane and see nature and then translate it into the rear fender on a car. He also knew that tail fins were a big idea, which worried him a little. What if they were too much of a stylistic leap for motorists to make? He'd never forgotten the experience of the "pregnant Buick." He was concerned, too, about his in-house audience, members of the executive committee and board of directors whose opinions would be solicited and taken into account before the car was finally approved for production.

With Harley's idiosyncratic guidance, a consensus clay model gradually emerged. The front end featured a subtle redesign of the so-called egg-crate grille that had come to identify a Cadillac in the 1940s—wide, horizontal, with crisscrossed chrome slats that created an architectural aspect, "like a Wilshire Boulevard building," according to Strother MacMinn, or, as Bob Gregorie saw it, "the public library in Washington, with pillars." Harley wanted the new front end to retain that strong Cadillac identity and at the same time be "more Tiffany," he instructed, more "jewel-like," and either "radically elegant" or "elegantly radical." Apparently, the design team knew how to express that in metal.

The model's back end was the pièce de résistance. The trend in postwar car design was toward an "envelope"-style body, which eliminated the traditional "applied" (nonintegrated) fenders of the late 1930s in favor of a full-width body that encapsulated and partially concealed the wheels. To better integrate Hershey's fins, however, the design team retained a modified version of applied fenders, which "made the back of the car look muscular," according to Michael Lamm, "like the rear haunch of a crouching animal getting ready to leap."

The ultimate corporate approval of the '48 fins may have come when a group of GM executives gathered to watch two prototypes being put through their paces at the Milford Proving Grounds. As the story goes, Alfred Sloan called Cadillac general manager John Gordon to his side, squeezed his arm, and said, "Now, Jack, you have a Cadillac in the rear as well as the front."

The whole process had been a boyhood dream come true for Hershey. He liked to tell the story of how his mother, Clara, a Detroit socialite, had purchased the third Cadillac that came off the assembly line in 1903 and how company founder Henry Leland had lent her his chauffeur to teach her how to drive it. His mother's 1918 Cadillac phaeton was the first car he ever sketched, and when she sold it he was so upset that he made a vow to himself that he would one day design Cadillacs. Now he was.

When the styling work was finished on the '48 models, Hershey threw a party at his farm for the entire Styling staff, and Harley was among the few who didn't come. The mood was jubilant as they joined in the preparation of an elaborate Italian meal in the large country kitchen and consumed a copious quantity of red wine. After dinner, a small group that included design chief Julio Andrade wandered out back to an old sheep shed, which Hershey had converted into a private studio where he was doing some commercial design work on the side. "It had nothing at all to do with automobiles," he explained later. "It was decorative brass and copper ware."

That didn't matter. They all knew GM had a strict policy against operating an outside business. There was only one exception to the rule: Harley had recently been granted permission to set up his own independent design company, the Harley Earl Corporation, under the provision that it would not compete directly with any GM division or subsidiary. The unique perquisite came in response to rumors, possibly spread by Harley, that Ford had approached him about becoming its head of design.

Andrade was one of the original Art and Colour team in the late 1920s, along with Hershey and a few others. For whatever reason, he ratted Hershey out on the sheep-shed design business. Shortly thereafter, Harley's assistant Howard O'Leary called Hershey and told him bluntly, "Frank, you're fired." Hershey was hurt and angry but blamed himself. "I was working so hard on my own business that I wasn't very much good to GM," he said later, adding, "It was a stupid thing to do."

He was still nursing his wounds a few months later when O'Leary called again and invited him to lunch at the Recess Club, a male members—only restaurant on the eleventh floor of the Fisher Building, the famed art deco skyscraper built by the brothers in 1928. "Harley feels very bad and he wants you to come back; he wants you to run his private industrial-design business," O'Leary said, explaining that it would only be for a couple of years and then he could return to the Styling Section, where he would probably be first in line for the job of chief designer for the whole department and, eventually, for a vice presidency. Hershey was surprised and tempted, but not enough. "I just got out of bed with him," he said. "I don't want to get into bed with him again."

"That was a mistake," he said years later. "I should have taken it."

13
DESIGNING
THE FUTURE

As Harley Earl marked his twentieth anniversary with GM in the summer of 1947, the Cadillac plant on Detroit's Clark Avenue was gearing up to begin assembling America's first production cars with tail fins.

Harley wasn't focused on the '48 models, however, or the '49s either, because the major styling work on them had been completed. His mind was fixed on cars the public wouldn't see until 1950 at the earliest—in particular, an experimental vehicle that was being developed in what he called his "hatchery," a top-secret studio with blacked-out windows and a misleading sign on the door to fool any interlopers. Only a handful of his most trusted designers were allowed access.

Code-named the XP-8, the vehicle amounted to little more than a grand idea at that point, "a car to show the world the promise of the future," as Michael Lamm put it. But Harlow Curtice, who had just been elevated to executive vice president of the corporation, believed that nobody could dream a car like Harley, so he'd agreed to finance the project to the tune of half a million dollars, or roughly ten times what he put up for the Y-job.

Harley's stock at the company had never been higher, as evidenced by the fact that after the executive committee allowed him to set up his own design company on the side, they let him hire Bill Mitchell, Cadillac's chief of design, to run it. Harley was earning more than $200,000 a year in salary and bonuses, with untaxed perks that included the use of company airplanes, the choice of any GM car he wanted, built to his specifications and maintained by a company mechanic, annual summer cruises to the Caribbean on Alfred Sloan's yacht, and extended trips to Europe every spring—primarily to attend the auto shows, but Sue always went along.

The Styling Section ranked as the largest and most successful industrial-design operation in the country, maybe the world. Its roster of in-house clients now included GM's Frigidaire home appliance division, which effectively extended Harley's design sensibility beyond the nation's garages and into its kitchens and laundry rooms. One team of stylists and interior specialists had just designed a new passenger train for GM's Electro-Motive division, which manufactured diesel locomotives.

Conceived as a promotional tool, the train took two years to build and consisted of four elegantly appointed cars, each topped with a laminated glass canopy, called an "Astrodome," the safety of which had been "tested in the windshields of thousands of bullet-swept warplanes," according to a GM brochure. The Sky View dining car provided "all the advantages of roof garden dining," the brochure boasted, while the Moon Glow observation car offered two cocktail lounges that were "furnished much like their counterparts in the smart supper clubs and hotels." In addition to the interior design, the Styling team created a striking deep blue-green exterior color scheme for the diesel locomotive and four domed cars, which embarked on a barnstorming tour through 180 cities in the United States and Canada in March 1947, billed as the "Train of Tomorrow." Nearly 6 million people either rode or walked through the train over a twenty-eight-month period.

Harley never stopped thinking about the future, and perhaps no single endeavor took up more of his attention in the postwar years than the plans for GM's Technical Center in Warren, Michigan. His role in the project was set down in December 1944, when Alfred Sloan called him and Charles Kettering together for an 8:00 a.m. meeting in Sloan's New York office. They needed to decide on an architect and submit their recommendation to the executive committee for approval at 9:00 a.m.

Sloan's secretary, Alice Goodson, transcribed their conversation for posterity and her notes may have captured more than any of them intended as the three old friends discussed the future of the company they had worked decades to build. They were barely seated when Kettering blurted out, "I think there is no better candidate than Albert Kahn. Let's just say to the committee that he's our choice. They won't argue. They all know Kahn. They like his work; it's the best this country has to offer."

Kahn was a logical choice, and a predictable one. The leading industrial architect of the day, he had built many of Detroit's most notable structures, including the Packard plant, Ford's Highland Park factory, the Fisher Building, the Detroit Institute of Arts, Edsel and Eleanor Ford's mansion at Gaukler Point on Lake St. Clair, and GM's own fifteen-story Detroit headquarters.

Agreeing that Kahn was a "marvelous" candidate, Sloan nonetheless urged, "Let's let Harley tell us his findings." Harley started to explain how he and an associate had consulted with deans of the leading universities noted for their architectural programs, including both Sloan's and Kettering's alma maters, MIT and Ohio State, respectively, but Kettering cut him off.

"You see, fellas, this is the problem to me," he said. "We are trying to find an architect when we've got one here who is the best in the world, and we know what his buildings are like; we work in them. I am worried we're going to get some fancy guy who will make us pay a fortune and he will come up with fancy buildings. We don't need fancy, Harley."

"Ket, I don't want fancy, dammit," Harley responded. "I want *significant*. I want those fellas at Ford and Packard and Chrysler to just be bowled over when they see what we did. And I want it to be the symbol of General Motors *in the future*. We keep showing this building we're in now as 'The General Motors building'—solid, sturdy, strong, like some New York bank. But Christ, we are not a bank. We are going to be the guys who shape the future. I think these buildings should give out that feeling to the press and the customers and to our people. Don't put 'em in a bank, Ket."

Sloan asked if Frank Lloyd Wright's name had come up in the discussions with the deans. It had, Harley said, "but no one had him high on the list, mostly because he is so difficult to work with. He's a tough old bird. Maybe they thought he and I would be a bad combination. I have a reputation for being a bit opinionated and headstrong." Sloan chuckled. "Why Harley, where would they ever get that idea?"

Harley said he favored a different local architect, Finnish-born Eliel Saarinen, who had designed the renowned Cranbrook Schools campus in nearby Bloomfield Hills, where he served as president of the Cranbrook Academy of Art and headed the graduate department of architecture and city planning.

Kettering scoffed: "A fellow who did a bunch of classroom buildings at Cranbrook is not prepared to design complex laboratories. . . . Saarinen wouldn't know beans about that kind of building inside." Harley countered that Kahn specialized in "very traditional buildings" but the Tech Center called for "something progressive rather than older." They went back and forth until Harley finally pushed the button that always worked with Sloan. "God, Alfie, we can't do something that looks old today," he said. "You wouldn't want me to do cars like that!"

At that, Sloan turned to Kettering. "I come to you if the subject is research or invention or ideas," he said. "There's no doubt about it, Ket; you are whom I put my undying admiration, trust and faith in. But when it comes to style or the aesthetics of things, I have to defer to Harley.

"I know what you are saying, Ket. Know that. But I feel Harley is right here. This is one of the few great opportunities we will ever get to do something, as Harley just said, 'significant.' I know that committee that's gathering in the next room would jump at the suggestion of Kahn in a minute. I know if I said, 'Let's give the job to Kahn,' that would be it, but on that whole committee there isn't an ounce of real awareness of what-is-what and who-is-who in architecture. And we are not doing this to please us, as if selecting an architect to do our own home. This is for a General Motors you and I have dreamed of and have wrestled with through these damned years of Depression and war and labor turmoil. These new buildings or this new facility is to be for a General Motors we bequeath to the next generation. You and I and Harley, we'll be gone, has-beens, names under portraits, names on gravestones, all but forgotten. But these buildings we set into being with this decision will be the flagship of this great corporation. We believe that it will be greater than we have ever known, and our legacy for all who come after, as lofty as all that sounds."

Read more than seventy years after the fact, Sloan's rhetoric sounds rehearsed, as if he and Harley had choreographed their side of the conversation in advance and the meeting was merely an attempt to get Kettering to accept what the two of them had already decided. But Kettering was as stubborn as Harley, and they went back and forth until Harley finally suggested they settle the matter with a competition—Kahn and Saarinen would be asked to submit a proposal and the best one in the eyes of the executive committee would win the contract. Sloan immediately pronounced it a great idea and Kettering grudgingly agreed to go along, saying, "I don't know how he'll feel about being in a contest, but I think that [Kahn's company] would want this job very much, and would win it. They have the experience, the expertise and they know us inside and out."

Harley wouldn't let the argument go. "Ket, they know the *older* General Motors. But they do not know the General Motors that's coming. We are going to stomp on Ford and Chrysler, believe me. And these new facilities are going to show the way. I say Kahn can't do it and that Saarinen will, just because he does not know our old ways as much. He will approach us from a new direction. I'll bet you a dinner at Delmonico's in New York on the outcome of this."

Seeking to end the meeting on that jocular note, Sloan asked whether he could join them at Delmonico's. "You're welcome," Harley said, "and will I enjoy that meal, with Ket paying for the best champagne. Have you ever bought me a meal, Ket?"

"It will be your treat, Harley," Kettering replied, "not mine."

There is no record of who picked up the tab or whether the dinner ever took place, but when ground was broken for the Technical Center on October 23, 1945, it was Eliel Saarinen, not Albert Kahn, who posed for photographers standing next to Harley, Sloan, and an unsmiling Kettering. Two years later, building construction still had not begun when Kettering retired from GM at the age of seventy-one, leaving Harley solely responsible for oversight of Saarinen and the $100 million project.

That summer, Harley took his mind off the future long enough to join Sue and their now college-age sons on what proved to be an elegiac journey through the past. Having grown up the daughter of a rancher in Banning, California, Sue delighted in taking her city-born boys on annual road trips to rustic guest ranches all over the West in the days when 80 percent of America's roads were unpaved. Harley rarely accompanied them because although he was an avid hunter and fisherman, he didn't care for horseback riding and he couldn't take that much time away from work. This time Sue and Jerry drove to a Wyoming dude ranch in an Oldsmobile that Harley bought specifically for the trip, and he made arrangements to meet them in San Francisco.

After a week at the ranch, Sue and Jerry connected with Jim, the older boy, in Cody, Wyoming. He'd spent two months in an Idaho logging camp doing the kind of hard, dangerous work his grandfather had endured in the Michigan pine forest sixty-five years earlier. Jim knew nothing of that history, however, because he and Jerry had met J.W. only once, when they were so young they had no memory of it.

The three of them then drove over the Sierra Nevadas, through the Tioga Pass, dipped down into Yosemite, and then picked up Harley in San Francisco for the last leg of the journey along the scenic Pacific Coast Highway to Los Angeles. The boys hadn't been there since they were little, and all they remembered of that visit was being led into their great-grandmother Taft's bedroom to give her a dutiful kiss. It was the only time they ever saw her. She died in 1938 at the age of ninety-seven.

On this trip, Sue and the boys spent most of their time with her parents, who still lived next door to the Hollywood hilltop house that she and Harley had built in 1925 and where Billy, the brother Jim and Jerry didn't know about, was born. Cecil B. DeMille still lived a hundred yards down the street. Harley visited separately with his father, brothers Art and Carl, and sister Jessie. "He had a particular affection for my mother," Jessie's son, John Sampson, recalled recently. "He stopped by whenever he came to town for the Los Angeles Auto Show."

To his nieces and nephews, Harley was the family's glamorous celebrity. "I had an uncle I could brag about," said Jessie's daughter, Virginia Ramshaw. She and her brother John would never forget the time Harley took them to dinner at Chasen's restaurant in Beverly Hills, where his star status qualified them for a table among the Hollywood elite in the middle of the room "while all the commoners sat around the perimeter," John said, adding, "But Harley didn't flash money; he was very shy about money."

He had good reason for that: money was a divisive issue in the extended family. Thanks to the success of Earl Automobile Works, J.W.'s children by his first wife, Abbie, had been able to attend private universities, establish professional careers, and experience life beyond the city of their birth. J.W. gave Jessie her own car, which she crashed, and an extended world tour as a graduation present.

Life was markedly different for his son and daughter by his second wife, Nellie. "Henry and Janelle could not go to college because after the stock market crash grandfather didn't have the money," their cousin Virginia explained recently. "I was very close to Janelle. She didn't ever talk about Harley, Art, or Carl. Uncle Henry worked at the dime store. In high school, he was drafted and served under General Patton in the Second Armored Division and was in a prisoner-of-war camp in Germany."

The disparity fed the resentment Nellie harbored for her step-children. Only Jessie maintained a relationship with her step-mother and half siblings, and she saw to it that her children did as well. She regularly brought bags of groceries to J.W. and Nellie and had helped arrange a surprise eightieth birthday party for her father at their home. Harley was not in town for the party, but he sent a gift that made an impression on everyone there. J.W. described the moment with a draftsmanlike exactitude in a letter to Harley dated February 6, 1946: "Jessie brought me a box five-feet-six inches long, five inches wide and five inches deep with those eighty roses, all long, with red buds," he wrote. "Many [guests] exclaimed they had never seen anything like it. Then came your phone call and that nearly bowled me over."

The letter made it clear that despite the enduring rift in the family, the bond between father and son remained strong. "Thanks ever and ever so much, and on top of all that, your checks," J.W. said in closing. "And now I stop and think and wonder why. Loads of love, Dad."

Harley outdid the roses during the Los Angeles trip, present-ing his dad with a new '47 Chevrolet, a no-frills black sedan that only a clergyman or funeral director could love. Given that J.W. was a devout Methodist church leader who wore a white shirt and tie every day, whether working in his tiny real estate office on Hollywood Boulevard or building a rabbit hutch in his backyard, it seems likely that Harley special-ordered the car af-ter carefully considering what his father might feel comfortable driving. It would have been unlike the car designer in him to do otherwise. But Nellie didn't see it that way. She grumbled that Harley could have afforded something nicer.

After a week of visiting old friends and favorite haunts, Harley sold the Oldsmobile to a local dealer and he and Sue and the boys hopped aboard the Super Chief streamliner and headed back to Detroit and the future, having taken what would turn out to be their last family vacation to Los Angeles.

The '48 Cadillacs didn't go into production until late February 1948, due to factory retooling delays, and they arrived in dealer showrooms a month later with little of the traditional fanfare. There had been no splashy unveiling at the Waldorf-Astoria in January; the industry did not mount the New York Auto Show for 1948 because only Cadillac had a new auto to show. The company's ads and brochures downplayed the car's most distinctive design feature, referring only to the rear fenders' "rudder-type styling." According to Bill Mitchell, it was "merely a humped up taillight really; it wasn't a fin at all." But Cadillac dealers, historically a conservative lot, were concerned when they first saw the new cars; nothing had prepared them for how radically different they looked from the prewar models. Their concern turned to alarm when longtime customers, after waiting six years for a new Caddy, reacted negatively to the never-before-seen rear fender treatment. Sales managers complained to the home office that the "fishtails" were driving people away. Calls were made demanding that the Styling Section fix the problem by fast-tracking a new rear fender design sans fins, a daunting prospect given that stylists had already incorporated them into the design of the '49 and '50 models. The ghost of the "pregnant Buick" seemed to hover in the hallways at GM headquarters. "We almost started a war inside the corporation," Harley recalled years later.

Before any drastic action was taken, however, something happened. As the new models began to appear on the streets, people stopped, looked, and decided they liked what they saw, including Frank Hershey's fishtailed fenders. "Their form, like that of a salmon, is entirely suited to smooth travel in one direction," said *Motor* magazine. "Static pictures can do scant justice to their natural look as they glide along the road." Some people did more than just look. It wasn't unusual to see a passerby stop beside a parked Cadillac and almost unconsciously run an admiring hand along the curve of the fender and over the rounded nub that housed the taillight.

After a sputtering start, sales accelerated to a record level by the end of the year. *Fortune* magazine later suggested it was the Cadillac that sold the public on tail fins, not the other way around. In an article headlined "The Cadillac Phenomenon," the magazine quoted a Cadillac competitor saying that if his company had introduced fins, "we would have been murdered."

Harley believed the tail fin caught on because Cadillac owners felt it "gave them an extra receipt for their money in the form of a visible prestige marking for an expensive car." In accordance with his three-year design cycle, the fins went unchanged for the next few model years as the Styling staff performed a series of face-lifts on other parts of the car. They lengthened the rear deck until there was nearly as much metal behind the driver as in front. They eliminated the center roof support, or "B-pillar," between the front- and rear-side windows, creating the so-called hardtop roofline that lent the two-door coupe the alfresco look of a convertible, but with the top up. They fashioned the first curved, one-piece windshield, a product of years of GM research and vision tests at the Dartmouth Eye Institute. More playfully, they added a pair of bullet-shaped front bumper guards that, when viewed head-on, resembled chrome-plated female breasts, which quickly earned the nickname "Dagmars," after a buxom blond TV personality of the day.

Cadillac engineers contributed a new high-compression 331-cubic-inch V-8 that moved *Mechanix Illustrated* magazine to declare, "With this engine, Cadillac, despite its large size, out-performs just about every car being made." Indeed, American race-car driver and racing-team owner Briggs Cunningham, a buddy of Harley's from West Palm Beach, Florida, promptly en-tered a Cadillac Coupe de Ville in France's legendary twenty-four-hour Le Mans Grand Prix, and the car finished in tenth place.

The end result was an automobile that perfectly captured America's sense of itself at the dawn of the 1950s—powerful, exceptional, and, in Harley's word, "significant." The new gener-ation of Cadillac was embraced by the burgeoning middle class, not as a symbol of wealth and privilege but rather as one of accomplishment, a car for the man who had earned his place in the world, not inherited it. At a time when the average family income was $4,200 a year and the lowest-priced Cadillac cost $3,000, polls indicated that a majority of Americans would buy a Cadillac over any other car if they could afford to. It didn't matter that only a fraction of them could; most believed that one day they would. In the wake of winning a world war, anything seemed attainable. "Probably never before has one material ob-ject become so much the focus for so many of the aspirations that propel the American ego," said *Fortune*.

African Americans aspired to equality more than anything else, of course, and according to *Ebony* magazine, owning a Cad-illac was "a solid and substantial symbol for many a Negro that he is as good as any white man." In a 1949 editorial headlined

"Why Do Negroes Buy Cadillacs?" the magazine declared, "To be able to buy the most expensive car made in America is as graphic a demonstration of that equality as can be found. It's the acme of dignity and stature." *Fortune* noted that Cadillac did not advertise in *Ebony* at the time and quoted one of its executives as saying, "You can never tell which man on the street will turn up with $5,000 to buy a Cadillac. And if he has had to cross over the tracks to get there, Cadillac doesn't worry."

Cadillac sales exceeded 100,000 in 1950, the first time a luxury car had reached that level. It was peanuts compared with Chevrolet's industry-topping total of 1.5 million, but nearly double the combined sales of the Packard, Chrysler, and Lincoln luxury models.

GM sold a record 3 million cars in 1950, nearly as many as the rest of the industry combined. The company produced not only the top-selling car in the luxury and low-priced categories but also the three bestselling mid-priced cars—Buick, Pontiac, and Oldsmobile, which ranked fourth, fifth, and sixth, respectively. The list offered empirical proof that Sloan's organizing principle of "a car for every purse and purpose" and Harley's "trickle down" design system that played to consumers' desire for social mobility made for an unbeatable combination.

The big story in the 1950 industry standings, however, was Ford's return to the number two position, ahead of Chrysler. In the wake of Henry Ford's death in 1947, his grandson Henry II had hired a team of young former Air Force procurement and logistics officers who called themselves the "Whiz Kids" and tasked them with setting up the modern-day accounting and purchasing systems that his grandfather so disdained. Henry II also brought in a veteran GM divisional vice president, Ernest R. Breech, to be his second in command, charged with massively reorganizing the company based on GM's decentralized model. Breech, in turn, recruited industrial designer George Walker, one of his golfing buddies, to consult with the styling department on the development of the company's '49 Ford.

Although Walker's firm had done some contract work for Nash Motors and Studebaker, it was primarily known for designing household consumer products. But Henry II picked its design for the company's namesake car over the one presented by Bob Gregorie's staff, which prompted the longtime styling chief to resign in a huff. The resultant '49 model stunned the industry by knocking Chevrolet out of the top spot for the first time since before the Depression, selling nearly 1.5 million units—a whopping 1 million more than the year before—and powering the company to $700 million in profits that year.

Henry II authorized Walker to expand Ford's styling department and to model it on GM's Styling Section, with separate studios for Ford, Mercury, and Lincoln. Walker began to style himself as a more flamboyantly dressed and outspoken version of Harley, encouraging reporters to refer to him as "the Cellini of chrome" in the way they had dubbed Harley "the da Vinci of Detroit." In an interview with *Time* magazine, Walker described what he called his "finest moment: 'There I was in my white Continental, and I was wearing pure silk, pure white embroidered cowboy shirt and black gabardine trousers. Beside me in the car was my jet black Great Dane, imported from Europe, named Dana von Krupp. You just can't do any better than that.'"

Even more provocatively, Walker began recruiting Harley's former and current designers, including Frank Hershey, whom he put in charge of the Ford design studio. It almost seemed as if Walker was playing a character from a 1950s western movie— the new fast gun in town, calling Harley out into the street.

If Harley was worried, he didn't show it. On December 29, 1950, the Friday leading into the New Year's weekend, GM issued a press release announcing that an "experiment in the automotive future—a low, sleek sports car with the dramatic sweeping lines of a jet air craft—was unveiled today by the Styling Section of General Motors."

It was the XP-8, rechristened Le Sabre and introduced to the press in the form of a gleaming full-size plaster model that only a trained eye could tell wasn't the real thing. Explaining that the actual roadworthy vehicle would not be finished for four months, GM distributed dramatic photographs of Harley standing next to the model, dressed in an elegant dark suit and brightly patterned tie, and gazing at what may have been the world's most prodigious tail fin that wasn't attached to an airplane or a very large fish. The car stood only 36 inches high at the cowl, and 50 at the top of the so-called panoramic windshield, the first with glass bent to wrap around the cockpit. The front fenders barely came up to Harley's knees.

Clearly, Harley had reconsidered his previous predictions that postwar automobiles would not take styling cues from aircraft design. The Le Sabre was named after the F-86 Sabre jet, the first supersonic fighter plane (originally code-named the XP-86). Its oval grille resembled the front air intake of its namesake, except that a button on the instrument panel would cause it to rotate 180 degrees to reveal a close-set pair of headlights. The rear deck tapered to a "jetlike center tail cone" with a "bomb-shaped hub." The flanking tail fins would be functional, the press release said, because each would house "aircraft-type 20-gallon rubberized fuel tanks," one for premium gasoline and the other for super-high-octane methyl alcohol, which would be injected into the combustion chambers through a second carburetor to provide "extra power boost at high speeds."

The press release likened the Le Sabre's interior to a "bomber cockpit" that would be equipped with thermostatically controlled electric seat warmers, which functioned on the same principle as "electrically heated flying suits used by airmen." The instrument panel would include controls to operate hydraulic jacks on each wheel "so that in the event of a blow out or flat, the driver could jack up the car without leaving his seat." And between the seats an embedded sensor device would detect the slightest drop of rain and instantly raise the convertible top and windows.

Harley described the car as a "laboratory on wheels" for testing mechanical and styling ideas, and he cautioned that many of the innovations were not financially practical for current production cars.

"However, if the time should come when some materials or some devices in this car get within range of the customer's pocketbook, we'll be ready.

"That is the point of building this car," he said. "To be prepared for the future."

14
THE GREAT
AMERICAN
SPORTS
CAR RACE

The press got its first look at the real Le Sabre on July 17, 1951, when Harley invited a handpicked group of automotive writers to the Milford Proving Grounds to see the car scream past the reviewing stand at 110 miles an hour. Afterward, he gave them a demonstration of some of its eighty innovations, including the rain sensor, which one of his assistants triggered with an eyedropper. Then each reporter was taken on what was likely the ride of his life. "A quick spin around the 3.8 mile track with its banked turn going by at 90 miles an hour is as smooth as an airplane banking gracefully in the sky," said the man from the *Detroit Free Press*, who proclaimed the car "Harley Earl's magnum opus."

A few weeks later, Harley took the Le Sabre to New York for its public debut as the pace car for the Watkins Glen Grand Prix, an annual road race that drew about 100,000 racing fans to a small village in the Finger Lakes region. The Le Sabre traveled in its own specially equipped trailer accompanied by its dedicated "engineer" (chief mechanic), Leonard MacLay, his assistant, Art Carpenter, and a GM photographer. Wherever the car and Harley appeared, crowds pressed in around them, to Harley's obvious delight. They were a photogenic pair—America's most spectacular automobile and the tall, tanned, elegantly attired designer who had imagined her. Dominick Fraboni, the owner of Watkins Glen Chevrolet, acted as Harley's host for the weekend, putting him up at his home and proudly introducing him to folks around town. "General Motors vice presidents didn't normally come to little dealerships like Watkins Glen," he later explained to a reporter.

The car almost didn't make the race. The day before, Harley took it out for a drive and as he slowed at a crossing the engine flooded and died. He tried repeatedly to restart it, getting madder each time the engine failed to respond. When it finally did, he floored the accelerator and, without lifting his foot, "dropped the transmission into drive," whereupon "the sudden burst of torque twisted the driveshaft like an aluminum beer can." Mac-Lay and Carpenter worked all night in Fraboni's shop to repair the damage in time for the race.

As Harley led the competitors in a parade around the course through the town that morning, he was struck by the number of foreign sports cars parked along the route, mostly British-made roadsters—Jaguars, Morgans, and MGs—with college-age owners showing them off. "He commented that American auto companies were lacking a sports car," said Fraboni, who rode in the Le Sabre with him. "When he saw that bunch of cars at the start-finish line, you could see that his wheels were turning."

The winning car that day was a white Cunningham C2 roadster built by Briggs Cunningham, whose cars also took second and fourth place, the latter car driven by Cunningham himself.

After the race, Harley went back to Detroit and began talking up an idea with his designers—a GM sports car, a two-seater convertible, but not like the Le Sabre, which was 17 feet long, 6 feet wide, and weighed 3,800 pounds on account of all its fancy engineering. The car he envisioned would be almost the opposite—light and nimble, simple, unadorned, and affordable for young people: an American version of a classic European roadster like the one he had just bought for his new daughter-in-law, Connie. The nineteen-year-old had come to live with Harley and Sue while her husband, Jim, served a tour of duty as an Air Force pilot in Germany, and she would never forget that car or the way Harley presented it to her. "He sent a company plane to get me in Palm Beach," Connie recalled shortly before her death in 2016, "and when I walked down the steps at the airport in Detroit, it was waiting for me there on the tarmac, a beautiful little MG, British racing green with white leather seats."

A team tasked with designing America's first sports car quickly got to work in Harley's top-secret, blacked-out studio. A misleading sign on the door said "Opel Project," and internal documents referred to the car as the EX-122.

After Watkins Glen, the Le Sabre appeared at the Canadian National Exhibition in Toronto and then sailed to France on the ocean liner *De Grasse* for the annual Paris Auto Show and a command performance at the headquarters of General Dwight Eisenhower, who was in his final months as Supreme Commander of NATO forces in Europe. MacLay took the soon-to-be president for a ride and entertained him with the rain sensor routine. The GM photographer snapped a picture of the man who had overseen history's largest deployment of air, land, and sea vehicles during D-day standing next to the car as its top went up, a delighted smile on his face and an eyedropper in his hand. Harley wasn't there that day, but he sent along autographed photos of himself behind the wheel. Ike sent back a note thanking him for the demonstration of the Le Sabre's "wizardry" and adding, "I was, to say the least, intrigued!"

Over the next year, the Le Sabre appeared at a succession of state fairs, municipal parades, and auto shows around the country, sometimes with Harley and sometimes solo. In one instance, they both were in Palm Beach but without MacLay, who had stayed behind in Detroit for reasons that are lost to time. Harley was taking Ford executive vice president Ernest Breech for a drive, with the top down as always, when a sudden south Florida rain shower came up. "Don't worry, we'll be okay," Harley said, confident that the rain sensor would do its job. But it didn't and they got drenched, which prompted an angry call to MacLay ordering him to get on the next flight down there to fix it. "That was one of the times I got fired," MacLay said later.

For Harley, the most satisfying stop on the Le Sabre road show may have been the car's appearance at the Los Angeles County Fair in September 1952 because it gave him the chance for a side trip to show it off at the GM-endowed Art Center School in Los Angeles, where one of his original Art and Colour staffers, Strother MacMinn, was on the faculty. Harley also hosted a press preview at the Beverly Hills Hotel, formally introducing the "car of tomorrow" to the city of his birth. "'Dream' Auto Unveiled by Engineer," read the headline in the *Los Angeles Times*, which mistakenly credited him with an engineering degree from Stanford but accurately described him as "a native son of Los Angeles, now a famed automobile designer."

◆

It was agreed from the get-go that the Le Sabre would be Harley's personal vehicle as well as the company's flagship, so, back in Detroit, car and driver once again became a familiar sight cruising along Lake Shore Drive on his daily commute between home and the office. "Le Sabre Takes Up Residence in the Pointe," reported the local *Grosse Pointe News*, with an accompanying photo of Harley and Sue sitting in the car in their driveway on a Sunday afternoon. Newspapers around the country gobbled up GM's publicity shots of the Le Sabre with Harley either behind the wheel or looming alongside. The PR department planted articles and "guest columns" under his byline, expounding on such subjects as "What Goes into Automobile Styling" and how the term "hardtop" came about. It's doubtful that he wrote any of them, however, since he rarely put anything down on paper, not even memos to staff. More likely, he dictated them to a PR staffer. A *Saturday Evening Post* article headlined "I Dream Automobiles" was authored "by Harley J. Earl as told to [*Post* editor] Arthur W. Baum." Harley told the magazine's 6 million readers by way of introduction, "I consider myself an ordinary garden variety American, and I think I can show enough common faults and foibles to prove it. Along with most people, I remember faces and forget names. Sometimes I overestimate the authority of two pairs and a fellow with three of a kind lets me have it in the customary eye. When I hit a golf ball I am sorry to say that it does not always stay on the fairway, and I have seen mallards fly off in excellent health after I have fired both barrels right at them. I don't like to write letters. I like baseball and I love automobiles."

He came across as all-American as one of the magazine's famous Norman Rockwell cover illustrations, like a Jimmy Stewart character in a Frank Capra movie titled *Mr. Earl Goes to Detroit*.

"My primary purpose for 28 years has been to lengthen and lower the American automobile," he said, "at times in reality and always at least in appearance. Why? Because my sense of proportion tells me that oblongs are more attractive than squares, just as a ranch house is more attractive than a square, three-story, flat-roofed house, or a greyhound is more graceful than an English bulldog. Happily, the car-buying public and I consistently agree on this."

No matter who really wrote the article, the Styling staff recognized the voice—minus the malapropisms and profanity. The comment "Let me say quickly that when I refer to myself I am merely using a short cut to talk about my team" was pure Harley, their publicly self-effacing team leader who had recently signed off on a press release that described him as "a man of towering genius."

GM's PR campaign was primarily intended to tout the company's styling supremacy, but in the process it turned Harley Earl into a household name. He became the de facto face of an increasingly faceless corporation, perhaps the only auto executive whom the average Joe would recognize on the street. And as much as Harley might deny it, he relished his late-blooming celebrity.

At fifty-nine, he was among the last of GM's old lions, the generation of executives that helped vanquish Henry Ford in the 1920s and kept the company profitable through the Depression. Their number was dwindling. Boss Ket and the Fisher brothers all were retired now. Big Bill Knudsen had rejoined the company as a board member after the war, but died in 1948, the same year Nicholas Dreystadt succumbed to throat cancer at age fifty-eight. Alfred Sloan was seventy-seven and slowing down, having ceded his day-to-day CEO responsibilities to GM president Charles E. Wilson, who was sixty-three and thus just two years shy of the mandatory retirement age of sixty-five recently set by the executive committee.

The age mandate wasn't retroactive, however, so it didn't apply to Sloan, whose successor, when he decided the time had come, was expected to be Harlow Curtice. That augured well for Harley because the two men had never hesitated to back his big ideas with blank checks, the latest of which was for an expensive reimagination of the traditional auto show.

After the industry decided to forgo its traditional New York show in 1948, Harley pushed the idea of going it alone, arguing that by mounting its own show GM could control the conditions, lighting, sets, and staging of the exhibition in a way that better presented its products.

GM's "Transportation Unlimited" exhibition was the first major postwar auto show. Held the week of January 20–27, 1949, in the grand ballroom of New York's Waldorf-Astoria Hotel, it served as the official debut of the tail fins, hardtops, and two-tone paint jobs that would dominate American automobile styling in the next decade. It also showed off products from GM's Frigidaire, Delco, and Electro-Motive divisions.

Harley followed up in January 1950 with the "Mid-Century Motorama," also at the Waldorf. The show's centerpiece, created by the Styling Section's Exhibit and Product design studio, consisted of an elaborate 1,500-square-foot revolving platform with five electronically synchronized turntables that displayed flamboyantly painted and trimmed models, including a two-tone ("cabana sand and over surf green") Oldsmobile Palm Beach Holiday with green alligator leather seats, and—even more jarring to modern sensibilities—a golden Cadillac Debutante with an interior fashioned from "the finest Somaliland leopard skin." GM publicity material pointed out that in its effort to obtain "perfectly-matching" skins for the car, the company went so far as to hire a furrier who spent months collecting nearly two hundred pelts, from which fourteen were selected as "the best that could possibly be attained." Styling's color department paired the leopard interior with a pearlescent "tawny yellow buff" exterior paint that was created by dissolving tiny moon-shaped fish scales and then spraying their pearly essence over the base coat. The glittering effect supposedly inspired George S. Kaufman and Howard Teichmann's 1953 hit Broadway comedy *The Solid Gold Cadillac*, which was later made into a movie starring Judy Holliday.

"Transportation Unlimited" and "Mid-Century Motorama" were warm-ups. What Harley envisioned as the auto show of the future was equal parts World's Fair exhibit, traveling Barnum & Bailey big-top performance, and Busby Berkeley movie musical, employing actors, singers, dancers, musicians, high-fashion models, and even a few animals in a lavishly choreographed celebration of the age of American abundance.

The Le Sabre would play a leading role, of course, since it had not been finished in time to make its official New York debut at the 1950 show. "People will stand in line, four abreast, completely around the city block, just waiting to get inside," Harley told a group of newly hired young stylists, sounding as if he were describing the world premiere of Cecil B. DeMille's latest Technicolor screen epic. "Once in the ballroom, it will be so crowded around the car that they will not be able to see it and will have to stay for the next show just to get a better view."

Each of the auto divisions would present their own one-of-a-kind "dream cars," Harley said. Like the Le Sabre, they would be eye-popping, heart-stopping creations, the kind of cars a movie star might drive but average folks could only fantasize about. "You know, when you go to Las Vegas to see a stage show, you don't expect to see your wife on the stage," he explained. "You expect to see a real floozy."

The advent of the Korean War scotched plans for the shows in 1951 and 1952, however, as a shortage of raw materials and defense contract commitments reduced the entire industry's production capacity to the point where it made little sense to spend money on promotional activity that would only increase consumer demand that already could not be met.

In the early spring of 1952, Harley showed a painted and fully trimmed mock-up of his EX-122 sports car to Chevrolet's chief engineer, Ed Cole, the division's new general manager, Thomas Keating, and GM executive vice president Harlow Curtice. They all agreed the car should be developed under the Chevrolet banner as the division's dream car at the next Motorama, in January 1953, with general production to begin as soon as possible after that. The tight timetable dictated that its body would be fashioned from a new structural material called GRP (for glass reinforced plastic) that GM had been testing. Also called fiberglass, the resin-based material was lighter than sheet metal and cheaper to use for a prototype body because it required no factory retooling.

A special committee meeting was called to come up with a name for the car, but after considering three hundred suggestions all they could agree on was that it should be a nonanimal name beginning with the letter "c." Myron Scott, the assistant director of Chevrolet's public relations department, took the job home with him that night and patiently searched that section of the dictionary until his finger came upon the name for a class of small, fast British warship—"corvette." For his extra effort Scott earned a permanent place of honor in GM annals.

No sooner had the name been settled than Harley's vaunted security system suffered a serious breach. "A friend of mine at GM sent me a picture of what he called 'our new Corvette,'" recalled Frank Hershey, who was Ford's chief of design at the time. "I flipped because it meant they were going to have something we didn't have."

He wasn't about to let that happen. "As design chief, I had the authority to do whatever I wanted to, and I had an extra room, so I bought an XK-120 Jag, took the same wheelbase, and roughed out a car. Nobody knew about it but the guys in my room. If [management] had found out about it, we never would have done it. It was all secret."

Hershey knew that Harley's head start meant the Corvette most likely would beat his sports car to the marketplace, but still he thrilled to the chase. And the fact that his old mentor didn't know he was coming up from behind made it all the sweeter.

GM's 1953 Motorama kicked off a weeklong run at the Waldorf on January 16, beginning with a traditional conference with automotive writers, whose numbers had grown since the war with the launching of a number of national automotive magazines, including *Road & Track*, *Car Craft*, *Motor Trend*, and *Hot Rod*. The latter two publications in particular celebrated the emergence of a car-crazy youth culture epitomized by a Los Angeles–based celebrity car customizer named George Barris, whose career rise mirrored that of Harley's in the early 1920s.

Harley had never before addressed the writers' gathering. He didn't like talking to large groups of people, supposedly because he was self-conscious about his stammer. "Harlow Curtice promised me I only had to get up and take a bow," he told them. "My work is really over. Whether it is good or bad, you fellows who haven't seen the show will know later. But I am very, very indebted to these guests of ours here today. For the last twenty-six or twenty-seven years, I have not gotten around to thanking them. This is really my first opportunity. The corporation has kept me more or less under cover.

"I want to thank you fellows for the fair way you have treated us in the Styling Section over all these years. I also want to thank the men who have written in telling us all the good things as well as the bad things, trying to coach us along. I hope you won't stop that. It means an awful lot more to me than you might think."

Inside the hotel's grand ballroom, thirty-eight automobiles were presented with the backing of a full orchestra, a fourteen-voice choral group, and a ballet troupe of two dozen dancers who put on a stage performance dramatizing "the story of engineering progress from the discovery of fire and the invention of the wheel to the present day," according to GM press material. Created by the noted Broadway choreographers Richard and Edith Barstow, the dance performance "is believed to represent the first effort to tell an industrial or engineering story through the medium of ballet," the company claimed. There was also a "Fashions First" revue that featured a parade of fashion models wearing opera gloves and evening gowns created by such leading designers as Christian Dior from fabrics that matched the color of the cars the women caressed.

As if all that weren't enough, the entire production—performers, technicians, stagehands, mechanics, and sixty tractor-trailer loads of cars and exhibits—was set to go on a three-month national tour after the Waldorf show, with weeklong stands in Miami, Kansas City, Dallas, San Francisco, and Los Angeles.

The New York show drew an estimated fifty thousand people the first day. They crowded around and stood on their tiptoes to get a better look at Harley's dream cars, especially his most famous "floozy," the Le Sabre, the automotive equivalent of Mae West. Pontiac's La Parisienne, a chauffeur-ready town car with a landau roof over the rear passenger compartment and a hand-lacquered jet-black exterior finish, seemed demure in comparison. Only the "roulette pink" leather bucket seats gave away its Harley Earl pedigree. Someone in Styling decided to outfit the car with a pair of "French" poodles—one dyed pink and the other blue—until the American Society for the Prevention of Cruelty Against Animals complained.

The two-seater Buick Wildcat and four-passenger Oldsmobile Starfire dream cars were billed as "sports convertibles" in keeping with an overall sporty theme set by the PR department. They boasted fiberglass bodies in brilliant colors, Le Sabre–style wraparound windshields, and elongated versions of Cadillac's P-38-inspired tail fins, a harbinger of bigger things to come.

The most dramatic design element of the Cadillac Le Mans was its lack of a rear seat, which made the "three-passenger" convertible two and a half feet shorter than a standard model and allowed GM ad copywriters to call it a "luxury sports car" even though it weighed approximately 4,000 pounds. The metallic silver-blue dream car sat five inches closer to the ground than Cadillac's top-of-the-line El Dorado, but—with the same massive grille, peaked snout, and sharply defined tail fins—it looked startlingly like a great white shark on wheels.

According to Harley, after seeing the Le Mans at the Los Angeles show, actor John Wayne walked up to him and announced that he wanted to buy one. Harley tried to tell him that it was just a show car and not for sale, and besides, he explained, it was made of fiberglass. "I don't care if it's made of *pudding*," the Duke replied. "I *want* one."

As it turned out, the least flashy dream car generated the most buzz. Plain white, with red leather seats, a manually operated black canvas top, and minimal chrome ornamentation, the Chevrolet Corvette didn't even have outside door handles or roll-up windows. Like the European sports cars that had inspired its creation, America's "first real sports car" came with canvas-and-Plexiglas side curtains that were to be stored in the trunk and snapped into place in the event of inclement weather. The car measured just 47 inches at the top of the wraparound windshield and weighed less than 2,900 pounds, with rounded fenders in front and back, recessed headlights covered by chrome "stone guard" mini-grilles, and jet-style taillight housings molded with vestigial fins.

The Corvette's most striking feature, however, was a low, rounded horizontal grille that framed a set of thirteen gleaming teeth, forming a face that was at once a first for a sports car and an instant classic.

The excitement surrounding the Corvette was such that on the second day of the show Harlow Curtice announced the company would begin production in June. An internal decision was made to continue with the fiberglass body, rather than switching to sheet metal as originally planned, and to set up a production line capable of turning out 10,000 cars per year. Ford dispatched a team of engineers to the Waldorf to check out

GM's new sensation. They were easy to spot as they practically crawled all over the car measuring every dimension.

Frank Hershey had managed to keep his sports car project hidden from upper management for a time, but word eventually got out when he brought a young engineer into his secret room to help lay out some key mechanical dimensions. That attracted the attention of Ford's chief engineer, Earle MacPherson, who was livid to learn that such a project had been undertaken without his knowledge. At Ford, styling was subordinate to engineering, the way it had been at General Motors before Harley broke the mold.

MacPherson's pique briefly threatened the project, as Hershey struggled to justify his clandestine undertaking to management. But GM's announcement about the Corvette settled the issue. Even though the sports car market was small—estimated at about 12,000 units a year at the time—Ford's top executives agreed that the Corvette challenge needed to be answered. Ford held an edge on Chevrolet among young hot rod, racing, and custom car enthusiasts whose preferred power plant was Ford's flat-head V-8, and the company couldn't afford to cede that territory to its longtime archrival.

So the race was on, with Hershey playing the tortoise to Harley's hare. Knowing his old boss's playbook better than anybody, he was confident his sports car could catch the Corvette in the long run, though not the short. He was given a May 1 deadline for the delivery of a full-size clay model and immediately clashed with his superiors over what kind of car it should be.

"They said they wanted a car that a banker could drive up to his bank and get out and people wouldn't point and say 'Look at that young hot-rodder,'" Hershey told Alexandra Earl years later. "They wanted a car that had 'dignity' but would still be a 'sports-type' car." They didn't want to call it a sports car, however, so they invented a new term for it, a "personal luxury car."

As Hershey and his team worked feverishly on the styling and mechanics of what was being referred to internally as the "Sportsman" or "Sportsliner," Ford division general manager Lewis Crusoe launched an intramural contest to come up with a better name, offering a prize that pointed up the absence of women in the ranks—a $250 Brooks Brothers suit. That was enough to garner some five thousand submissions, ranging from Runabout, El Tigre, Coronado, and Detroiter to Hep Cat and even Beaver. Crusoe himself suggested Savile because he purchased his suits at expensive men's stores on London's famed Savile Row.

The prize went to a young Ford stylist named Alden Giberson, who submitted the name of a powerful creature from Native American myth. "'Thunderbird' was the best damn name," said Hershey. "It was as American as you can get." In addition to honoring the country's original occupants, it practically dictated an ad line for a sports car. "'Sounds like thunder; flies like a bird,'" Hershey enthused forty years later. "You just couldn't beat it. General Motors wishes they had thought of that name. What is a 'Corvette'? A small navy mine sweeper?"

The first Corvettes started coming off a temporary production line in Flint on June 30, 1953. They were basically handmade, and due to the late start and some quality issues with the fiberglass body sections, which were molded by a company in Ohio, only 300 were manufactured that year, all of them white with red leather seats.

Automotive writers praised the Corvette's styling and performance, noting its top-end speed of 110 miles per hour and acceleration rate of zero-to-sixty in eleven seconds, which was considered fairly quick in those days. *Road & Track* may have paid it the ultimate compliment: "The Corvette corners like a genuine sports car."

When it came to sales, however, the Corvette sputtered at the starting line. In a misbegotten attempt to create an exclusive image for the car, Chevrolet division managers decided to limit its availability during the first production run to VIP customers only, which included GM executives, business leaders, politicians, and celebrities such as John Wayne, who was allotted one apparently to make up for his disappointment over not being able to buy a Cadillac Le Mans. As a result, of the more than 1 million people who saw the Corvette at the Motorama shows, only 180 were able to purchase one by the end of the year. In January 1954, Chevrolet switched production to a St. Louis plant and began turning 50 cars a day; however, it quickly had to cut back due to a lack of demand. As *Motor Trend* noted, "The long gap between initial publicity and availability has cooled the desires of many buyers."

It was more than the wait that discouraged customers. Harley had conceived and designed the Corvette with young people in mind. He'd seen his sons' college friends driving racy, inexpensive foreign sports cars for lack of a domestic alternative. He remembered being their age and winning a road race in his father's New Jersey–made Mercer Raceabout. He thought America should be making a rambunctious, rebellious car like that again. There was a market for it. So it seemed oddly discordant when Chevrolet chose to introduce the Corvette at the Motorama shows with a short promotional film that featured a well-dressed, obviously well-to-do couple in their mid- to late thirties—"Mr. and Mrs. America," according to the narration—cruising along manicured boulevards past stately mansions in what appeared to be Grosse Pointe.

When the Corvette hit the showrooms, it turned out that Mr. and Mrs. America cared more about outside door handles and roll-up windows than sports car authenticity, and the young people for whom the car was intended couldn't afford its $3,000 to $4,000 price tag. As a result, Chevrolet struggled to sell a total of 700 Corvettes in its first two model years, sparking talk inside the company about discontinuing the car.

The Ford Thunderbird made its debut as a show car at the Detroit Auto Show in January 1954 and went on sale to the public the following December, making it a 1955 model. Like the Corvette, it was low and light, with a rounded horizontal grille and minimal external trim. "I didn't want to have a lot [of] gewgaws on it," said Frank Hershey. "It was designed to be simple but elegant; the T-Bird was a dignified sports car." Even so, he couldn't help copping one of Harley's least dignified trademarks, a set of chrome "Dagmars" affixed to the front and rear bumpers, the latter serving as portholes for the twin exhaust pipes.

In contrast to the Corvette's softly rounded shape, the T-Bird was sleek, crisp, and sharply creased, with a straight through-line from the front fenders to the back. Its roll-up windows and detachable fiberglass hardtop sealed the rain out of the cockpit (the early Corvettes' snap-on side curtains leaked like crazy). And driving enthusiasts vastly preferred its new 292-cubic-inch V-8 and optional three-speed manual transmission to the Corvette's tired six-cylinder engine and two-speed "Powerglide" automatic.

Hershey and his team gilded the power plant with chrome manifold covers engraved with an ancient Thunderbird insignia and topped it off with a formidable-looking four-barrel carburetor and chrome air filter that sat so tall in the engine compartment they had to design the hood with a center air scoop to accommodate them. He was certain they had created a real Corvette killer the day Henry Ford II called him to say he was sending over a guest who wanted to tour the styling department and check out the new car he'd been hearing about. The guest turned out to be actor Tyrone Power. "He went crazy about the Thunderbird," Hershey recalled. "He said, 'I'm going to buy one in reserve in case I wreck the first one.'"

Ford planned a production run of 15,000 T-Birds for 1955, but after taking more than 3,000 orders during the car's first ten days on the market, the company upped its projection and wound up producing more than 16,000 for the year.

As one automotive writer put it, Frank Hershey's T-Bird "walked a finely drawn line between sportiness and class, managing to bridge the tastes of a wide spectrum of buyers of different ages, income levels, and social strata. In looks, price, and positioning, the Thunderbird was an inherently desirable car, which also made it a fine showroom traffic-builder."

Apparently, that wasn't enough for Ford's top executives. Barely a month after the T-Birds first appeared in showrooms, Hershey began hearing rumors that the higher-ups were talking about killing the car because they didn't think it would ever be profitable enough to justify the investment. A two-seater wouldn't sell to single-car families, they said. Henry Ford II complained that his golf clubs wouldn't fit in the trunk. The company would be better off making a bigger car and just calling it a Thunderbird.

Hershey was upset but not surprised. "The company was in such a mess at the time," he said. "It was amazing they could build a car at all."

His antipathy toward management was partly a character trait and mostly directed at the Whiz Kid executive team that Henry II had hired after the war to bring a system of financial controls to the company. They definitely had done that, but from his perspective they were glorified bean counters without a molecule of gasoline in their bloodstreams. He particularly disliked Robert McNamara, the Ford division controller who was rumored to be on track to become general manager. Hershey said, "They were grooming Mac, who didn't know anything about automobiles, and didn't like automobiles, and had no right to be in the automobile business. But he thought he did."

Hershey recalled an encounter with McNamara late one night when he was working on a new dashboard instrumentation design. "From now on there is no reason to keep designing new instrument boards all the time," McNamara told him. "We're going to make one board and use it in every car."

"If you want to stop people from buying Ford cars, then just do that," Hershey replied impertinently as he proceeded to lecture the ranking executive. "Don't you know there is a little boy in every man, Mac, and they like to think they are in command of the car? And do you know what makes them think they are in command of that car? All those instruments on the board. What do you see when you are driving the car? Ninety-nine percent of the time you are sitting behind that instrument board and it wants to be pleasant and informative and make you feel like you are in control. Mac, I don't think you've ever been a kid."

In response, McNamara "glared at me and got up and walked

out," Hershey said. "I knew eventually we were going to lock horns."

Shortly thereafter, Ford division general manager Lewis Crusoe ordered the Thunderbird design team to start working on a bigger, four-seat version for the 1958 model year. It was one of the last directives Crusoe issued before McNamara took over as general manager. One of the first things McNamara did was discontinue Hershey's employment. "The Thunderbird got me fired," he said.

Instead of killing the Corvette, the Thunderbird helped save it by proving to GM that the sports car market was larger than anyone had thought. Ford sold 53,000 of the two-seater "Little Birds" between its introduction and the end of 1957, and Corvette sales increased in each of those years. Even after Ford withdrew from the sports car race with the introduction of the four-seater "Square Bird," in 1958, Chevrolet continued to lose money on the Corvette for another two years.

The Corvette survived when the T-Bird didn't because it was Harley's baby, the product of his passion. And no one—not Harlow Curtice and not Alfred Sloan—was going to kill it as long as he was alive.

15
THE
HOT ONE

The U.S. economy was firing on all cylinders in 1955, with the gross national product growing at a rate of 7.1 percent, a median family income that had more than doubled—to $5,100—since the war, a rapidly expanding middle class, a booming housing market, and a federal budget headed toward surplus territory.

It was a moment in the nation's history that would be conjured again and again in coming decades by politicians and writers waxing nostalgic about the days when America was great. "We were young and proud," Detroit's own Bob Seger would sing thirty years later in the voice of an aging assembly line worker. "Back in '55, we were makin' Thunderbirds."

Mostly, they were making Chevrolets. GM's low-priced line had been the number one seller since Ford's surprise first-place finish in 1949. But the margin of victory had dwindled each year until 1954, when the race ended in a virtual dead heat with both companies claiming victory by a few thousand units. That set the stage for a grudge match in 1955, when Ford introduced a flashy new series called the Fairlane, after Henry Ford's famed Fair Lane estate in Dearborn.

The Fairlane looked like something Harley Earl's Styling staff might have designed, what with its copycat chrome Dagmars and wraparound windshield, as well as a checkmark-shaped chrome strip running from headlight to taillight along each side, neatly dividing the body into sections tailor-made for two-tone paint combinations. The top-of-the-line Crown Victoria Skyliner flaunted a chrome molding that ran up the B-pillars and across the roof, the front half of which was made of smoked acrylic glass that provided the driver with a view of the sky. Auto writers described the molding variously as a "basket handle" or a "tiara," and one of them noted that the acrylic roof section looked impressive but "tended to bake the passengers like ants under a magnifying glass."

There had never been anything particularly flashy about the Chevrolet. Its trademark emblem looked like a bow tie, after all, and the company had promoted it for years as a sensible, affordable family car with ads and commercials steeped in the milky goodness of Mom, apple pie, and Sunday afternoon drives in the country. "See the USA in your Chevrolet. . . . America's the greatest land of all," Dinah Shore belted out at the open and close of her weekly Chevrolet-produced network TV show. Despite the Styling staff's best efforts, under the aegis of the division's conservative managers the 1952–1954 Chevrolets were so unexciting that one critic joked they looked as if they were "designed by Herbert Hoover's haberdasher." Chevrolet's chief engineer, Ed Cole, called them "grandmother cars."

The advent of the Corvette shook things up at Chevrolet. As Harley's Chevrolet studio chief, Clare MacKichan was able to purchase one of the first batch of two hundred at cost. "I had number one hundred and ten, I think. And I'll never forget the day I went down to pick up my car at the Chevrolet dealer on Jefferson Avenue, and there was a car that was *not* a Chevrolet;

it was something from another world as far as the [dealership employees] were concerned. And it was really a sensation when I drove it home. I think every kid from ten miles around came to look at it, to ride in it, and this happened all over the country."

MacKichan hoped to create that same youthful excitement with a completely restyled Chevrolet for 1955. Working with Harley and Ed Cole, who had collaborated closely in the development of the Corvette, MacKichan and his Styling team executed what Harley called a "cross-up," which meant an abrupt change in direction from where everyone else was heading. They veered away from Harley's well-known preference for soft, rounded shapes and sculpted a car that was more sharp corners than smooth curves, with a flat, squared-off hood and rear deck set nearly flush with the front and back fenders, forming a plateau. They called it the "shoe-box" body.

"One of the things we wanted was a simplicity of design and a smoothness," said MacKichan. "At the time there was a tendency to over-chrome the car, and we tried not to do that." That meant no bulbous chrome bumper guards or Dagmars and only a minimal, tasteful application of side trim. Chevrolet was the only GM line that had not yet sprouted some form of tail fins, and MacKichan kept it that way. Harley dictated the "face" of the car. "He had been to Europe shortly before that so he had the idea that we wanted a small Ferrari-style front end with egg crate within a small grille."

Ed Cole and his engineering team brought a revolutionary new engine to the mix. The 265-cubic-inch "small block" V-8—the first Chevrolet V-8 since 1917—was smaller, 41 pounds lighter, and more powerful than anything Ford had to offer, making it an instant favorite among hot rodders and a perfect addition to Chevrolet's underpowered Corvette, which was being left in the dust by the V-8-equipped Thunderbird.

When all was said and done, the '55 Chevy "was a totally new car," MacKichan said. "There wasn't one nut or bolt carried over from the '54. We knew it was going to be a success; we were sure of it."

GM president Harlow Curtice recognized early they had a potential game changer on their hands, especially with the sport coupe hardtop and convertible versions, which the Styling staff regarded as their crowning achievement for the 1955 model year. When Curtice learned GM was set to manufacture its 50 millionth car in the fall of 1954, he made sure it was a Bel Air sport coupe with every option, including the new "Turbo Fire" V-8, "Powerglide" automatic transmission, air-conditioning, power brakes, power steering, power seats, and a signal-seeking radio. He arranged with Harley to have the 50 millionth car finished in a glittering "anniversary gold" inside and out and underneath, so even the chassis glinted. The seats were covered in gold vinyl and a fabric woven through with gold metallic thread.

The two inveterate showmen then turned the assembly process into a public event, with the press invited to record the moment—9:50 a.m. on November 23, 1954—when "GM's 50-millionth body met its 50-millionth chassis" and line workers added on more than seven hundred parts plated in 24-carat gold, including bumpers and wheel covers. The completed car was rolled to a specially built platform as a band played "See the USA in Your Chevrolet," and Curtice boasted to the gathering that 50 million cars represented "more than any other country or combination of countries has ever produced."

With that, Harley had finally made good on his boast to Lawrence Fisher at that Hollywood cocktail party thirty years before: he'd designed a Chevrolet that looked like a Cadillac, and a solid gold one to boot.

GM subsequently celebrated the 50 million landmark with all-day open houses at 125 factories and facilities, and the commemorative golden Bel Air hardtop became part of the 1955 Motorama road show, which drew more than 2 million attendees.

The '55 Bel Air arrived in dealer showrooms priced at just under $2,200 fully loaded, available in twenty-three different two-tone paint combinations and backed by a national ad campaign heralding it as the "Hot One." Said *Motor Trend*, "We find it hard to believe it's a descendant of previous Chevrolets."

"That car probably had more impact on the Chevrolet Division than any one it's ever done since," said Dave Holls, who was one of the youngest designers in the Styling Section at the time. "Because [prior to that] no self-respecting young man would be caught dead in a Chevrolet; it was just everything that was dull and dumb. And then, all of a sudden, here comes that neat little car with a Ferrari grille and overhead valve engine and a power pack you could buy for $40. And it looked good and it went like a scalded weasel, and boy, all of a sudden Chevy was the 'in' thing. If ever there was a time when the kids went 360 degrees from Fords to Chevys, it was 1955."

The "Hot One" had barely rolled onto the streets when a new kind of music aimed specifically at teenagers began blaring from car radios all across the country. "As I was motorvatin' over the hill, I saw Maybellene in a Coupe de Ville," sang twenty-nine-year-old Chuck Berry, who'd written the song while earning $94 a week as a GM assembly line worker in Chicago. His lyrics told of a working-class guy pursuing a cheating girlfriend who was fleeing in a car that was fancier than his, but not faster. "Cadillac a-rollin' on an open road, nuthin' will outrun my V-8 Ford."

"Maybellene" was the first popular song to capture the zeitgeist of an exuberant youth culture that was seizing on fast cars and rock 'n' roll as a means of breaking from the strictures of the past and escaping the grim memories of Depression and war that had enveloped the previous generation. Suddenly the American songbook was injected with references to tailpipes, four-barreled carburetors, and drive-in romance. Berry even offered a sly commentary on the car-crazy consumerism and easy credit terms of the day in his follow-up hit "No Money Down," which placed his protagonist at a Cadillac dealership trying to trade in "that broken-down, raggedy Ford."

Well, Mister, I want a yellow convertible four-door de Ville
With a continental spare and a wide chrome wheel. . . .
I want air condition, I want automatic heat.
And I want a full Murphy bed in my back seat.

In the dozens of teen-oriented car songs that followed there would be an occasional appearance by a "hot rod Lincoln" or a "little Nash Rambler," but the road was ruled by Chevys, Fords, and Cadillacs, and nothing could outrun General Motors.

Chevrolet outsold Ford by more than 250,000 cars in 1955. In naming Harlow Curtice its Man of the Year, *Time* noted that the United States had "rolled through [the year] in two-toned splendor to an all-time crest of prosperity," much of which "was directly attributable to the manufacture and sale of that quintessential American product, the automobile."

As president of the first corporation in history to earn net profits of more than $1 billion in a year, Curtice had "assumed the responsibility of leadership for American business," the magazine said, quoting him as declaring, "General Motors must always lead."

GM didn't just lead; it dominated. Its five auto divisions produced 50.8 percent of the record 7.9 million cars sold in America in 1955. Its output was more than double that of Ford, more than triple that of Chrysler, and more than ten times that of the smaller independent companies. Indeed, GM sold more than twice as many Chevy Bel Airs as all the Studebakers, Packards, Hudsons, and Nash Ramblers combined.

Together, GM, Ford, and Chrysler—the so-called Big Three—controlled 94 percent of the U.S. car market, an imbalance that made it nearly impossible for smaller companies to compete, forcing them to combine operations to survive, until only two remained of the dozens that existed prior to the Depression: Studebaker-Packard, an uncomfortable merger of the once proud firms, and American Motors Corporation, a similarly coerced combination of Hudson Motors and Nash. George Romney, now the president of American Motors, would spend the rest of the decade in fourth place railing against the anticompetitive practices of the big companies and pushing for a government breakup of GM. Alfred Sloan worried about the potential regulatory consequences of GM exceeding a 50 percent market share, but Harlow Curtice did not share his concern, prompting the joke inside the company—"The boss says we're still losing five out of ten sales."

Numbers didn't tell the whole story of GM's dominance, however. Thanks to Harley, the company had gained an inordinate measure of influence over the look of virtually all makes and models of American automobiles. By the mid-1950s, every design department in the industry had adopted his system, his techniques, and even his theories. Every studio was filled with—if not directed by—men he had trained. Former GM designer Eugene Bordinat was now the number two man at Ford styling. Virgil Exner, formerly chief of the Pontiac studio, had just been made director of styling at Chrysler. Elwood Anderson, formerly chief of the Chevrolet studio, was director of styling at American Motors. Richard Teague held the same position at Packard. "I guess you could say that everybody in the automobile design business in those days came from under [Harley's] tutelage," said Clare MacKichan. "I'm trying to think of somebody that didn't, and I don't know of anybody."

Harley's reputation and GM's success attracted the best young designers coming out of the best art and industrial-design schools. "I couldn't believe I was going to General Motors," said Norman James, who arrived fresh from Pratt Institute in 1954. "GM had an aura of the Yankees."

"Chevrolet sold more cars than anyone else in the world, so they were doing the greatest good for the greatest number of people," said Robert Cumberford, a product of the Art Center School of Design in Los Angeles. "It seemed like the right place to be."

"There was a very strong esprit there," said Glen Wintershied, another graduate of the Art Center School. "The feeling was, 'We're the best; we work for the best.' Harley Earl was the father of American styling."

Most of them had not been born when Harley designed the first LaSalle with a team of three back in 1926. Now they were part of a staff that numbered nearly nine hundred and was spread through seventeen design studios and a dozen technical shops and departments, with responsibilities that included mounting the annual Motorama shows and contributing to the design and decor of the new Technical Center, which was nearing its move-in date.

With so much to oversee, Harley had brought Bill Mitchell back from running his outside design firm and named him director of styling with the promise that he would be promoted to vice president when Harley retired in three years. Mitchell and the studio design chiefs—MacKichan, Ned Nickles (Buick), Art Ross (Oldsmobile), Paul Gillan (Pontiac), and Ed Glowackie (Cadillac)—schooled the younger designers in how to avoid getting fired. Rule Number One, they counseled, was never disagree with the boss, a point they sometimes illustrated with an anecdote about the time Harley supposedly had all the designers seated in a circle around a car as he expounded on how the heavy bumpers made it look lower. "And you boys all agree, don't you?" he said. None of them did, but no one said so, which proved smart. "And if anyone doesn't [agree]," he continued, "then he should stand up so we can take a look at the sonofabitch."

Another oft-cited example of Harley's peculiar style of consensus building had him popping into one of the design studios on a Saturday and launching into a caustic critique of the design operations at Ford, where George Walker had just been named vice president of styling, a title that had previously belonged only to Harley. "Why, all they have over there at Ford is a bunch of yes men," he said, turning to Bill Mitchell and adding, without a trace of irony, "Isn't that right, Bill?" To which Mitchell responded correctly, "Yes, it is, Mr. Earl."

The punishment for breaking Rule Number One was usually swift, as a young Chevrolet designer named Duane "Sparky" Bohnstedt learned when he pushed back on something the boss said during a visit to the studio. "I never want to see that guy's face again," Harley told Howard O'Leary as he left. The kindly O'Leary had mitigated many such spontaneous terminations over the years, often saving the employee's job by doing nothing and giving them a few days off while Harley's temper cooled. This time he took the boss at his literal word and instead of firing Sparky, a decorated World War II bomber pilot, he stashed him in a studio in a building across the street where Harley wouldn't see him. The ploy worked for several months, until Harley happened to be passing through the other building and came face-to-face with Sparky and thereupon fired him for not being fired in the first place.

Harley's Rule Number Two was, as everyone quickly learned, there's no such thing as too much chrome. "He thought the more chrome a car had, the more expensive it looked," said designer Chuck Jordan.

"He called it 'entertainment,'" said designer Bernie Smith. "The need for entertainment was high on his priorities in car design. He'd say, 'It feels like you need something of interest over here. The customer needs some entertainment. It looks too plain; you have to get something going on.' Chrome was a great entertainment device to draw attention to an area."

Despite the commercial and critical success of the '55 Chevy, Harley pushed for more chrome during the subsequent face-lifts, insisting on heavier bumpers and more side trim on the '56 and '57 models, replacing the understated Ferrari-style grille with wider, thicker grilles that looked "more Cadillac." He introduced tail fins the first year, heightened them the next, and festooned the rear quarter panels with a fantail-shaped expanse of chrome and brushed aluminum, until the crisp clean lines of the '55 were cluttered with "entertainment."

"The '55 Chevy was a real designer's car; we all loved it," Smith lamented. "As designers, we didn't like the '57," said Chuck Jordan.

Perhaps no one disliked Harley's devotion to chrome more than Bill Porter, who had joined the staff armed with an undergraduate degree in fine art and painting, a master's in industrial design, and a firm belief that GM Styling had become "the center of evil, vulgar and overstated design."

In Porter's opinion, the problem had begun with Harley's Le Sabre. "It was as if he took a collection of airplane parts, put them in a box, poured in some glue and shook it up," he said. "I thought his application of aircraft imagery to automobile design was wasteful and inappropriate. Cars are not airplanes. But Le Sabre took everybody by storm, and once you did that you had a whole new design vocabulary. It was a vulgar vocabulary and it was coming from Harley Earl. For some reason or other, he had this dichotomy in his personality. He'd hire top people and at the same time have them doing the most vulgar and awful bombs-and-fins in the production studio. I felt I had to do something about it. I was idealistic. There were other guys who felt the same way."

None of the young Turks expressed those feelings to Harley, however, not even Bill Mitchell, who admitted years later, "We were putting on chrome with a trowel in the 1950s." They said nothing at the time because they all knew what happened to people who broke Rule Number One. "[Harley] was a terrifying figure," said Porter. And besides, they knew it was unlikely that anything they said would have persuaded him to change what he was doing. He didn't give a damn what a bunch of junior designers thought. GM was leading and all the other companies were following. The marketplace was telling him that chrome and bright colors were what midcentury Americans were look-ing for in their automobiles and, by god, he was going to keep giving it to them.

So he continued to order up more decorative entertainment, and because he did, Ford, Chrysler, Studebaker-Packard, and American Motors did, too, until even the little Nash Rambler sported a heavy chrome grille as garish and awkward-looking as a teenager's new set of braces.

The creative fissure that had opened between Harley and his younger designers was an underlying theme of an article that appeared in the *Atlantic* in April 1955. Titled "Jukebox on Wheels" and written in the first person by longtime Studebaker styling consultant Raymond Loewy, it was an acid-tongued take-down of the current state of American automobile styling. Loewy didn't mention Harley or GM by name, but he didn't need to.

"Every really creative and imaginative stylist and many en-gineers I know seem to be frustrated in their work today," he wrote. "Designers today are briefed to 'give the public what it wants,' and 'what the public wants' is being translated into the flashy, the gadgety, the spectacular."

Noting that the automobile "has become so potent a force that it is very nearly the symbol of American thought and morals to people who don't know us," Loewy argued that the major com-panies and their stylist minions were destroying America's hard-won image around the world. "Nothing about the appearance of the 1955 automobiles offsets the impression that Americans must be wasteful, swaggering, insensitive people. Automotive borax offers gratuitous evidence to people everywhere that much of what they suspect about us may be true. Our values are off beat, our ostentation acute, *if* the 1955 automobile is any reflec-tion of ourselves and our taste."

The article descended into a series of rhetorical questions through which Loewy laundered his opinion: "Is it responsible to camouflage one of America's most remarkable machines as a piece of gaudy merchandise? . . . Is it possible that they don't know the merchandise is gaudy? . . . Aren't manufacturers doing disservice to this country if they mass-present the automobile in such misleading vulgarity? . . . Aren't they depressing the level of American taste by saturating the market with bad taste? . . . Is it necessary? . . . Are we proud of them? . . . What do you think?"

While not disagreeing with Loewy about the trend in styling, Harley's young designers thought the article read like a howl of frustration from a man whose work, though often critically acclaimed, had never moved the American public the way the '55 Chevy had. After all, those jukeboxes weren't playing any hit songs about Studebakers.

16

GLORY
DAYS

The General Motors Technical Center in Warren, Michigan, was officially completed on September 19, 1955, nearly eleven years after Alfred Sloan, Charles Kettering, and Harley Earl met in Sloan's office to discuss the selection of an architect.

With Kettering now retired, Sloan soon to follow, and Eliel Saarinen, the original architect, five years deceased, Harley was in a sense the last man standing of the group that had posed for photographers at the ceremonial groundbreaking. He had successfully pushed for Saarinen's son and business partner, Eero, to be awarded the contract to relaunch the project after Eliel retired due to ill health in 1948. The younger Saarinen had expanded and improved on his father's plan and brought the job in at an estimated cost of $125 million, to the satisfaction of everyone except, of course, Boss Ket.

For months the classified advertising sections of the Detroit newspapers had been filled with notices for hundreds of job openings at the Tech Center—for stenographers, custom automobile painters, metal experimental body builders, body draftsmen, senior layout and engineering artists. In anticipation of more than four thousand new workers who were expected to be coming into their community, Warren residents recently had approved a reorganization of their municipality into a full-fledged city.

For Styling staffers accustomed to working in the tight corners of the Argonaut Building in downtown Detroit, arriving for the first time at the Tech Center felt a bit like landing on another planet. "We were awestruck," said Bernie Smith. "The place went on forever." The complex was vast, encompassing eleven miles of roads, 85 acres of parking, and 155 acres of landscaped lawn with shaded pedestrian walkways, all bounded by a broad perimeter of thirteen thousand newly planted trees that company literature promised would grow into "a virtual forest, a green belt that will protect it from encroachment of highways or buildings."

In keeping with Kettering's original idea for a "campus of thought," Eero Saarinen grouped the offices, laboratories, and technical shops for the Styling, research, engineering, and manufacturing staffs in separate clusters along three sides of the central lake, like individual schools within a university, each with its own administration building. According to the architect, the center was "designed at automobile scale and the changing vistas were conceived to be seen as one drove around the campus."

The school of Styling was hard to miss. The reflective aluminum dome of the auditorium was the first thing people saw as they came through the main gate on Mound Road. The Styling administration building had a lemon-yellow-glazed brick end wall and *Bird in Flight*, a twenty-foot bronze abstract by French sculptor Antoine Pevsner, positioned at the entrance. In the lobby, a two-level suspended stairway of white terrazzo was set against a black-glazed brick wall, making it appear to float in the air as it rose from a reflecting pond. "It was just startling to me," said Bernie Smith. "I didn't have words to describe it. I felt like I had died and gone to designer heaven."

Architectural design critics and scholars were effusive. "A dazzling demonstration of what a glamorous American modernism could be," one of them wrote after a visit to the main research building, where suspended slabs of emerald-pearl Norwegian granite formed a grand spiral stairway in the center of the lobby:

> Shimmering reflections and sensuous textures contributed to the theatrical scene, creating the unlikely but undeniable effect of ennobling the General Motors researchers as they descended to greet their waiting visitors or ascended to their studios. The experience was like a performance, and the spaces seemed to have more in common with the grand foyers of European palaces or opulent opera houses than they did with the mundane waiting rooms of a midwestern automobile manufacturer.
>
> Here, as in the nearby Styling dome, where a perfectly proportioned circular disk of modulated light . . . floated above the viewing area, transforming the cars into moviestars or objects of veneration in a sacred space, the architects seemed to take their cue from Hollywood, with its aura not only of visual luxury but also of glamour and make-believe.

Clearly, Saarinen had created his midcentury modern masterpiece with Harley looking over his shoulder and talking in his ear. In fact, as staffers explored their new surroundings, they wondered if the entire complex had been erected as an unstated

monument to Styling. That would explain Harley's office. The
1,225-square-foot space was located directly above the lobby at
the northwest corner of the administration building, with glass
outer walls on two sides providing a commanding view of the
Styling dome, lake, and fountains—indeed, of the entire complex. The original plan was for the Styling staff to create the
interior, but Saarinen asked to do it as his final design at the
center, and Harley agreed.

The result was an executive office like no other in the world,
composed of soft curves rather than straight lines and right an-
gles. The interior walls were covered by a serpentine spline of
cherrywood slats that resembled the front of an old-fashioned
rolltop desk, except vertical, and undulated the length of the
room, enveloping a cantilevered, curvilinear cherrywood desk
and several seating areas, creating the impression that the room
was itself a sculpture, with the furniture, walls, and glass flowing together as if to form the passenger compartment of a car.
From the driver's seat, Harley could look out the panoramic
windshield and with the touch of a finger control the lights, curtains, music, television, temperature, and telephone.

"No officer of the corporation before, at that time or since has
ever sat behind a more remarkable desk or overlooked so grand
an empire," said interior studio chief George Moon. "It was the
throne room for the man who was at that time the king of this
industry."

The Harley Earl Suite, as it was called, included a bathroom with a shower and a large closet in which Harley kept a
full wardrobe—dozens of suits, shirts, ties, pairs of socks and
shoes, in a full range of colors—because he liked to freshen up
and change clothes at midday in preparation for his afternoon
meetings and visits to the design studios.

When he wasn't traveling, he usually ate lunch in his private dining room on the third floor of the Styling building, adjacent to a cafeteria for the general staff and an executive dining area for the studio chiefs and department heads. Saarinen's original decor in Harley's private dining room was of a piece with that of the executive room—light, monochromatic, and elegantly modern, with rare gray-green English harewood wall panels and natural beige Berber wool carpeting. Shortly after the move-in, however, Harley asked George Moon and his interior department to come up with something less low-key.

They spent eight weeks producing "an infinitely detailed model," Moon recalled. "There was nothing to be spared, to be left to the imagination; nothing was too good for this model. We created dishes, flatware, lighting—all in correct scale." They unveiled it to the boss with typical Styling flair, inviting him into a darkened room where the model sat on a revolving turntable set at his eye level and then slowly dialing up the model lights.

"Fellas, that's great," he said, chuckling at the drama of their presentation. "I want it built just like that, no changes. If anyone wants to change one item, you send them to me." Moon took that to mean he'd been given "an unbudgeted, Priority One" assignment. "I'd dare say we were to spend more on that four hundred square foot space than any space, anywhere . . . within General Motors."

It would become known as the Blue Room for the deep-blue silk wall covering and the matching upholstery of dining chairs created by the famed Danish designer Finn Juhl. Moon and his team developed a six-sided, solid teak dining table that measured 10 feet across, with two settings per side, including a "host seat" from which Harley could electronically summon the waitstaff, control the music, lights, and curtains, and rotate the large lazy Susan in the center of the table. Reflector lights concealed in a centerpiece of green plants illuminated a dropped, gently arched ceiling of brushed aluminum that created the feeling of an umbrella over the table and gave the room a "sort of night club expectancy and intimacy," said a writer from *Interiors* magazine. "It was a fantasy world befitting the man at the center of General Motors' industrial Versailles," said another writer.

As a final touch, Harley hung blue-tinted portraits of Sloan, Kettering, and Harlow Curtice on the fabric wall. They were perhaps the only GM executives to whom he felt truly subordinate. But since they didn't have offices in the Tech Center, he was—literally and figuratively—the biggest man on the thought campus, and as the complex quickly became GM's primary corporate showcase, a parade of notable personages beat a path to his glass door, hoping for a private tour of the auditorium and studios and maybe even an intimate lunch in the Blue Room. "No room in all of the General Motors Technical Center saw more visitors," said Moon.

Eleanor Roosevelt was one of the first, followed by Gary Cooper and his wife, Spencer Tracy, Mr. and Mrs. Jimmy Stewart, Walt Disney, Douglas Fairbanks Jr., and many more. For a lucky few, the visit included the presentation of a personalized car. Air Force general Curtis LeMay, the commander in chief of the Strategic Air Command and a friend of Harley's from his prewar days as the commander of Selfridge Field, was given a blue Cadillac convertible with white leather seats and four chrome general's stars on each door. Harley's friends the Duke and Duchess of Windsor received a new Cadillac limousine every year, either a deep wine or burgundy color, with the House of Windsor crest embroidered on the backs of its beige wool broadcloth seats and its roof raised six inches to accommodate British royal head-wear. Dale Robertson, the star of the Buick-sponsored TV series *Tales of Wells Fargo*, was given a white Roadmaster convertible outfitted with hand-tooled natural saddle leather seats, pony-skin floor covering, a pair of .30 caliber carbine rifles mounted on the center console, and a matching set of ivory-handled Colt .44 revolvers fastened to the doors. (Robertson sold the car after the series was canceled in 1962.)

Such expensive perquisites were not restricted to visiting dignitaries and celebrities. When Chevrolet studio chief Clare MacKichan was recovering from an illness in late 1955, Harley arranged a surprise makeover on his Corvette as a get-well gift. MacKichan returned to find the car repainted metallic blue, "with white racing stripes which ran over the hardtop and came down the back," matching metallic blue upholstery, a blue con-vertible top, and a set of expensive Dayton wire wheels. Accord-ing to MacKichan, he blew the Corvette's engine downshifting shortly thereafter, and Ed Cole, Chevy's newly named general manager, told his chief engineer, "Why don't you take Mac's car and put that [new] engine in it? And while you're at it, put in the new four-speed transmission, and the fuel injection, too."

MacKichan and his fellow design chiefs operated in a bubble of privilege even off campus, where their distinctly decorated cars and generous expense accounts guaranteed them special attention wherever they went to blow off steam from the pres-sure that built up at work. They were the princes of Motor City, received as royalty at the Recess Club, the Rathskeller, and Topinka's on the Boulevard, where Buick studio chief Ned Nick-les held court nightly from his reserved corner table, picking up the tab for any senior Styling staffer who might stop by.

"It was like *Mad Men*," eighty-eight-year-old Bernie Smith

recalled in a recent interview. "The places were all dark and served good drinks. All the designers I knew back in those days were heavy drinkers or heavy smokers, or both. We'd go to a little cocktail lounge called Hintz's down on Van Dyke Street and have a two-martini lunch. My boss Art Ross had two or three ladies on the side. He would go out to dinner around five and come back around eight or nine, three-fourths gone and all wound up with all these ideas driven by drink, and expect us to stick around when all we wanted to do was get out of there."

Alcohol contributed to the early retirement of Howard O'Leary, and Bill Mitchell's booze-fueled exploits were legendary. Among the most famous was the time he went missing from a party at George Moon's house and was found the next morning stuck fifty feet up in a tree. The police and fire department were called to get him down.

Harley was a big believer in parties as morale boosters. He let each design studio throw its own annual celebration at the restaurant or hotel of its choice, and the studios competed to see who could spend the most money. He hosted a Christmas party in the Styling Auditorium for the broader staff, handing out big boxes of candy to every employee, with purses and perfume for the women. He threw a picnic in the summer, with softball games pitting the metalworkers against the wood shop and the designers against the sculptors. There was a rodeo one year, with steer bulldogging and a Wild West show starring Harley in an elaborate silk cowboy outfit. It was at these events that the staff saw his other side—softer, relaxed, playful. Staffers who interacted with him frequently were surprised that he recognized them out of context, even if he didn't have their names down pat. "He always called me Ernie," said Bernie Smith.

When the Tech Center formed an intramural softball league

and began playing games in a vacant field across Mound Road, "Harley went out and hired some pro ballplayers to come and work at various places in the shops," recalled designer Dick Ruzzin. "With them playing on our team, design won all the time. He did that with the bowling team, too; hired semipro or pro bowlers. He had a strong competitive spirit that was strategically organized. Whatever the task, he would lay his grid over it and boom!"

Prior to the opening of the Tech Center, the Styling staff consisted almost entirely of men. There were no female designers, clay modelers, or layout artists, only secretaries, stenographers, and "mail girls." The situation was mirrored throughout corporate America at that time, and the auto industry was especially male dominated. So it came as a shock when Harley announced in the summer of 1955 that Styling had hired seven young women fresh out of Pratt Institute's school of industrial design to work alongside the men as full-fledged GM designers. Equally shocking was the unprecedented publicity blitz that preceded their arrival. Dubbed the "Damsels of Design," they were paraded before the press, photographed half to death, and encouraged to talk to reporters, something that no male designer had ever been allowed to do.

"The day we arrived, somebody told us, 'We're taking you up to see Harley Earl,'" recalled Ruth Glennie, who'd driven to Detroit directly from Pratt with her classmates Sue Vanderbilt and Jan Krebs. "We asked, 'What should we say to him?' and they replied, 'You just say, 'Yes, Mr. Earl.'" At their first meeting, Harley told them that a car "is like a house" and their job would be to think about "what you can do there, everything you react with inside the car, how you can make it better, safer."

"Yes, Mr. Earl," they said, not fully understanding what he

meant. A GM press release explained why they'd been hired, and it had nothing to do with gender parity in the workplace. "Not too many years ago, the woman's influence on automobiles was limited to a stern voice from the back seat," it began. "Today, besides sharing the driver's seat with men, women cast the deciding vote in the purchase of seven out of ten cars."

"We simply lucked out when Harley got it into his head to use us as a sales ploy," Sandy Longyear chuckled. "He was sitting around thinking, 'How can I get women to buy these cars?'"

Not that any of them complained, even though the "damsels" moniker and much of the news coverage made them cringe. "We were given a marvelous opportunity; you'd have to be stupid not to realize it," said Glennie. "We were very well paid. Five thousand dollars a year was unbelievable at that time. It was three times what I could make as a draftsman, and the same as the men because Michigan law said you could not discriminate." Longyear pointed out that they were actually "discriminated *for*, because we could eat in the executive dining room and men at our level could not."

Five of the women were assigned to the auto design studios and two went to Frigidaire design. Harley placed Sue Vanderbilt in the Cadillac studio, and because she proved particularly poised he often chose her to greet famous visitors and show them around in his stead. Though she wasn't related to the robber-baron family, he thought her name impressed. An article in the *New York Mirror* later described her as "slim, trim, with large brown eyes, reddish brown hair and the dimpled face of a little girl." It didn't mention that she first felt an affinity for industrial design while sitting at her father's workbench in the family garage. "Pounding nails into a block of wood at about age six was the beginning of a special respect for tools and materials from wood to metal," she recalled. When she went to sign up for a mechanical drawing course in college, she was told it wasn't open to women. "Women don't do that; they don't take mechanical drawing," an administrator said. To which Vanderbilt replied, "Then why is a woman teaching it?" She turned out to be the only female student in the class.

As the sole women in their respective design studios, the "Pratt girls," as they called themselves, naturally bonded. Vanderbilt shared a two-bedroom house with Glennie, Krebs, and Dagmar Arnold. Longyear moved in when Krebs moved out to be closer to her boyfriend, who lived downtown. They were young and on their own, making great money in a glamorous profession they had trained for, and they loved cars. Longyear dropped more than $3,000 on a black Corvette with red seats. They were not damsels in distress hoping for a man to rescue them. "We were all saving each other," said Glennie. And they didn't see themselves as gender pioneers in the workplace.

It didn't take them long to figure out what Harley had meant when he told them they should think of a car as a house. It turned out that they were tasked with designing the interiors of the cars and excluded from working on the exteriors, which was solely the purview of their male counterparts. In the Styling hierarchy, exterior design outranked interior design. The women were being kept in the house. Longyear said she bristled when she heard Harley say, "To really be good, a designer has to have gasoline in his blood."

Interviewed decades later, however, neither she nor Glennie nor Vanderbilt expressed any resentment toward their male coworkers, and they insisted that GM management had not treated them "any differently than the men." For their part, most of the men accepted the newcomers as fellow professionals, even though they weren't used to working with women. Some tried to modify their typical male behavior out of deference to what they assumed were female sensibilities. They weren't always successful. When Buick division managers were first shown the model of an all-black interior for a sporty new model, marketing director Rollie Withers looked at the floor-mounted stick shift topped with a bright red knob and declared, "I like everything but that horse's cock sticking up in the middle there." Realizing in that instant that Peggy Sauer, a designer, was sitting across from him and beginning to blush, Withers dug himself in deeper by blurting out an apology: "Oh, shit. I'm really fucking sorry." Everybody laughed, Sauer included.

Bill Mitchell, Harley's director of design, found nothing funny in the situation, however. "No woman stylist will ever be photographed standing next to one of my cars," he hissed to his male colleagues. As an unabashed misogynist and the number two person in Styling, Mitchell could have made life hell for the women, but he was held in check by his devotion to Harley, who had promised him the vice presidency when he retired in two years. So Mitchell decided to bide his time.

For her part, Sue Vanderbilt had nothing but praise for Harley. "In spite of stories that you hear, Mr. Earl was always a gentleman with the women, and more a father figure maybe than a boss. And he loved having all the girls around and having his picture taken with them. He commanded a great deal of respect, and whatever he said, we did."

Even if they didn't like it, as was the case with their first big assignment, the so-called *femme* cars. As a GM press release explained, "Mr. Earl gave them a free hand to choose special colors and interiors for ten GM hardtops and convertibles—

without male guidance. The result was a feminine fashion show that bubbled with originality."

"It was really a publicity stunt sort of thing that forced us to scratch our heads about what was supposed to be feminine in a car," said Ruth Glennie. "Was it more spaces to store things?"

Harley's original idea was for the *femme* cars to be featured in the Motorama shows, but the decision was made to mount an additional showing in the Styling Auditorium. The "Spring Fashion Festival of Women-Designed Cars" was open only to the "women of the press," who covered it accordingly. "The setting was a veritable symphony of spring with 90 canaries making music and twice that many potted white hyacinths filling the air with fragrance," wrote Jessie Ash Arndt, the "women's editor" of the *Christian Science Monitor*, who praised Ruth Glennie's "Fancy Free" Corvette for its seats with a "pinched waist" and umbrella "tucked away in an ingenious pocket"; Sandy Longyear's Pontiac Bonneville "Polaris" for its picnic supplies compartment between the front seats and the "sportable" radio that could be lifted out of the dashboard; and Sue Vanderbilt's "Saxony" Cadillac convertible equipped with a Dictaphone.

Harley made an appearance at the show. "I don't know why the ladies shouldn't be represented in this designing of cars," he told the women. "So many talented girls are entering our field of design that in three or four years women may be designing entire car exteriors." But as if to reassure the Bill Mitchells of the world, the last line of a GM press release about the event quoted Harley as saying, "We'll never let women designers offend men's tastes, because it's still the men who pay—most of the time."

Sue Vanderbilt was the only one of the women who spent

more than a few years at GM, logging nearly thirty. Reminiscing about her damsel days years later, she lamented that Harley's progressive move to hire the first generation of female industrial designers had not worked out as they all hoped and none of the Pratt girls ever got to design the exterior of a car. "We've had a misconception about interior designers, [that] you just se-lect fabrics and sew things together, as interior 'decorators' do," Vanderbilt said. "But there's a lot more to it than that, and that's what we tried to tell the press over and over again. We weren't there just to decorate. Unfortunately, the projects that were pub-licized were 'decorating.' We did not have a chance to redesign an instrument panel. We just suggested color."

Change was afoot in 1956. The Motorama featuring the *femme* cars drew 2.5 million attendees, but the record cost of more than $10 million to send scores of people and 115 tractor-trailers traipsing around the country for four months had the corporate financial folks questioning whether it was an efficient use of pro-motional funds compared with national TV advertising. There was talk of cutting back or even killing the annual show. Alfred Sloan's retirement in April left Harley without his staunchest supporter. On May 16, the morning of the Tech Center dedica-tion, Harlow Curtice revealed to reporters that the company was experiencing a significant falloff in sales from the record perfor-mance of 1955. And as Harley led a group of VIPs through the Styling Auditorium and design studios that afternoon, he didn't realize that long-simmering creative tensions between him and the staff were about to boil over and threaten his thirty-one-year reign.

17
INSURRECTION

As Cadillac assistant design chief Chuck Jordan drove past the Plymouth plant on Mound Road, a few miles from the Tech Center, he spotted cars parked tightly together behind a cyclone fence in a field off to his right. He couldn't make them out clearly because they were partially obscured by the overgrown grass and the August afternoon sunlight reflecting off their windows. He pulled over to get a better look.

What he saw when he got close enough thrilled him and unnerved him at the same time. "There were all these '57 Plymouths backed up against the fence and all I could see were fins," he recalled. They were taller than the tail fins on any Cadillac, rising nearly as high as the rooflines. "But it was more than fins," he said. "The cars were really sleek and lean and they had that simplicity and dash that our cars didn't have."

Jordan had taken a lunchtime drive to collect his thoughts on the growing dissatisfaction among the GM design staff. Few were proud of the '57 models that were about to be shipped to dealers, and some were downright embarrassed by the work they'd just completed on the '58s.

They blamed Harley Earl. He seemed stuck in the past, fixed on gross images of bombs and bullets and still talking about headlights set close together and centered Le Sabre–style in the nose of the hood, as if the '55 Chevy Bel Air had never happened. It made no sense. They were surrounded by perhaps the largest collection of exquisite, cutting-edge modern design in the world—from dancing water fountains to floating staircases to office furniture sculpted by European masters—yet none of it seemed to be reflected in the cars they were designing. The incongruity between the work and the workplace was jarring.

Every studio had a Harley story to tell. At one point, when the Pontiac design team failed to execute a design to his liking, he abruptly swapped them with the Oldsmobile team "to shake things up." He then browbeat the Pontiac conscripts into festooning the rear quarter panel of the '58 Oldsmobile with chrome "speed lines" that resembled staves on a page of sheet music, inspiring some wag in the studio to cut out black musical notes and pin them to the clay model in an act of mockery. The rear end wound up with no visual relationship to the front, which wasn't surprising, given that they'd been designed by two different groups of people. It was just that sort of bifurcation in the design process that Alfred Sloan originally hired Harley to fix.

In the Buick studio they'd developed two wildly divergent ideas for the rear quarter panel of the '58 Buick Special. One was an update of the "sweep spear" side trim that first appeared on the '49 Roadmaster, consisting of a thin chrome molding that ran the length of the front fender, dipped down across the door, and then curled up around the rear wheel well. The other was a thick oblong configuration of chrome and stainless steel that was fully five feet long and featured a forward-pointing chrome tip shaped like the business end of a spade.

As they broke for lunch one day, someone pinned a detailed, airbrushed rendering of each design on an actual-size side view of the car. While they were out, Harley stopped in to look around and saw the two designs tacked one above the other.

"You know, boys, I think you've finally got it," he said when he returned unannounced later that day. It took a moment for them to understand what had happened: he thought the two renderings he'd seen earlier were actually a single design, with the spade positioned over the spear, which would cover most of the quarter panel with chrome. Looks were exchanged and eyes rolled, but no one corrected his impression, and when he instructed them to add the misbegotten combination to the clay model, it seemed to confirm what some had suspected for months—the legendary Harley Earl at long last was losing it.

Chuck Jordan's mind was racing as he hurried back to the Tech Center. Harley was on one of his extended trips to Europe and wouldn't return for at least three weeks. When he did, of course, he would immediately conduct a command inspection of their progress on the '59 design program, which he had practically dictated and none of the staff particularly liked. It would not be pleasant. Everything they'd been working on since he left looked heavy and cumbersome compared with what he had just seen. He went straight to Bill Mitchell, whose office shared the undulating wall with Harley's. "Bill, you better come down and look at what the Plymouth guys are doing for '57," he said.

"The word got around in a matter of minutes," said Bernie Smith. "We all hopped in our cars. There wasn't a single designer who didn't go down there. There were probably thirty of us in half a dozen to a dozen cars."

They rolled up in a caravan, walked over to the fence, and looked out onto a field of fins. They "shot up out of the grass," said Dave Holls. "The cars [had] absolutely razor-thin roofs and wedge-shaped bodies, and it was just unbelievable. We all said, 'My god, they blew us out of the tub.'"

It was a sobering moment. They were accustomed to being

number one. GM had led the industry in styling for their entire careers—indeed, since they were boys drawing pictures of cars in the margins of their schoolbooks. The company's postwar dominance had led to an atmosphere of arrogant complacency, a feeling among the designers that they were "so far ahead of Ford and Chrysler that we weren't even breathing close to them," said Holls. "[We] could almost trot along and stay ahead."

Not anymore, apparently. The cars parked in the field were the most dramatic examples yet of Chrysler Corporation's so-called Forward Look, a $500 million restyling of its five divisions—Plymouth, Dodge, DeSoto, Chrysler, and Imperial—begun two years earlier under the direction of styling vice president Virgil Exner. A gifted designer, "Ex" had been one of Harley's earliest protégés in the Art and Colour Section until he went to work for Studebaker in 1938. Harley supposedly cried when he left.

To the men at the fence, the most radical aspect of Exner's Forward Look was how the through-line of the fender rose steadily from front to rear, reaching its highest point at the tail end of the car. That violated one of Harley's cardinal rules, which held that the fender line should always hit its high point at the base of the A-pillar by the windshield and then slope gently all the way to the back. The industry had been doing it Harley's way for decades, and they'd never seen it done differently, until now. Exner's rising fender line gave the cars a unique wedge profile and made the upswept tail fins look even taller than they were.

"That woke everybody up," said Bernie Smith. They realized that while they'd been busy fashioning chrome accouterments, the industry's perennial third-place finisher had blown past them, and they would be trying to catch up for the next two years.

Back at the Tech Center, Jordan and Mitchell agreed that they needed to act fast; they couldn't wait for Harley to return. There was nothing they could do about the '58 models; that transport truck was too far down the road to turn around. Mitchell decided the best course of action was to continue working on the '59 design program that Harley had approved and at the same time launch an entirely new effort in every studio so they would have an alternative to show him when he walked in the door. It was a gargantuan undertaking, and one fraught with peril. They were, after all, about to mount a mutiny against a man who fired people for walking funny.

As the director of the department, Bill Mitchell drew the dirty job of breaking it to the boss. The whole place was on tenterhooks the morning Harley returned. As planned, Mitchell intercepted him in his office, told him what they'd all seen down on Mound Road, and then took him there to see for himself. Finally, Mitchell accompanied him into every studio to show him the progress on the pre- and post-fence designs. Harley mostly nodded and listened. The staff had never seen him at a loss for words, so it was impossible to get a reading on what he was thinking. He was quiet—too quiet, they thought.

Afterward, Mitchell made the rounds of the studios by himself, saying only, "The boss agrees that we're doing the right thing; we need to change course and go in a new direction." Still, the staff waited nervously for Harley's reaction—the inevitable shouting, the profanity, the firings. To their astonishment, it never happened. Instead, "We didn't see as much of him after that," said Smith. "And when he did come into the studio it was almost always with Mitchell, who did most of the talking."

Relieved and reenergized, they threw themselves into the new '59 design program, hoping they'd drawn their last Dagmar. The Cadillac team had no intention of trimming down their trademark rear fender treatment, however. Chuck Jordan and Dave Holls set to work on the tail fin to end all tail fins.

18
NOT
FADE
AWAY

J. W. Earl died on January 6, 1957, three weeks shy of his ninety-first birthday. General Motors announced his passing in a press release, calling him "an early California automotive pioneer." Survived by his wife Nellie, seven children, twelve grandchildren, and ten great-grandchildren, the former Michigan lumberjack was buried in Rosedale Cemetery in Los Angeles near his first wife, Abbie, Harley's mother.

J.W. had never made it to the GM Technical Center for a tour of the Styling dome and Harley's office, but he did attend the 1956 Motorama when the show stopped in Los Angeles. He wore his trademark white shirt, tie, suit, and vest, and he was grumpy with reporters who bugged him with their questions about his son, the famous car designer.

The '56 show turned out to be the last of Harley Earl's traveling extravaganzas. Television advertising had exploded, growing from $12.3 million in annual billings at the beginning of the decade to $1 billion in 1955, with cars ranking as the most advertised consumer product. The annual road show had become an anachronism, the twentieth-century equivalent of a wagon train creaking across the prairie.

While GM managed to maintain its industry lead in 1957, Ford outsold Chevrolet for the first time since 1949, and Chrysler's new, amply finned Forward Look Plymouth knocked Buick out of third place. With the Big Three automakers experiencing a 30 percent drop in sales, a recession was all but certain.

American Motors emerged as one of the few bright spots in the sales picture. On the brink of bankruptcy, the number four carmaker bounced back with the Rambler American, which it introduced at the 1958 Chicago Auto Show as "the one car that the modern American demands."

Offered only as a two-door sedan, the Rambler was more than two feet shorter and half a ton lighter than the standard-size Chevrolet, Ford, or Plymouth, which made it "easier to park, garage and maneuver in traffic," according to the company's eight-page promotional brochure. American Motors chief executive George Romney dubbed it a "compact" car to avoid calling it "small," and played up its greater fuel efficiency by constantly referring to competitors as "gas guzzlers." Long the industry's lone voice crying out about big cars and their bad gas mileage, Romney gave a speech to the Motor City Traffic Club of Detroit in 1955 called "The Dinosaur in Our Driveway." He complained, "Cars nineteen feet long and weighing two tons are used to run a 118-pound housewife three blocks to the drugstore for a two-ounce package of bobby pins and lipstick."

With a base price of $1,789, the Rambler was the lowest-priced car made in America, and arguably the least alluring—plain and plump, with none of the glittering jewelry that buyers had come to expect from Detroit. But the indefatigable Romney spun the car's frumpiness into an asset, calling it "an automobile for the American people that appeals as much to their native intelligence as their ego."

The Rambler got an unexpected promotional boost when a pop music group called the Playmates released a novelty record titled "Beep Beep," which rose to number four on the pop charts on its way to selling more than a million copies. For anyone who'd heard Chuck Berry's "Maybellene," the song told a familiar story, but with a twist:

> *While riding in my Cadillac, what to my surprise,*
> *A little Nash Rambler was following me, about one-third*
> *   my size.*

The driver of the Rambler beeped his horn to pass, but the Cadillac owner sped up to prevent him. They were doing 120 side by side when the Rambler suddenly sped away, with the driver hollering out his window:

> *"Hey, buddy, how do I get this car out of second gear?"*

"Beep Beep" was an apt metaphor for the state of the auto industry in 1958. As Detroit struggled to sell its big cars in the midst of an economic downturn, more than 430,000 small, inexpensive foreign cars were shipped into the United States, nearly a quarter of them Volkswagens. Henry Ford II and Chrysler chairman K. T. Keller initially sneered at the invaders, with Ford calling them "little shit boxes" and Keller harrumphing, "Chrysler makes cars for people to sit in, not piss over."

The VW quickly became the top-selling import, "rolling over France's Renault Dauphine like the Wehrmacht routed the

French army," in the words of one writer. Despite its peculiar buglike appearance, its noisy, rear-mounted, 57-horsepower engine, and its dark connection to the Third Reich, the affectionately nicknamed Beetle found favor with white middle-class suburbanites, especially housewives, in the market for an affordable second family car.

"There is no longer any doubt about it," *Road & Track* magazine said in October 1956, "the little 'people's car' has done what no other import has ever been able to do. It has gained an unmistakable wheel-hold in the garages and hearts of the American car-buying public."

With no national advertising, Volkswagen relied on word of mouth and the kindness of reporters who were unable to resist a story about a plucky little car that could. For every writer who said the Beetle was ugly and underpowered, two touted its low cost ($1,495), fuel efficiency (35–40 miles per gallon), and engineering. *Popular Mechanics* went so far as to drive a VW into a lake to test the claim by some owners that the passenger compartment was so tightly sealed the car could actually float. It did.

"This German car has amazing performance and roadability," wrote the magazine's test driver, who pronounced it "a thoroughly practical, dependable, economical and worthwhile car for anybody interested in low cost transportation."

Fortune praised the VW for its static styling and lack of flash, calling it "an utterly honest car." On college campuses and high school parking lots, students staged "Beetle stuffings" to see how many people could be crammed into a VW passenger compartment and trunk. A high school in Oregon set a record for thirty-three, but that didn't last long. Bad Beetle jokes proliferated. In one, a donkey asks a VW, "Hey, what are you?"

"I'm a car," the VW replies. "What are you?"

"In that case," says the donkey, "I'm a horse."

In a remarkable turnabout, Americans were talking about a car conceived by Adolf Hitler with the same affection they'd once reserved for Henry Ford's Model T; the Beetle had become the postwar Tin Lizzie.

Harley had seen the small-car revolution coming even before Volkswagen opened its first U.S. sales office in Englewood Cliffs, New Jersey, in late 1955. Looking down from his office window, he noticed the increasing number of European imports that were beginning to appear in the staff parking lot, mostly sports cars at first, then more and more small four-passenger sedans. The owners obviously weren't college students; they were young professionals, some no doubt married with kids. He concluded that the typical two-car family of the future would have a small car sitting in the driveway next to a standard-size coupe or sedan. To help make that point to the executive committee, he arranged a photo shoot on the large patio next to the Styling Auditorium, with more than thirty staffers standing next to their vehicles.

After the pictures were taken, the owners lined up their cars and began a procession around the complex, drawing people in the buildings to the windows. Then one impatient driver decided to pass another, and the parade instantly turned into a road race that would be remembered by participants and spectators alike as "the Styling Grand Prix." But Harley's photos didn't convince the division managers that the company needed to jump into small-car production in a big way, as he had hoped. Only Chevrolet general manager Ed Cole, his collaborator on the Corvette, expressed any interest in exploring the development of an American small sedan. Instead, GM began importing Opels and Vauxhalls from its European subsidiaries.

With Volkswagen and American Motors cast as modern-day Davids doing battle with Detroit's three Goliaths, it didn't take long for industry writers and critics to begin questioning the practice of annual model change. "Detroit thinks this year's car is guaranteed to become so unstylish in four years that you won't be able to stand the sight of the thing," wrote journalist John Keats, whose caustically humorous 1958 bestseller *The Insolent Chariots* characterized the industry's latest offerings as "not reliable machines for reasonable men, but illusory symbols of sex, speed, wealth and power for day-dreaming nitwits."

Harley may have sown the seeds of an antistyling narrative inadvertently with a comment he made to *Industrial Design* magazine in October 1955. "Our big job [as car designers] is to hasten obsolescence," he told writer Jane Fiske Mitarachi. "Since 1934, the average car ownership span has gone from five years to two years. When it is one year, we will have a perfect score."

Though few if any of his fellow automobile designers would have disagreed that their work was aimed at getting people to buy new cars more often, many were surprised that he had stated it so bluntly. Given that he was the man who invented the system that made annual model change possible, it appeared to critics that he had let the proverbial cat out of the bag. Hastening obsolescence sounded like a bad thing for consumers.

Industrial designer Brooks Stevens subsequently coined the term "planned obsolescence" in a speech to the Minneapolis Advertising Club, explaining that it was the logical result of the consumer's natural desire "to own something a little new, a little better and a little sooner than is necessary" and the manufacturer's "duty to engage in continual research and product development to provide the market with the best and the newest."

Unfortunately, planned obsolescence sounded even worse than hastened obsolescence, more intentional, and Stevens's version caught on as a derogatory term that suggested the big companies were making chumps of their customers. GM pushed back. The issue was "widely misunderstood," a top executive told the *New York Times*, explaining that its annual model change actually was an example of "dynamic obsolescence" because "we obsolete our products by making them better." Critics countered that styling change didn't make cars better, it just made them look different.

Harley must have been amused by the debate. After all, Americans were in love with automobiles—with the idea of them— long before the Duryea brothers and Ransom Olds rolled their first gas-powered buggies out onto the streets and, in GM's terminology, obsoleted the horse. That love of cars had fueled the creation of hundreds of companies that built thousands of factories that employed millions of workers who produced history's greatest economy and won a world war. So he thought the idea that GM or any other company could bamboozle Americans into buying cars they didn't want or need was as nonsensical as it was naïve.

He likewise scoffed at the notion that tail fins had been foisted on unsuspecting car buyers, as critics like Raymond Loewy and John Keats seemed to believe. The plain truth was that Frank Hershey had sketched a picture that blended an ingenious fighter plane with a beautiful sea creature; the GM Styling staff then turned his drawing into the rear fender of a Cadillac; and car buyers responded enthusiastically to changing versions of it for ten years, or tail fins would have disappeared. That's the way car styling worked, with designers constantly trying to anticipate what Americans would want their automobiles to look like three years in the future. And every stylist knew that a lot could happen to affect the consumer's buying habits between the day a design was approved and the day the finished car rolled off the assembly line. It wasn't a job for the faint of heart. As Harley once said, only half joking, "I'd rather try crossing a river on a path of bobbing soap cakes than make predictions about the car of tomorrow. The footing would be far safer."

The Edsel was a perfect case in point.

Preceded by weeks of ads featuring a blurry image of a mystery car and the headline "The Edsel Is Coming," the first new brand of American automobile introduced since 1938 arrived in showrooms on September 4, 1957—"E-day"—carrying a lot of expectations.

The Ford Motor Company had spent a reported $250 million developing the car and establishing a separate Edsel division, which would offer eighteen different models in ninety possible color combinations through a network of nearly 1,200 exclusive new dealerships. Edsel executives boldly predicted sales of at least 200,000 cars in the 1958 model year and were privately holding out hope for 300,000.

"The smart money both in and out of Detroit is solidly behind Ford's new Edsel," said automotive writer Eugene Jaderquist. "It's about as sure to succeed as a straight flush in a two-handed stud game."

In a filmed address to his troops the week of the launch, Ford chairman Henry Ford II called the Edsel "the only truly new car on the American road," and added, "From a more personal perspective, I believe the car accurately represents the ideals and principles of automobile styling which were so strongly held by my father, in whose honor it is named." Behind the scenes, however, his mother, Eleanor, Edsel's widow, and other members of the Ford family were appalled that his name had been chosen over eighteen thousand other suggestions and as a result would be "spinning on hubcaps." A public relations representative from the company went to see Eleanor at Gaukler Point to smooth things over, but she refused to speak to him.

A lot was riding on the Edsel's succeeding. The company's research indicated that when Ford owners moved up to a medium-priced car, only 26 percent of them chose the company's sole medium-priced offering, the Mercury, while the rest most often switched to a Pontiac, Oldsmobile, or Buick. In contrast, 82 percent of Chevrolet owners stayed within the GM family when they traded up. In interviews with 1,600 car owners in Peoria, Illinois, and San Bernardino, California, researchers were surprised to hear 88 percent of them say they didn't like GM because it was too big while at the same time 80 percent said they liked GM cars. And a surprisingly high number said they thought the Oldsmobile was the most attractive GM car and put the Buick down as a close second.

As a result, the Edsel was priced, engineered, and styled to appeal specifically to traditional Buick and Olds customers— young executives with families on their way up the corporate ladder. The company set the Edsel's debut for September 4, a month ahead of the competition, to maximize attention, and launched a $10 million marketing campaign that included an hour-long CBS television special called *The Edsel Show* that starred four of the most popular entertainers of the era—Bing Crosby, Frank Sinatra, Rosemary Clooney, and Louis Armstrong. Saturation TV commercials highlighted the car's two most distinctive features, an oddly elliptical vertical grille and a "Teletouch" transmission, which operated electronically when the driver pushed buttons located in the hub of the steering wheel.

If you watched television, listened to the radio, or read the newspaper in the summer of 1957, it was hard *not* to know the Edsel was coming. "Barring war or depression, the Edsel's pushing, brawling entry into the U.S. car market should be a first-class show," wrote the ever enthusiastic Eugene Jaderquist.

Instead, it was an embarrassment. Thousands of customers came to the shiny new Edsel showrooms the first day, looked, and walked away. The push-button transmission seemed like an impractical gimmick that was bound to break. The unorthodox grille was described variously as looking like a horse collar, a toilet seat, a vagina, or "an Oldsmobile sucking a lemon." Aside from that and its lack of tail fins, an Edsel didn't look much different from a '58 Oldsmobile or Buick, which the GM Styling staff thought were the two ugliest cars they'd ever designed.

Within a month, Edsel dealerships began to fail. On November 27, the only one in Manhattan closed. By January 1958, it was clear to industry experts that the Edsel was doomed. In fact, by one account, it had been dead on arrival. At a celebratory dinner dance on the eve of E-day, Ford division general manager Robert McNamara supposedly told Fairfax Cone, the head of the big ad agency that had hired additional staff to handle the Edsel account, that Ford had already decided to "phase out" the car. "Of course, you are going to have to lay all these people off," he said.

The debacle would go down as one of the most costly blunders in manufacturing history for reasons that seem clear in hindsight. The research that led to the Edsel's creation was conducted between 1955 and 1956, when car sales were booming. But by the time the first Edsels emerged from the factory, priced between $3,000 and $4,000, a recession had made buyers more cost-conscious and large shipments of inexpensive foreign imports were being deposited onto the docks of New York Harbor. A grille that wasn't the butt of jokes or a name that didn't need to be explained probably would not have made any difference in the outcome. The Edsel division sold only 62,000 cars in its first year, almost 140,000 short of management's prediction.

The U.S. economy began to recover in May 1958, but the damage had been done. GM barely managed to sell 2 million cars that year, down from 4.7 million in 1955. And to the surprise of no one on the design staff, the company's two biggest losers were Oldsmobile and Buick. The latter fell to sixth place, with its worst sales performance since before the war. Cadillac sales were the lowest in four years. Chrysler fared worse, with sales dropping by nearly 50 percent, indicating that perhaps the Forward Look's moment had passed. It turned out that the cars were plagued by engineering problems. At the same time, American Motors doubled its market share on the strength of the Rambler, and foreign imports gained an 8 percent share of the U.S. market.

All the controversy and criticism marred what should have been Harley's victory lap as he neared his mandatory retirement date in November. Still, he seemed sanguine about the approaching transition. If he was disappointed to be going out on a down note with the '58 models, he didn't show it. Whatever hurt or anger he may have felt about the staff insurrection, he appeared to have dealt with it and moved on. He was never one to dwell in the past; only the future mattered to him. Besides, the uprising had proven beyond a doubt that his handpicked successor was up to the job; Bill Mitchell had handled a difficult situation as well as any experienced chief executive could. He'd acted decisively and executed beautifully. The 1959 cars, produced under the duress of a drastically shortened time line, were a credit to the design teams. The department was in good hands going forward.

Harley's own corporation looked to be in good shape as well. He'd moved the industrial-design firm to a 10,000-square-foot office building he built on Mound Road just south of the Tech Center. Touted in a press release as "the most modern design studio in the world," it boasted contracts with U.S. Rubber, Aluminum Company of America (Alcoa), and Westinghouse, and it employed at least a dozen designers under the direction of his sons Jim and Jerry, with Harley functioning primarily as the landlord, leasing the building to them.

Harley and Sue seemed to be set for life. In addition to income from the design company, his GM stock, and a consulting contract with the company that would pay him a million dollars over the next fifteen years, they'd built up a portfolio of real estate holdings thanks to Sue, who had proven to be an astute investor.

Over the decades, the former sweethearts from Hollywood High, a rancher's daughter and a carriage maker's son, had forged a formidable domestic partnership, the kind that was held up as the ideal in those days. In exchange for his putting in however many hours it took to provide them with an enviable standard of living, she did practically everything for him except pick out his wardrobe.

"She managed the household so no matter how vexing the day, he came home to a warm, well-run house, was served a good dinner, and stored up energy for the next day's hassles," said her daughter-in-law Connie. "She handled all their social arrangements, being careful that they did not impinge on his work schedule. She was also very attuned to the social complexities of the auto industry hierarchy and helped him maneuver through the corporate world." Indeed, at a fancy industry dinner shortly after the war, Sue sat next to Henry Ford II, who was known to be looking for a new Styling chief, and schmoozed with him the entire evening, making sure everyone in the room noticed. She delighted in taking credit when the executive committee subsequently offered Harley the long-term contract that allowed him to start the outside design company and gave him the million-dollar postretirement consulting contract. Harley never disputed that her dinner performance had done the trick.

It was Sue who decided they would retire in Florida, where they had vacationed in the winter for years. She couldn't wait to be done with Detroit weather, and she didn't want to go back to California because "the water there is too cold." So she purchased a modest two-bedroom house at 995 South Ocean Boulevard in Palm Beach, just north of "Millionaire's Row" (now "Billionaire's Row"). It was right on the sand, across the road and around the bend from the Marjorie Merriweather Post estate (now Donald Trump's Mar-a-Lago). Sue had the house painted pink, her favorite color.

As Harley's days drew down at GM, he mostly worked through Mitchell, keeping tabs on certain projects from a distance, telling his soon-to-be successor what he thought and trusting Mitchell would pass those opinions on to the design teams as he saw fit. He took particular interest in the development of Chevrolet's upcoming rear-engine compact car, which Ed Cole had named the Corvair, and the revived Motorama, which was to be scaled back to just two exhibitions in 1959, in New York and Boston.

At a ceremony in the Styling lobby, with Alfred Sloan looking on, Harley presided over the unveiling of a portrait he'd commissioned in honor of his corporate mentor "whose genius conceived this industrial campus," according to the inscription. The portrait still hangs on the wall in the lobby.

When the studios completed their work on the '59 cars, he circled them on the patio and gathered all the designers together for his annual pep talk. Since everyone knew it would be his last, staffers from other departments and buildings came to listen.

"How many of you guys are under thirty years old?" he asked the designers at one point. Hands went up. "I'd like all of you guys to step over here to my left. And all you others step over here to my right.

"Now, you guys on my left are the creators," he said. "You come up with most of the new creative ideas. And you guys over here on the right are the finishers; you know how to turn those ideas into a workable design."

He seemed to be saying, in his inimitable way, that both groups were necessary to a successful design operation. Some of the older men wondered whether he was telling them they were over the hill creatively, while a number of the younger designers thought he was saying he understood what happened with the '58 models and he should have listened to them more.

His last official appearance was at the presentation of the '59 cars to the board of directors and members of the executive committee under the lights in the Styling Auditorium. He dragooned several of the women designers into service as car show models, to open doors and explain interior features to gray-haired men "with names like DuPont and Firestone," Ruth Glennie recalled years later. "I remember that they really had Mr. Earl on the hot seat about the fins. They kept asking him, 'Why do they have to be so high? Why do you have them at all?' We were shocked because we'd never heard anyone talk to him that way."

Harley's chief inquisitors that day were Frederic Donner, who'd recently been elected chairman of the board, and John

Gordon, who'd just been named president and chief executive officer, replacing Harlow Curtice, who was retiring. The two longtime GM executives had risen through the ranks in the company's New York headquarters, where they'd established reputations as fervent cost cutters and earned the joint sobriquet "Donner and Blitzen." The *New York Times* later described Donner, an accountant, as a "bean counter" in a headline and characterized Gordon, in his obituary, as an executive "who worried about saving fractions of pennies."

Not surprisingly, neither man had any love for Harley and his expensive operation. Gordon's bad feelings dated back to 1946, when as the newly named general manager of the Cadillac division he instructed Bill Mitchell to lower Frank Hershey's original P-38-inspired rudder-style fins on a clay model by three-quarters of an inch. He didn't learn until it was too late that Mitchell had tricked him into thinking they had.

Throughout his four-year tenure at Cadillac, Gordon objected to the tail fins to no avail. They were too popular with the public and he had too little clout on the executive committee for Harley to pay him any mind. Gordon had stewed ever since. Now he was getting his last licks in.

The cars in the auditorium that day were Styling's response to Virgil Exner's Forward Look cars, which Chuck Jordan had first seen on Mound Road in the summer of 1956. They all featured clean lines, razor-thin, pillar-free rooflines, and dramatic tail fin treatments. But the Cadillac stood out from the rest in its breathtaking audacity: 7 feet wide, 19 feet long, weighing more than 5,000 pounds, with fins rising sharklike from the rear fenders to a height of 42 inches, as sharp-edged and pointed as chef's knives, embedded with twin bullet-shaped taillights.

"We probably overcooked the design," said Chuck Jordan.

"Still, it was tame compared to what it could have been. I can remember when the fin on the clay model was higher than the coupe roof." Jordan and designer Dave Holls acknowledged later that their design was in part a declaration that *nobody* was going to out-fin Cadillac. "It was our year of total excess," said Holls.

By the time the public got a look at the '59 lineup, Harley and Sue had sold their house in Grosse Pointe Farms and decamped to Palm Beach, where they could step out of their home and wade into the warm ocean or stroll down the beach for lunch at the tony Bath and Tennis Club. In the afternoon Harley played golf at the Everglades Club, one of the oldest and most exclusive private clubs in the country, while Sue engaged in competitive canasta and dime-a-point bridge in the clubhouse with her friends. Harley bought her a '59 Pontiac Bonneville convertible and had the shop at the Tech Center paint it pink and reupholster the interior in pink and white with maroon carpets and a plum-colored dashboard. They eventually replaced the so-called Pink Lady with a Corvette that matched Harley's, except his was electric blue and hers was pink.

A glamorous and popular couple, they were invited to most of the town's myriad charity balls, and though they rarely went, they always sent a check. Their social life consisted mostly of dinners with friends, and they were usually home by eleven o'clock.

It was a languid, luxurious life, punctuated by summer vacations in Europe, sometimes with a grandchild or two in tow, and fall trips back to Detroit, during which Harley spent time duck hunting in Canada and visited the Styling studios at the Tech Center as part of his consulting agreement. Bill Mitchell took him around to see what each design team was doing. "He never criticized the cars," Dave Holls recalled. "It was mostly like seeing his old friends and all that, and he was as nice as he could be." During one such visit, however, the news that Harley was about to enter the Pontiac studio provoked an unexpected reaction. Designer Sparky Bohnstedt, who had been brutally fired by Harley several years before and had only recently returned, bolted from the room to avoid coming face-to-face with him again.

"I looked around and Sparky was gone," said Bill Porter. "I asked somebody where he was and they said, 'He's back in the men's room puking his guts out.' The guy was a famous bomber pilot and the mere mention of Harley's name made him vomit."

On November 19, 1959, General Motors—indeed, the entire car industry—was rocked by the news that Harlow Curtice had shot and killed one of his best friends, former GM executive Harry Anderson, in a hunting accident on Saint Anne's Island in Ontario, Canada. According to news accounts, the two recent retirees were sitting side by side in a blind when Anderson unexpectedly stood up just as Curtice swung around to fire at a flight of ducks passing overhead. The shotgun blast "tore away the top of Anderson's head," according to one newspaper account. Curtice would never recover emotionally. He died three years later, a broken man.

The incident added a sobering coda to GM's most productive and colorful decade. With Sloan, Harley, and Curtice gone, the reign of the bean counters had begun, and one of the first orders of business was to get rid of the fins and the heavy chrome. The Styling staff was all for it. They'd become embarrassed by the leading role they'd played in what designer Dick Teague dubbed "the Golden Age of Gorp."

"People always ask me why we did those [1959] fins, and

269

I say, 'It was the right thing to do at the time,'" Chuck Jordan said. "It got us out of this stale state we were in, and got the blood circulating. The '59 was like letting a tiger out of the cage and saying, 'Go!'"

Within two years, fins had disappeared from all GM cars except the Cadillac. Bill Mitchell argued for lowering—but not blunting—the Cadillac's fins gradually over a period of several years rather than lopping them off abruptly. After eleven years, they had become the defining design feature of the car, and loyal Cadillac customers still expected them.

By 1965, fins had vanished from the automotive landscape, but they remained embedded in the national psyche. For better or worse, the '59 Caddy tail fin would endure as perhaps the defining single image of the 1950s in America.

The new decade brought a sea change to the industry, with Harley's "longer, lower, and wider" precept giving way to smaller, cleaner, and—albeit begrudgingly—safer. As American Motors' Rambler became the nation's fourth-best-selling car, the Big Three finally introduced small four-passenger sedans in 1960—the Chevrolet Corvair, the Ford Falcon, and the Plymouth Valiant. The Corvair was named *Motor Trend*'s Car of the Year for its revolutionary rear-mounted, air-cooled engine, its trans-axle, and four-wheel-independent suspension, but it sold only moderately well, averaging about 250,000 cars a year for the first three years.

Chevrolet introduced a sleek new Corvair coupe for the 1965 model year. *Car and Driver* magazine said it was "undoubtedly the sexiest looking American car and possibly one of the most handsome in the world." But the restyled Corvair collided with a new book written by a thirty-one-year-old Harvard Law School graduate named Ralph Nader.

Titled *Unsafe at Any Speed: The Designed-In Dangers of the American Automobile*, the book alleged that a design defect in the suspension system of the 1960–63 Corvairs had led to rollovers that caused numerous serious injuries and deaths. Corvair sales dropped by nearly 90 percent over the next two years as customer lawsuits piled up and news coverage drove Nader's book to the top of the bestseller lists, launching his career as a consumer advocate.

But only the first chapter of *Unsafe at Any Speed* dealt with the Corvair. The rest was a broad indictment of the industry, General Motors, and even the automobile itself. As Nader wrote hyperbolically in the book's opening sentence, "For over half a century the automobile has brought death, injury and the most inestimable sorrow and deprivation to millions of people."

With a muckraker's zeal, he attacked the big companies for allowing styling decisions to take precedence over engineering and safety considerations, noting that "styling changes added on average about $700 to the consumer cost of a new car, compared to an average twenty-three cents per car spent on safety."

He cited a study based on accident and autopsy reports of more than 200 pedestrian fatalities in New York City during 1958 and early 1959, showing that the victims' bodies had been "penetrated by ornaments, sharp bumper and fender edges, headlight hoods, medallions, and fins."

Saying that the '59 Cadillac tail fin "bore an uncanny resemblance to the tail of the stegosaurus, a dinosaur that had two sharp rearward-projecting horns on each side of the tail," Nader listed the gory details of the carnage they'd inflicted. A California motorcyclist had hit the rear bumper of a Cadillac stopped in traffic and was "hurled onto the tail fin, which pierced his body below the heart and cut him all the way down to the thigh bone in a large circular gash." A nine-year-old girl was riding her bicycle near her home and bumped into the tail fin of a parked 1962 Cadillac, "which ripped into her body below the throat," causing her to die of a "thoracic hemorrhage." A thirteen-year-old Chicago boy was chasing a fly ball on a summer day when he "ran into a Cadillac fin, which pierced his heart and killed him."

In February 1966, shortly after *Unsafe at Any Speed* was published, Alfred Sloan died of a heart attack at the age of ninety. Perhaps it was a mercy that he didn't live to see the company dragged over the coals during the resultant Congressional hearings into auto safety and to hear GM chairman James Roche apologize to Nader for the company's hiring of private investigators to dig up compromising information about his private life.

On September 16, 1966, President Lyndon B. Johnson signed the National Traffic and Motor Vehicle Safety Act and the Highway Act, which both houses of Congress had passed unanimously, requiring the establishment of new vehicle safety standards, and the creation of a new agency, the National Highway Traffic Safety Administration (NHTSA), to enforce them and supervise safety recalls. "In this century, more than one and a half million of our fellow citizens have died on our streets and highways; nearly three times as many Americans as we have lost in all our wars," Johnson said. "I'm proud at this moment to sign these bills—which promise, in the years to come, to cure the highway disease, to end the years of horror and give us years of hope."

The auto safety legislation spurred by Nader's book has been credited with saving 3.5 million lives in the ensuing years, and the *Unsafe at Any Speed* episode ranks as perhaps the worst public relations disaster in GM's history. When the last Corvair came off the production line at the Willow Run plant on May 14, 1969, network newscasts covered the story, noting Nader's role in the car's demise and comparing it to the Edsel.

(Three years later, the NHTSA released the results of a two-year study that concluded: "The handling and stability performance of the 1960–1963 Corvair does not result in an abnormal potential for loss of control or rollover and it is at least as good as the performance of some contemporary vehicles, both foreign and domestic.")

◆

Detroit suffered a devastating blow to its image in July 1967 when the city's implacable racial problems hit the front pages of newspapers around the world.

In response to the Black Bottom race riots of 1943, the city had launched a postwar urban renewal project on the Lower East Side that critics quickly branded "Negro removal." Five thousand buildings were demolished, supposedly to eliminate blight but also to make way for a network of new federally funded highways, including the Edsel Ford and Walter Chrysler freeways, that cut through Black Bottom and Paradise Valley and obliterated them. A lack of low-cost replacement housing forced thousands of the city's poorest black citizens into neighboring Virginia Park, a predominantly Orthodox Jewish community, setting off a wave of white flight.

It was there, on July 23, that an early-morning police raid on an unlicensed bar on Twelfth Street, the main commercial thoroughfare of the new black ghetto, set off a rash of looting, gunfire, and arson that quickly overwhelmed the city's police and fire departments, prompting Governor George Romney to call up the Michigan National Guard. President Johnson sent in 4,700 troops from the U.S Army's 102nd and 87th Airborne Divisions. "Troops Seal Off Nests of Snipers; Death Toll Grows; Copters Called In," blared a banner headline in the *Detroit Free Press*, as TV newscasts all over the country showed pictures of rioters chanting "Burn, baby, burn," and tanks rumbling through streets with paratroopers under the command of Lieutenant General John Throckmorton following behind, armed with M-16 rifles and fixed bayonets.

By the time order was restored after five days, the official tally of damage stood at forty-three deaths, at least a thousand injuries, more than two thousand arrests, and nearly seven hundred businesses burned to the ground.

Detroit never recovered. White flight doubled in 1967, to over 40,000, and then doubled again in 1968. And the city once hailed as the "Paris of the Midwest" and the "Arsenal of Democracy" eventually came to be defined by stark photos of the abandoned Packard plant—a hollowed-out husk, weed-choked and strewn with rubble, the industrial age version of a Roman ruin.

◆

In late March 1969, Harley Earl sat in a large carved oak chair at the Country Club of Detroit in Grosse Pointe Farms, where he and Sue maintained a membership and always stayed when they came back to town. He was giving a sort of lion-in-winter interview to Barbara Holliday of the *Detroit Free Press*, and at seventy-five, he looked every inch the elder statesman of automobile styling. "Just in from shooting ducks on Walpole Island, he was impeccably dressed in a Navy blue jacket, gray slacks, handsome white shirt with a tiny blue windowpane check and an expensive-looking blue tie," she observed.

He was in town for one of his biannual visits to the design studios, he told her. "I've learned to be a good consultant," he chuckled. "I don't suggest unless they ask me. But I get a look at what's coming out in the next two or three years and I can't wait."

For the better part of two hours he entertained her with stories of growing up in the rustic hills above Hollywood, designing expensive car bodies for silent movie stars, and coming to Detroit on the train to work for Alfred Sloan and the legendary Fisher brothers.

"Right now people are wondering what to do," he said near the end of their conversation. "Cars are getting so safe you can hardly use them. But it will be interesting to see how many lives they save with these new devices. I'm definitely for safety, but I'd start over with the fundamentals. Get some of the space program scientists and have them build some fundamental safety features that will really help to sell, that aren't just window dressing."

As they got up to go, he told her, "Mr. Sloan made this [consulting] deal with me until I'm 80. It was quite a compliment. What could I do at 80? These days I go duck hunting, fish for marlin off the shores of Bimini, go deer hunting—all the things I didn't have time to do when I was working."

Several weeks later, a day after he and Sue had dinner in Palm Beach with Bill Mitchell and his wife, Harley suffered a massive stroke. Sue's longtime English housekeeper, Iris Ashton, heard him fall in the bedroom and found him lying on the floor with his eyes open but unable to speak or move. He remained silent and motionless in the hospital for several weeks.

One doctor compared what he was experiencing to that of a person floating in a dreamlike state at the bottom of a swimming pool: perhaps seeing vague shapes and hearing muffled sounds but with no ability to communicate, and not likely to ever get better. Another doctor used the word "vegetative."

"When they told Sue there was no hope, she never went back to the hospital," said Connie Earl. "She didn't want to remember him that way. She wanted him to always be the guy who was going out to play golf."

Connie kept up a bedside vigil. "One day he seemed to slam his hand down on the bed in frustration," she said. "It was the only thing I saw him do."

Harley died at 3:00 a.m. on April 10, 1969. A contingent of GM executives and designers, including Bill Mitchell, flew down from Detroit to attend his memorial service at Bethesda-by-the-Sea Episcopal Church in Palm Beach. Afterward, Connie and a friend took his ashes up in a small Cessna to scatter them over the ocean. But just as they opened the door, the friend fumbled the urn and a good bit of Harley ended up inside the plane, though most of him made it to the water eventually.

Sue lived out her life in Palm Beach. She sold the house on South Ocean Boulevard in 1984 and moved into a high-rise condo, where she died on May 10, 1988, from complications due to old age. She was ninety-two, and according to family members, her last words were *"Hasta la vista."* A few days later, Connie Earl went up in a small plane once more and scattered her mother-in-law's ashes over the ocean in front of the pink house.

◆

In the years following Harley's death, many members of his Styling staff were asked by writers and researchers to share their memories about their time with him at General Motors. None spoke with more affection or regret than Frank Hershey. He was in his eighties, an automotive legend in his own right, and destined to be remembered as the "Father of the Thunderbird," which had turned out to be the last car he worked on.

"I am the only classic designer left in the world," he said, referring to the pre-Depression era of Duesenbergs, Marmons, and Pierce-Arrows, all of which he had helped design as a young man in the early 1920s, before he met Harley.

"I want to tell you one thing," he told art historian C. Edson Armi. "I have a dream which I dream about once a week or every two weeks. I've been doing this for the last five or six, maybe ten, years. I dream about being back in the good old GM Styling Department. I never dream about being back at Ford. Only General Motors. And Harley Earl is there. Sometimes [Bill] Mitchell is there, but always Harley Earl.

"I didn't know how good I was having it, if you know what I mean. I would give anything to be able to go back there and drop back into the old days. Knowing what I know now, I would never have left . . . the biggest regret of my life is that I screwed up so badly at the end. I broke a promise to Harley, and I paid dearly for it."

On May 8, 1991, Hershey told Alexandra Earl that her grandfather "was a complicated man, and he was difficult. He was a tough guy. But I think he had his fears. Look at the responsibility he had. No wonder he bellowed once in a while. He was bellowing at himself sometimes. He had responsibility for the biggest corporation in the world, at a time when a bad design could almost break the company."

He told her that he didn't realize "until years later" that he had been Harley's favorite, and was sorry that he never told his old boss how he felt about him. So finally, forty-odd years after the fact, he got it off his chest.

"Harley was a very sentimental person inside," he said. "But he didn't think sentimentality was a good thing to show; he thought it was unmanly. I'd like to tell him that I loved him, although he'd probably slap me if I did. I'd like to tell him that he ought to feel proud. He did a helluva job."

◆

In a fond editorial about Harley's passing, the *Detroit Free Press* took the opportunity to eulogize what became his most recognized—though not necessarily his most important—contribution to American life.

"Fins," the newspaper said, "were ebullient expressions of devil-may-careness, the hoisting of the flag to honor the end of the war and a hope of better days to come. They were outrageous, impractical and splendid."

The same could be said of Harley.

ACKNOWLEDGMENTS

I could not have written this book without the support of the following people: Alice Martell, my agent for more than thirty years; Hollis Heimbouch, my editor at HarperCollins for going on a decade; and Sheri Rosenberg Kelton, my manager and the newest member of Team Bill; my friends John Mettler, Bill and Nancy Cason, Michael and Deborah Rybak, Dennis McDougal, Pat Broeske, Jeff Kwatinetz, Sherman Allan, Chris Mills, Ninon Aprea, Kim Morgan, and Bryn Freedman; my sisters, Mary Kaveney, Ann Wiethucter, Kate Sundermeyer, and Martha Brooks; and my children, Matthew, Colin, and Halle. Special thanks to Christo Datini and Larry Kinsel at the GM Heritage Center and GM Media Archive for their assistance with research and photographs, and to Los Angeles realtor Richard Stanley, who was an invaluable source of information about the history of the Earl family in Hollywood as well as the classic period of American car design.

NOTES

Much of the information in this book is drawn from interviews I conducted over the last four years with members of the Earl and Taft families, and with men and women who worked for Harley Earl during his later years at General Motors. Most of the quotes about his early years at GM are taken from interviews conducted by journalist Michael Lamm, the co-author (with Dave Holls) of *A Century of Automotive Style: 100 Years of American Car Design*; art historian C. Edson Armi, the author of *The Art of American Car Design: The Profession and the Personalities*; researcher David Crippens, whose taped interviews with numerous now deceased GM designers are housed as a collection, the Automotive Design Oral History Project, at the Benson Ford Research Center at the Henry Ford Museum in Dearborn, Michigan; and automotive writer Stanley Brams.

A great deal of research material was provided by the General Motors Design Archives and Special Collection in Warren, Michigan, notably a nearly 600-page unpublished manuscript by the late George Moon, "An American Versailles: Eero Saarinen and the General Motors Technical Center—A Privilege Remembered," and Brams's unpublished manuscript, "The Skillful Men: An Intimate Record of the Styling Section at General Motors—1928 to 1954." I also drew upon the reporting of the *Detroit Free Press* and *Detroit News*, as well as the following books: *Chrome Colossus: General Motors and Its Times*, by Ed Cray; *The Story of Hollywood: An Illustrated History*, by

Gregory Paul Williams; *The Arsenal of Democracy*, by A. J. Baime; *Freedom's Forge*, by Arthur Herman; *Ford: Expansion and Challenge, 1915–1933*, and *Ford: Decline and Rebirth, 1933–1962*, both by Allan Nevins and Frank Ernest Hill; *Henry and Edsel: The Creation of the Ford Empire*, by Richard Bak; *The Fifties* and *The Reckoning*, both by David Halberstam; *My Years with General Motors*, by Alfred P. Sloan Jr.; *Chrysler: The Life and Times of an Automotive Genius*, by Vincent Curcio; *Billy, Alfred, and General Motors: The Story of Two Unique Men, a Legendary Company, and a Remarkable Time in American History*, by William Pelfrey; *Auto Opium: A Social History of American Automobile Design*, by David Gartman; *The Automobile Age*, by James J. Flink; *Breaking the Banks in Motor City: The Auto Industry, the 1933 Detroit Banking Crisis and the Start of the New Deal*, by Darwyn H. Lumley; and the website carofthecentury.com, which is curated by Richard Earl, Harley's grandson.

The history of the Earl and Taft families is largely taken from personal correspondence and three personal narratives: *The California Pioneer Family of Ariel Merrick Makepeace Hazard*, by Warde Eugene Parker; *The Journal of Mary Hazard, 1841–1938*; and *The Recollections of George W. Hazard*. The latter two can be found on Ancestry.com.

PROLOGUE: DEDICATION DAY

3   "an architectural feat": "The Maturing Modern," *Time*, July 2, 1956, 52.

CHAPTER 1: PIONEERS

9   When the first loggers arrived in Michigan: Bill Loomis, "Shanty Boys, River Hogs and the Forests of Michigan," *Detroit News*, April 8, 2012.

9   Michigan's pine forest: Maria Quinlan, "Lumbering in Michigan,"
       Michigan Department of Natural Resources, Michigan.gov.

10   the loggers spent the entire winter: Loomis, "Shanty Boys."

10   Jacob William Earl: Earl family records, interviews.

11   Mary Hazard was born in Detroit: *The Journal of Mary Hazard,
       1841–1938*; *The Recollections of George W. Hazard*; and Taft and
       Earl family records and correspondence.

16   The city of Los Angeles: Nathan Masters, "From Plaza Abaja to Per-
       shing Square: LA's Oldest Park Through the Decades," www.kcet.org.

16   "the first Anglo-Saxon child": Sally Taft Teschke, "When Hollywood
       and I Were Babies: An Oral History by Sally Taft Teschke," *Los An-
       geles Times*, December 2, 1934.

16   The Earls eventually followed: Michael Lamm, "Harley Earl's Califor-
       nia Years, 1893–1927," *Automobile Quarterly* 20, no. 1 (April 1982): 39.

17   Their slowness wasn't the only problem: Joel A. Tarr, "Urban
       Pollution—Many Long Years Ago," *American Heritage* 222, no. 6
       (October 1971).

18   "would benefit the public health": Ibid.

20   "It never kicks or bites": Vincent Curcio, *Chrysler: The Life and
       Times of an Automotive Genius* (New York: Oxford University Press,
       2000), 127.

21   Olds's new Detroit factory: William Pelfrey, *Billy, Alfred, and Gen-
       eral Motors: The Story of Two Unique Men, a Legendary Company,
       and a Remarkable Time in American History* (New York: AMACOM,
       2006), 58.

21   "Rows upon rows of special machinery": "The Automobile World and
       Its Doings," *Detroit Free Press*, May 4, 1904, 35.

22   "build a motorcar for the multitudes": David L. Lewis, "Henry Ford:
       A Fresh Perspective," *Michigan History*, March–April 1996.

23   "As a group they were": John B. Rae, "Why Michigan?," *Michigan
       History*, March–April 1996, 11.

CHAPTER 2: HOLLYWOOD AND HARLEY

25   Trees weren't all that Whitley had planted: Gregory Paul Williams,
       The Story of Hollywood: An Illustrated History (Los Angeles: BL
       Press, 2005), 62.

25   "a God-fearing suburb": Ibid.

26   "a self-contained oasis": Christy Borth, "Harley J. Earl: The Man
       Who Invented the Modern Car," *Ward's Autoworld*, June/July
       1969, 34.

26   "We lived a country life": Teschke, "When Hollywood and I Were Babies."

26   "Hollywood was a very moderate": Ibid.

26   Sally and her six siblings: Ibid.

27   Every June, he packed up: Earl family records and correspondence.

27   "The automobile is essential": Charles L. Palmer, "The Automobile Outlook," *Harper's Weekly* 5, part 2 (1906).

28   changed the name of his business: Earl Automobile Works catalog, courtesy of the Earl family.

30   "My father made a very tough steel": Harley Earl, as told to Arthur W. Baum, "I Dream Automobiles," *Saturday Evening Post*, August 7, 1954, 17.

30   Harley wanted to try his hand: Michael Lamm and Dave Holls, *A Century of Automotive Style: 100 Years of American Car Design* (Stockton, CA: Lamm-Morada Publishing, 1996), 86.

31   "Harley was sixteen and I was fourteen": Ibid.

31   a chance encounter on a Hollywood street: Williams, *The Story of Hollywood*, 62.

32   "They popped up like gypsy encampments": Ibid., 64.

32   They shot their short: Ibid., 65.

33   "We delighted in watching movies": Teschke, "When Hollywood and I Were Babies."

34   anti-movie prejudice: Williams, *The Story of Hollywood*, 73.

35   Griffith's follow-up: Ibid., 87.

36   "I liked to fell over": Stanley Brams, taped interview with Harley Earl, January 1953.

36   "the love of motion and speed": Cecil B. DeMille, foreword to "Cars of the Stars and Movie Memories," *Floyd Clymer's Historical Album* no. 1 (1954).

37   "poor but worthy young men": Julian Smith, "Transports of Delight: The Image of the Automobile in Early Films," *Film & History: An Interdisciplinary Journal of Film and Television Studies* 11, no. 3 (September 1981): 59–67.

37   On October 8, his mother: Earl family records and interviews.

37   "But he fought it": Lamm, "Harley Earl's California Years, 1893–1927," 40.

CHAPTER 3: THE COMPETITORS

40   Henry Ford was so pleased: David L. Lewis, *The Public Image of Henry Ford: An American Folk Hero and His Company* (Detroit: Wayne State University Press, 1976), 114.

41 Twenty thousand workers found employment: Charles K. Hyde, "The Dodge Brothers, the Automobile Industry, and Detroit Society in the Early Twentieth Century," *Michigan Historical Review*, Fall 1996, 63.

41 The Dodges chose not to compete: Robert L. Rosekrans, "Bandits, Bullets, Battles—Dependability Is Born Amid Violence as Old Betsy Chugs on Stage," *Dodge News*, January 1964, 4–5.

42 The Dodge brothers became millionaires: Hyde, "The Dodge Brothers," 71, 75–78.

44 "easily the greatest industrial domain": Lewis, *The Public Image of Henry Ford*, 161.

45 "the king of the carriage makers": Pelfrey, *Billy, Alfred, and General Motors*, 36.

48 "The ideal for which": Alfred P. Sloan Jr., *My Years with General Motors* (New York: Doubleday, 1963), 64, 69.

48 "It always seemed to me": James J. Flink, *The Automobile Age* (Cambridge, MA: MIT Press, 1988), 190.

49 "The growth in the motor vehicle market": Ibid., 131.

49 "When first-car buyers returned": Sloan, *My Years with General Motors*, 163.

49 "Mr. Ford's concept": Ibid.

CHAPTER 4: THE CADILLAC KID

51 "Perhaps the most startling local models": Lamm, "Harley Earl's California Years," 42.

52 "seems to surpass even the wonderful creations": "Some Class to This Body," *Los Angeles Sunday Times*, May 11, 1919.

53 "Those were the days": Barbara Holliday, "Harley Earl, the Original Car Stylist," *Detroit Free Press*, May 25, 1969.

54 "When my dad came back": Ibid.

55 "Dad felt he was too old": Ibid.

55 "They'd come in with a Rolls Royce": Ibid.

57 A onetime writer for *Motor* magazine: Kim Morgan, "The Roaring Road to Ruin: Wallace Reid," SunsetGun.com, 2013.

58 Reid had a reputation: Ibid.

59 "rarely showed reserve or restraint": Lamm, "Harley Earl's California Years," 44.

59 "Could you have lunch": Brams, interview with Harley Earl.

60 "Manager Harley Earl": "Doll Up Cars for Company," *Los Angeles Times*, April 16, 1922.

61 "He once chartered": Lamm, "Harley Earl's California Years," 45.

61   "I can make a car": C. Edson Armi, *The Art of American Car Design: The Profession and the Personalities* (University Park: Pennsylvania State University Press, 1988), 6.

62   "Mr. Fisher saw Mr. Earl": Sloan, *My Years with General Motors*, 316.

62   "The idea was to approach": Ibid., 269.

62   "Up until this time": Maurice D. Hendry, *Cadillac: Standard of the World: The Complete Seventy-Year History* (New York: E. P. Dutton, 1973), 131.

63   "The Hispano-Suiza was the apple": Holliday, "Harley Earl, the Original Car Stylist."

64   "They walked around": Ibid.

64   a "prissy" kid: Ed Cray, *Chrome Colossus: General Motors and Its Times* (New York: McGraw-Hill, 1980), 149.

64   "a functional, frill-less man": "Alfred P. Sloan Jr. Dead at 90; G.M. Leader and Philanthropist," *New York Times*, February 18, 1966.

66   "When we got to Detroit": Holliday, "Harley Earl, the Original Car Stylist."

67   "Knowing Harley, I doubt": Hendry, *Cadillac*, 131.

68   "longer and lower than other production cars": David Gartman, "Harley Earl and the Art and Color Section: The Birth of Styling at General Motors," *Design Issues*, Summer 1994, 13.

68   "Happy as a boy who succeeded": "Harley Earl, of Car Factory in Los Angeles, Home Again," *Los Angeles Times*, May 15, 1927, 113.

CHAPTER 5: BATTLEGROUND DETROIT

72   "How are you getting along?": Brams, interview with Harley Earl.

73   "I personally thought it was a sissy name": Holliday, "Harley Earl, the Original Car Stylist."

73   "I think you had better work": Sloan, *My Years with General Motors*, 270.

74   "Mr. Sloan never gave orders": Brams, interview with Harley Earl.

74   "I didn't know how to build anything": Holliday, "Harley Earl, the Original Car Stylist."

75   "Edsel, you shut up": David Halberstam, *The Reckoning* (New York: William Morrow, 1986), 100.

75   But the night before the planned unveiling: Richard Bak, *Henry and Edsel: The Creation of the Ford Empire* (Hoboken, NJ: John Wiley & Sons, 2003), 133.

75   "Ford could be elected President": Allan Nevins and Frank Ernest Hill, *Ford: Expansion and Challenge, 1915–1933* (New York: Charles Scribner's Sons, 1957), 395.

77   "history's worst case of product planning": Daniel Gross, *Forbes Greatest Business Stories of All Time: 20 Inspiring Tales of Entrepreneurs Who Changed the Way We Live and Do Business* (Hoboken, NJ: John Wiley & Sons, 1997), 88.

78   "Detroit was macho in those days": "Reminiscences of Frank Q. Hershey," Automotive Design Oral History Project, Benson Ford Research Center, Henry Ford Museum, Dearborn, Michigan.

79   "Father made the most popular car": Peter Collier and David Horowitz, *The Fords: An American Epic* (San Francisco: Encounter Books, 2002), 90.

79   "We've got a pretty good man": Bak, *Henry and Edsel*, 111.

80   "I've got no use": Halberstam, *The Reckoning*, 100.

80   "The new Ford automobile": Nevins and Hill, *Ford: Expansion and Challenge*, 450.

81   By June, Chevrolet had produced: Ibid., 449.

81   a look at "Henry's new car": Ibid., 459.

82   Henry Ford's impromptu model change: Ibid., 458.

83   "The Marmon had a hollow": Alexandra Earl, taped interview with Frank Hershey, May 9, 1991, provided by Alexandra Earl.

83   "But I gave up college": Ibid.

84   "These were rough-and-tumble guys": Ibid.

84   "Having come from California": "Reminiscences of Clare MacKichan," Automotive Design Oral History Project, Benson Ford Research Center, Henry Ford Museum, Dearborn, Michigan, 7.

86   "I roared like a Ventura sea lion": Earl and Baum, "I Dream Automobiles," 18.

87   Harley was "practically suicidal": Alexandra Earl, interview with Hershey.

88   1.8 million Model As: Cray, *Chrome Colossus*, 266.

89   "stand out like a toucan": Thomas L. Hibbard, "Early Days in GM Art and Colour," *Special-Interest Autos*, July–August 1974, 42.

89   Adam Opel AG: "General Motors Starts European Campaign; Sloan and Aides Arrive to Advise Opel Agents," *New York Times*, October 17, 1929.

CHAPTER 6: ASSEMBLY LINES TO BREADLINES

91   Hundreds of unemployed: Joyce Shaw Peterson, *American Automobile Workers, 1900–1933* (Albany: State University of New York Press, 1987), 135.

92   "dragged like a dead weight": Allan Nevins and Frank Ernest Hill,

NOTES

288

Ford: Decline and Rebirth, 1933–1962 (New York: Charles Scribner's Sons, 1962), 7.

93   Laid-off workers overwhelmed: Peterson, *American Automobile Workers*, 137.

93   In Henry Ford's hometown: Ibid.

94   "Why should we bail out Mr. Ford?": Darwyn H. Lumley, *Breaking the Banks in Motor City: The Auto Industry, the 1933 Detroit Banking Crisis and the Start of the New Deal* (Jefferson, NC: McFarland & Company, 2009), 112.

95   "would not contribute a single dime": Francis Gloyd Awalt, "Recollections of the Banking Crisis in 1933: The Detroit Episode," *Business History Review*, Autumn 1969, 347–71.

97   "Finally it became obvious": Lumley, *Breaking the Banks in Motor City*, 131–32.

97   "an industrial fascist": David Farber, *Sloan Rules: Alfred P. Sloan and the Triumph of General Motors* (Chicago: University of Chicago Press, 2002), 92.

97   "It's good that the recovery": Lewis, "Henry Ford: A Fresh Perspective," 15.

98   A virulent anti-Semite: Bak, *Henry and Edsel*, 146–47.

98   Henry had embarrassed himself: Ibid., 102–3; Nevins and Hill, *Ford: Expansion and Challenge*, 138; Carol Gelderman, *Henry Ford: The Wayward Capitalist* (New York: Dial, 1981), 178, 180.

99   "a man with a vision distorted": Steven Watts, *The People's Tycoon: Henry Ford and the American Century* (New York: Vintage, 2005), 269.

100 "no organization, no specific duties": Henry Ford, *My Life and Work* (Garden City, NY: Doubleday, 1923), 63.

100 "There is no bent of mind": Ibid., 62.

100 As GM sales dropped: Cray, *Chrome Colossus*, 266–67.

100 "After the crash": Alexandra Earl, interview with Hershey.

101 "knobs and handles plated": Ronnie Schreiber, "GM's First Concept Car and the Influential Result: 1936 Cadillac V16 Aerodynamic Coupe by Fleetwood," TheTruthAboutCars.com, July 27, 2014.

102 "a dream of the Roaring Twenties": Hendry, *Cadillac*, 167.

103 "Go out there and tell me": Lamm and Holls, *A Century of Automotive Style*, 98.

103 "a full-sized airbrush rendering": Ibid., 99.

104 "had the LaSalle mock-up onstage": Ibid.

CHAPTER 7: A MAN OF STYLE AND "STATUE"

105 "He had kind of pale blue eyes": "Reminiscences of Richard Teague,"

Automotive Design Oral History Project, Benson Ford Research Center, Henry Ford Museum, Dearborn, Michigan, 38.

105 "He was a terrifying figure": Author interview with Bill Porter.

105 "were physically scared of him": Alexandra Earl, interview with Hershey.

106 "a stretch of three months": Author interview with Bernie Smith.

106 "This was Christmas Eve": "Reminiscences of William L. Mitchell," Automotive Design Oral History Project, Benson Ford Research Center, Henry Ford Museum, Dearborn, Michigan.

106 "Harley had selected": Borth, "Harley J. Earl," 35.

107 "I picked up a pencil": "Reminiscences of Irvin W. Rybicki," Automotive Design Oral History Project, Benson Ford Research Center, Henry Ford Museum, Dearborn, Michigan.

107 "It's tough to be creative": Hibbard, "Early Days in GM Art and Colour," 44.

107 "The really good guys": Author interview with Porter.

108 "I saw him chew some guys out": "Bill Mitchell, General Motors Head of Design, Part I," corvetteactioncenter.com.

108 "He was ruthless": "Reminiscences of Strother MacMinn," Automotive Design Oral History Project, Benson Ford Research Center, Henry Ford Museum, Dearborn, Michigan, 28–29.

108 "You loved automobiles": "Reminiscences of Frank Q. Hershey."

109 "When he wanted something": "Reminiscences of William L. Mitchell."

110 "I want that line": Armi, *The Art of American Car Design*, 25.

111 "I sometimes wander": Earl and Baum, "I Dream Automobiles," 19.

112 "No one was to get publicity": Hibbard, "Early Days in GM Art and Colour," 43.

112 "isolated the staff": Armi, *The Art of American Car Design*, 19.

113 "manipulated and intimidated": Ibid.

113 "Hello, Alfred, how are you?": Gartman, "Harley Earl and the Art and Color Section," 3.

114 "Sue did what she wanted": Author interview with Connie Earl.

114 "He was what he was": Ibid.

115 "Dad was a hired hand": Author interview with Jim Earl.

116 "Money was always a consideration": Ibid.

116 "they looked like they had wooden trees": Lamm and Holls, *A Century of Automotive Style*, 103.

117 "He wore clothes that nobody wore": Author interview with Connie Earl.

117 "Oh, he was flamboyantly dressed": "Reminiscences of Frank Q. Hershey," 88.

CHAPTER 8: "WHAT WILL I TELL MR. SLOAN?"

119   Upon learning in June 1932: Peter F. Drucker, *Adventures of a Bystander* (New York: John Wiley & Sons, 1944), 268–69; Cray, *Chrome Colossus*, 278–79.

122   "dark paneled walls": Lamm and Holls, *A Century of Automotive Style*, 103.

122   "As you walked into that room": "Reminiscences of Frank Q. Hershey."

123   "There would be guys drafting lines": Armi, *The Art of American Car Design*, 177.

125   "They had proved a point": Sloan, *My Years with General Motors*, 275.

126   "to explore areas beyond what": "Reminiscences of Strother MacMinn"; see also "Reminiscences of Clare MacKichan."

127   "It was his insistence": "Reminiscences of Clare MacKichan."

127   "There was Sloan": "Reminiscences of William L. Mitchell."

128   "For sheer taste": Griffith Borgeson, *Errett Lobban Cord: His Empire, His Motor Cars: Auburn, Cord, Duesenberg* (New Albany, IN: Automobile Heritage Publishing, 2005), 144.

130   "I remember they had it all finished": "Reminiscences of Frank Q. Hershey."

133   "Art in industry": *Modes and Motors* (Detroit: General Motors Corporation, 1938), deansgarage.com.

CHAPTER 9: HELPING MAKE GERMANY GREAT AGAIN

135   As early as 1922: "Berlin Hears Ford Is Backing Hitler," *New York Times*, December 20, 1922, 2.

136   "It can only be said": Edwin Black, "Hitler's Carmaker: The Inside Story of How General Motors Helped Mobilize the Third Reich," *Global Research*, May 5, 2007.

137   "hundreds of thousands of people's comrades": German Propaganda Archive, Calvin College, Grand Rapids, MI, www.bytwerk.com.

139   "Are you sure your wife": Alexandra Earl, interview with Hershey.

139   "You had to step up": Ibid.

140   "Where do I send it?": "Reminiscences of Frank Q. Hershey."

CHAPTER 10: "I WOULDN'T BUY THAT SONOFABITCH"

145   He even started his own school: Lamm and Holls, *A Century of Automotive Style*, 106.

146   "played upon consumers' desire": David Gartman, *Culture, Class,*

and Critical Theory: Between Bourdieu and the Frankfurt School (New York: Routledge, 2013), 63–64.

147 "I don't give a goddamn": "Reminiscences of William L. Mitchell."

147 "to go and find out": Armi, *The Art of American Car Design*, 193.

148 "Earl's real talent lay": David Gartman, *Auto Opium: A Social History of American Automobile Design* (Oxford: Taylor & Francis, 1994), 85.

149 "No, Bob," he said: Lamm and Holls, *A Century of Automotive Style*, 102.

150 "This country has been good to me": A. J. Baime, *The Arsenal of Democracy: FDR, Detroit, and an Epic Quest to Arm an America at War* (New York: Mariner Books, 2014), location 1171 of 7201, Kindle.

151 "If we get into war": Arthur Herman, *Freedom's Forge: How American Business Produced Victory in World War II* (New York: Random House, 2012), 8.

151 "They'll make a monkey": Baime, *The Arsenal of Democracy*, location 1174 of 7201, Kindle.

151 "Can you build": Cray, *Chrome Colossus*, 316.

152 "Mr. Ford, this is terrible": Baime, *The Arsenal of Democracy*, locations 1294–97 of 7201, Kindle.

153 "the greatest production problem": Ibid., location 1335.

153 "Talk to your men": Ibid., location 1356.

154 "I fell in love with those tail fins": Alexandra Earl, interview with Hershey.

CHAPTER 11: DETROIT'S WAR

155 "What is America": Herman, *Freedom's Forge*, 13.

156 "When Hitler put his war": Gregory D. Sumner, *Detroit in World War II* (Charleston: History Press, 2015), 28.

156 "Detroit must now become": Baime, *The Arsenal of Democracy*, location 2223 of 7201, Kindle.

156 William Knudsen's eighteen months: *Freedom's Arsenal: The Story of the Automotive Council for War Production* (Detroit: Automobile Manufacturers Association, 1950), 79.

157 Chrysler president Keller operated: Michael W. R. Davis, *Detroit's Wartime Industry: Arsenal of Democracy* (Charleston: Arcadia, 2007), 29.

158 $12 billion worth: General Motors Annual Report, 1943; General Motors Annual Report, 1945.

158 "If the corporation ever": Cray, *Chrome Colossus*, 317.

159 "You've got pilots": Stanley Brams, "Car Makers' Styling Section and the War Effort," Military.com.

159 "Colored cloth was used": Ibid.

160 "We have the Wildcats": Ibid.

164 "It's got to be done": Drucker, *Adventures of a Bystander*, 270.

165 On June 20, 1943: "Martial Law at 10 P.M., U.S. Troops Move In," *Detroit Free Press*, June 22, 1943.

165 Nicholas Dreystadt found: Drucker, *Adventures of a Bystander*, 270–71.

167 Newspaper editorials characterized: Bak, *Henry and Edsel*, 254.

169 "The best thing for me to do": Ibid.

169 "Grandfather is responsible": Baime, *The Arsenal of Democracy*, location 2227 of 7201, Kindle.

169 "A powerful force": Ibid.

170 "one of the most tragic figures": Ibid.

171 "The services you will render": Ibid.

171 "This thing killed my father": Ibid.

171 Eleanor conspired with Clara: Ibid.

171 A month after D-day: Ibid.

CHAPTER 12: THE BIRTH OF FINS

173 Half of the 26 million passenger vehicles: Cray, *Chrome Colossus*, 319.

173 "The car of the future": Edward R. Grace, "Your Car After the War," *Saturday Evening Post*, November 14, 1942, 13.

174 "The higher the prices of automobiles": Cray, *Chrome Colossus*, 324.

174 "until a considerable period of time": Karl Ludvigsen, "The Truth About Chevy's Cashiered Cadet," *Special-Interest Autos*, January–February 1974, 16.

176 "Unless we get a more realistic": Farber, *Sloan Rules*, 239.

177 "We would lay out ideas": Armi, *The Art of American Car Design*, location 3399 of 7042, Kindle.

178 "simply locked away and forgotten": Ludvigsen, "The Truth About Chevy's Cashiered Cadet," 19.

178 "She sits bestride the world": David Halberstam, *The Fifties* (New York: Open Road Media, 2012), location 2102 of 17039, Kindle.

178 "Never in all the history": Cray, *Chrome Colossus*, 323.

179 "lower than the keels": Bak, *Henry and Edsel*, 268–69.

179 "Cadillac fever is of epic proportions": Hendry, *Cadillac*, 274.

180 "more customers than cars": Charles H. Whyte, "The Cadillac Phenomenon," *Fortune*, January 1955, 108.

180 "to make the far fin": Lamm and Holls, *A Century of Automotive Style*, 111.
181 "made the back of the car": Ibid.
182 "decorative brass and copper ware": Armi, *The Art of American Car Design*, location 3419 of 7042, Kindle.

CHAPTER 13: DESIGNING THE FUTURE
185 "tested in the windshields": *Train of Tomorrow* (promotional brochure), General Motors Corporation, 1947.
186 "I think there is no better candidate": George Moon, "An American Versailles: Eero Saarinen and the General Motors Technical Center—A Privilege Remembered," General Motors Design Archives and Special Collection, Warren, Michigan.
194 "we would have been murdered": Whyte, "The Cadillac Phenomenon," 181.
194 Harley believed: Earl and Baum, "I Dream Automobiles," 19.
195 "Probably never before has one material object": Ibid., 106.
195 "a solid and substantial symbol": Jason Chambers, *Madison Avenue and the Color Line: African Americans in the Advertising Industry* (Philadelphia: University of Pennsylvania Press, 2008), 44.
197 "my white Continental": "The Cellini of Chrome," *Time*, November 4, 1957.

CHAPTER 14: THE GREAT AMERICAN SPORTS CAR RACE
200 "A quick spin around the 3.8 mile track": Leo Donovan, "Staid Reporters Cheer Le Sabre," *Detroit Free Press*, July 18, 1951.
201 "General Motors vice presidents": Charlie Coon, "Idea for Corvette Was Born in Watkins Glen," *Star Gazette* (Elmira, NY), September 6, 1996.
201 "dropped the transmission into drive": Michael Lamm, "1951 GM Le Sabre: The Future Was Then," *Special-Interest Autos*, March–April 1997, 27.
202 "He sent a company plane": Author interview with Connie Earl.
204 "by Harley J. Earl as told to [*Post* editor] Arthur W. Baum": Earl and Baum, "I Dream Automobiles," 16.
206 "Mid-Century Motorama": David W. Temple, *Motorama: GM's Legendary Show and Concept Cars* (North Branch, MN: CarTech, 2015), 30–34.
207 "the best that could possibly be attained": Ibid.
207 "People will stand in line": Norman J. James, "Of Firebirds and

Moon Men: A Designer's Story from the Golden Age," history.gm heritagecenter.com.

209 "A friend of mine at GM": Alexandra Earl, interview with Hershey.

210 "Harlow Curtice promised me": "Remarks of Harley Earl," Auto News Writers' Conference, Waldorf-Astoria Hotel, New York City, January 16, 1953.

213 Frank Hershey had managed: Aaron Severson, "Little Bird: The 1955–1957 Ford Thunderbird," AteUpWithMotor.com, July 4, 2009.

213 "They said they wanted a car": Alexandra Earl, interview with Hershey.

215 "The Corvette corners": Mike Mueller, *The Complete Book of Corvette: Every Model Since 1953* (Minneapolis: Motorbooks, 2006), 29.

215 "The long gap between initial publicity": Ibid., 28.

216 "I didn't want to have a lot [of] gewgaws": Alexandra Earl, interview with Hershey.

217 actor Tyrone Power: Ibid.

217 "walked a finely drawn line": Aaron Severson, "Gaudy but Glamorous: 1958–1966 Ford Thunderbird," AteUpWithMotor.com, July 17, 2008.

219 Lewis Crusoe ordered the Thunderbird: Ibid.

CHAPTER 15: THE HOT ONE

221 "tended to bake the passengers": Chad Tyson, "1955 Ford Fairlane Crown Victoria," *Keith Martin's American Car Collector*, November–December 2017.

223 in the fall of 1954: David W. Temple, "GM's 50-Millionth Car: A Golden Opportunity," dwtauthor.blogspot.com/2011/07/1955-chevrolet-bel-air.html, July 26, 2011.

224 "We find it hard to believe": Mike Mueller, *Chevy 55-56-57* (Osceola, WI: MBI Publishing, 1993), 10.

224 "That car probably had more impact": "Reminiscences of Dave Holls," Automotive Design Oral History Project, Benson Ford Research Center, Henry Ford Museum, Dearborn, Michigan.

225 "rolled through [the year] in two-toned splendor": "Man of the Year: First Among Equals," *Time*, January 2, 1956.

226 "The boss says we're still losing": Halberstam, *The Reckoning*, 327.

227 "I couldn't believe I was going to General Motors": Author interview with Norman James.

227 "Chevrolet sold more cars than anyone else": Author interview with Robert Cumberford.

227 "There was a very strong esprit there": Author interview with Glen Wintershied.

228 breaking Rule Number One: Author interview with Porter.

229 "He thought the more": Ron VanGeldersen, interview with Charles M. Jordan, deansgarage.com, 2006.

229 "He called it 'entertainment'": Author interview with Smith.

231 "Every really creative": Raymond Loewy, "Jukebox on Wheels," *Atlantic*, April 1, 1955.

CHAPTER 16: GLORY DAYS

235 "Shimmering reflections": Alice T. Friedman, *American Glamour and the Evolution of Modern Architecture* (New Haven, CT: Yale University Press, 2009), 119–32.

238 "sort of night club": "Interiors of the Styling Building in GM's Technical Center," *Interiors*, January 1957, 80–89.

241 "The day we arrived": Author interview with Ruth Glennie.

242 "We simply lucked out": Author interview with Sandy Longyear.

242 "slim, trim, with": Sidney Fields, "Lady Auto Makers: Designs on Future," *New York Daily Mirror*, May 2, 1960.

242 "Pounding nails into a block of wood": "Reminiscences of Suzanne Vanderbilt," Automotive Design Oral History Project, Benson Ford Research Center, Henry Ford Museum, Dearborn, Michigan.

244 "I like everything": Author interview with Smith.

245 "The setting was": Jessie Ash Arndt, "Behind That Wheel," *Christian Science Monitor*, April 7, 1958.

CHAPTER 17: INSURRECTION

247 "all these '57 Plymouths": VanGeldersen, interview with Jordan.

249 "shot up out of the grass": "Reminiscences of Dave Holls."

CHAPTER 18: NOT FADE AWAY

253 Romney dubbed it a "compact" car: Patrick Foster, *George Romney: An American Life* (Grapevine, TX: Waldorf, 2017), 124–25.

254 a quarter of them Volkswagens: Ralph Kinney Bennett, "Small Car, Big Shadow," *American*, March 13, 2009.

255 "There is no longer any doubt about it": HowStuffWorks.com/1945-1959-volkswagen-beetle4.

255 *Popular Mechanics* went so far: "But It's Noisy," *Popular Mechanics*, October 1956, 158.

257 "Detroit thinks": John Keats, *The Insolent Chariots* (Greenwich, CT: Fawcett, 1958), 38.

257 "Our big job [as car designers]": Jane Fiske Mitarachi, "Harley Earl

and His Product: The Styling Section," *Industrial Design*, October 1955.

257 "to own something a little new": Brooks Stevens, "Planned Obsolescence—Is It Fair," *Rotarian*, February 1960.

258 "we obsolete our products": Joseph C. Ingraham, "Auto Men Restyle Motive of Change," *New York Times*, November 6, 1960.

259 a reported $250 million developing: Michael Beschloss, "Hubris, and Sputnik, Doomed the Edsel," *New York Times*, June 6, 2015.

259 "The smart money both in": Eugene Jaderquist, "Why the Edsel Will Succeed," *True's Automobile Yearbook*, 6 (1956), edsel.net/succeed.

260 when Ford owners moved up to a medium-priced: Ibid.

261 "Barring war or depression": Ibid.

261 "lay all these people off": Beschloss, "Hubris, and Sputnik, Doomed the Edsel."

265 "How many of you guys": Author interview with Smith.

265 "Mr. Earl on the hot seat": Author interview with Glennie.

266 The *New York Times* later described Donner: "Bean Counter Donner Reshaped GM in the 1960s," *New York Times*, September 14, 2008.

266 "saving fractions of pennies": Youssef M. Ibrahim, "John F. Gordon, 77, Ex President of GM," *New York Times*, January 7, 1978.

268 Designer Sparky Bohnstedt: Author interview with Porter.

268 On November 19, 1959: "Harry Anderson Victim in Tragedy," *Detroit Free Press*, November 19, 1959.

276 "I want to tell you": Armi, *The Art of American Car Design*, locations 3584–96 of 7042, Kindle.

276 On May 8, 1991: Alexandra Earl, interview with Hershey.

277 "ebullient expressions of devil-may-careness": "A Legacy of Style," *Detroit Free Press*, April 2, 1969.

INDEX

Michigan Manufacturer and Financial Record, 41
Michigan National Guard, 273
Michigan Quarterly Review, 37
Milford Proving Grounds, 200
military-industrial complex, 151, 178–79
Mills, Ogden, 94
Minneapollis Advertising Club, 257
Minter, Mary Miles, 57
Mitarachi, Jane Fiske, 257
Mitchell, Bill, 106, 108–10, 127, 129, 144, 154, 158, 172, 175, 177, 180, 185, 193, 228, 230, 240, 244–45, 249–51, 262, 264, 266–69, 274–76
Mix, Tom, 56–57
Modes and Motors (booklet), 133–34
Moon, George, 236–38, 240
Mooney, James, 136, 140
Morgan sports car, 201
Motorama, 206–16, 224, 228, 245–46, 252–53, 264
Motor City Traffic Club, 253
Motor magazine, 57, 194
Motor Trend, 209, 215, 224, 269
movie industry, 32–37, 55–58, 116–17
Munich Conference (1938?), 141
Murphy, Frank, 92–93
Murphy, Walter M., Company, 83
Museo Histórico de la Revolución, 42
Mussolini, Benito, 138, 141
My Life and Work (Ford), 100, 135–36, 138

Nader, Ralph, 269–72
Nash, 197, 226
Nash Rambler, 225, 231
Nash Rambler American, 253–54, 262, 269
National Automobile Chamber of Commerce, 49
National Automobile Show, 21, 27, 42
National Defense Advisory Commission, 150–51
National Highway Traffic and Safety Administration (NHTSA), 271–72
National Traffic and Motor Vehicle Safety Act (1966), 271

NATO, 202
Nazi Party (Germany), 135–41
Nestor Film Company (*later* Universal), 32, 34
Nevins, Allan, 92
New Deal, 114, 151
New York Auto Show, 66–67, 128, 133–34, 193, 206
New York Mirror, 242–43
New York Times, 64, 81, 81, 97, 99, 135, 174, 258, 266
New York World's Fair (1939–40), 144, 159
Nicholas II, Czar of Russia, 43
Nickles, Ned, 228, 239
"No Money Down" (song), 225
Normand, Mabel, 56

Oakland (*later* Pontiac), 45, 47
Olds, Ransom E., 19, 21–23, 39, 156, 258
Oldsmobile, 21–23, 27, 45, 47, 77, 123, 146, 160, 196, 228, 248, 260–62
Oldsmobile Palm Beach Holiday, 206
Oldsmobile Starfire, 211
Oldsmobile Viking, 77, 87–88
O'Leary, Howard, 72, 77, 82, 107, 183, 229, 240
Opel, 124, 136, 138–40, 142, 256
Opel Kadett, 139

P-38 fighter plane, 153–54, 176–77, 266
Packard, James, 23
Packard Clipper, 157
Packard Motor Company, 29, 43, 50, 54, 61, 77, 87, 121, 131, 156, 186, 196, 226–27
Packard Six, 62
Packard Twin Six, 43
paint, 49, 59, 206, 221, 224, 231
Paramount, 34
Paris Auto Show, 64–65, 130–31, 202
Patton, George S., 41–42, 161, 192
Payne, Robert, 178
Pearl Harbor attacks, 155
Peerless Motors, 43, 77, 91
Perry, Oliver Hazard, 11

ABOUT THE AUTHOR

W ILLIAM KNOEDELSEDER is the *New York Times* bestselling author of *Bitter Brew: The Rise and Fall of
Anheuser-Busch and America's Kings of Beer,* as well
as the critically acclaimed *Stiffed: A True Story of MCA, the
Music Business, and the Mafia.* His book *I'm Dying Up Here:
Heartbreak and High Times in Stand-Up Comedy's Golden Era*
is the basis for the Showtime series of the same name. He lives
in Woodland Hills, California.